If All We Did Was to Weep at Home

Susan Estabrook Kennedy

Minorities in Modern America
Editors: Warren Kimball
David Edwin Harrell, Jr.

INDIANA UNIVERSITY PRESS
Bloomington and London

IF ALL WE DID WAS TO WEEP AT HOME:

A HISTORY OF WHITE WORKING-CLASS WOMEN IN AMERICA

Manufactured in the United States of America

Library of Congress Cataloging in Publication Data

Kennedy, Susan Estabrook.
  If all we did was to weep at home.

  (Minorities in modern America)
  Bibliography: p.
  Includes index.
  1. Women—United States—Social conditions.
  2. Labor and laboring classes—United States. 3.
  Social mobility—United States. I. Title. II. Series.
  HQ1410.K45   301.41'2'0973   78-20431
  ISBN 0-253-19154-8   1 2 3 4 5 83 82 81 80 79

For my students,
especially
Ralph Steinberg
Mark Winograd
Lynn Caveney Keiner
David Wick
Martha May
Stefanie Newberry

Contents

.

Foreword

The idea for this series of books took shape a decade ago, when the editors were colleagues at the University of Georgia. Our memorable luncheon gatherings, which frequently included Willard Gatewood, Melvin Herndon, Charles Alexander, Bob Griffith, Roger Nichols, Emory Thomas, and Will Holmes, were filled with anecdotal testimonials about our own histories. The two of us were fascinated by one another's provincialism—one having become a young adult before meeting a northerner or a Jew or a Catholic, the other having moved to Georgia without ever riding a mule or attending a revival. It has increasingly occurred to us that what one teaches about American history and what students learn in American history courses are strongly related (probably rightly so) to the location of one's university. Students in Alabama who have never seen a subway, or much of an urban ghetto, or a first-generation immigrant still flock to courses on the Civil War. And New Jersey classes are filled with students who have never seen a cotton field, a Klansman, or a mimosa tree. So one person's American history centers on the Taft-Hartley Act, while another's defines the Wheeler-Howard Act, the Tennessee Valley Authority, or the gay rights movement as the central issue of the American experience. We need to understand ourselves, but if we would know our country, we must do more.

This series of books studies one key level of American loyalties, the numerous and often ill-defined minority groups that exist in fact or in myth. In the broadest sense humans identify with the common sufferings and aspirations of all mankind. On a second level we relate our self-interest to our nation. When confronted with a foreign environment (as the editors experienced during their Fulbright years in India and Spain), even those of us who would not think of ourselves as superpatriots become self-consciously aware of how American we are. At the other end of the spectrum, all of us identify our self-interest in personal and family terms. In short, all of us have complex loyalties, but most Americans identify with some group (or groups) larger than family and smaller than nation, groups defined by section, class, race, sex, or ideology. It is that identification which shapes our most immediate value judgments.

Nearly thirty years ago Walter Prescott Webb argued that the closing of world frontiers spelled the end of the individualistic days of Western civilization. The fluidity of a society in economic boom would be replaced by the stasis of a society that emphasized order and stability. Men in the West would increasingly come to identify with groups, slowly abandoning the emphasis on individualism and all its free-wheeling implications. Webb's view, of course, contradicts the more commonly held belief that most people have always seen themselves as part of some important larger group. Whichever assertion is correct, the history of America is a unique case study in the survival and molding of group loyalties. Remarkable and important as the rise of nationalism in the United States has been, all Americans—even the most affluent and powerful—have, in some sense, remained hyphenated. The founding fathers' vision of a competing and compromising balance of minorities has come much closer to being realized than has the later ideal of a melting pot.

The most common focus of group unity has been ethnic. Race or place of origin was particularly central to the lives of the late arrivals in America, who found that ethnic groups generally shared homogeneous economic, social, and cultural values. But Americans have consciously sought to go beyond the confines of ethnic-group loyalty. The ethnic dimension has become less central, particularly in the mainstream of American life, where millions of people care little about their genealogies. But other important associations have been formed. Regional loyalties seem ineradicable. Many people also identify themselves with an economic class. At times that identification has been quite broad—the poor or the middle class—but more often people hold a stronger identification with a specific economic group, such as industrial workers or the urban poor. Finally, some people's view of the world is shaped primarily by intellectual and cultural values. One might be poor and black and southern and yet live as a Christian zealot, a Marxist, or a cynic. In short, all of us are many things, but at any given time we are likely to hold some loyalty supreme, or at least vitally important. It is those loyalties, those minority-group identifications, which this series seeks to examine, explain, and evaluate.

It is no secret that "The Women's Movement" has failed to capture the support of all women in America even while it has captured the attention of the news and entertainment media, presidential politicians, and academics. When confronted with this fact, the movement's leaders retort that women who deny the legitimacy of their cause are "victims of social programming." But that is a political statement, not an explanation. Moreover, it is a statement that white working-class women frequently interpret as a slur on their intelligence, efforts, and dedication.

The title of Part One of Susan Estabrook Kennedy's poignant study of working-class white women, "She Must Be Married Because She Don't Work," captures the essence of the conflict. Middle-class feminists claim that working-class women have accepted a set of outdated values imposed on them by a male-dominated society. Specifically, they see freedom from work as a way for males to maintain their dominance. But many working-class women still see freedom from work as a positive goal. The former group views work in social and psychological terms, as a source of meaning in life. The latter group sees work in economic terms; for example, the issue of equal pay for equal work is not a moral one; it is simply a question of a paycheck. Perhaps, as Kennedy suggests, the growing awareness of the 1970s, when combined with contemporary economic pressures (more and more middle-class women are working and admitting that they are doing so just for the paycheck), will bring these two groups of women together.

As students of history we must gain some understanding of the roots and development of such different perceptions of women's values and goals. Yesterday's reform is often today's problem, and the history of working-class women illustrates that point. Seventy years ago, American reformers, frequently led by middle-class women, fought for the laws that would protect working women from being exploited and mistreated. Today, many of those laws seem, to some, to restrict rather than protect women. But before Americans can agree to revise or eliminate such institutions, they must understand what they are, why they came to be, and what will result from such changes. Those protections were designed primarily for white working-class women, and until that group is understood by others—as well as by themselves—change for them will continue to mean the imposition of someone else's values. Professor Kennedy, who teaches at Virginia Commonwealth University in Richmond, Virginia, has provided us all with a compelling, evocative, and sensitive portrait of white working-class women, which is sure to deepen our understanding and appreciation of what may be the largest group of anonymous heroines in American history.

WARREN F. KIMBALL
Somerset, New Jersey

DAVID EDWIN HARRELL, JR.
Birmingham, Alabama

Introduction

In the United States in the 1970s, a white working-class woman lives somewhere between the terrors of poverty and the security of the middle class. Throughout American history, the lives of these women have been marked by a continuing struggle for survival for themselves and their families, together with great societal pressure to remove themselves upward, out of their working-class status and into the economic, social, and emotional safety of the middle class. So consistently has tenure in the working class been regarded as a temporary condition that working-class women have generally not developed a sense of their own place or of their history as a collective entity. Frequently, they did not know who they were and thought of themselves as in-the-process-of-becoming something else, something better. These women so identified with middle-class values that they attempted to hide their poverty, their lifestyles, and their employment, seeking instead to struggle toward at least the outward appearances of middle-class respectability. Moreover, those who chronicled the activities of these women in the past often did so in efforts to bring about reform which would remove the women from the danger, fears, and potential degradation of their own class and raise them into a more socially acceptable order.

A primary task in developing a history of America's white working-class women, therefore, is one of definition and discovery. This is not an "established" field of historical research such as political or diplomatic studies, nor has it yet enjoyed a major share of the more recent interest in social history. At best, the history of working-class women might draw upon the larger studies of women in general or upon working-class studies which have heretofore paid most attention to men. Even the term "working-class women" does not evoke immediate recognition—or agreement—when the concept is discussed. In fact, it is frequently easier to say who a working-class woman is *not* than to establish who she is.

Many scholars, archivists, and casual observers assume that any employed female must be a working-class woman. And much of the recent discussion of low and inequitable pay for women workers has reinforced this conception. But some women have been employed at jobs too prestigious or professional, or at salaries too high, to qualify them for working-class status. The teacher, the white-collar worker, the professional nurse may earn low wages but be regarded as middle class for reasons which are not economic. In addition, history shows that one of the major objectives of most working-class women has been to remove themselves from the paid labor force, to become a working-class woman who does not work for wages as part of a program to become a middle-class woman who does not work for wages. Therefore, working-class women may or may not be employed. If they are employed, the nature of their employment usually has something to do with their working-class status. For those who do not hold paying jobs, their working-class status might be determined by that of the principal man in their lives, usually a father or husband.

Similar confusion clouds the issue of destitution as determining membership in the working class. During the colonial period and early days of the new American nation, it was difficult to establish any hard and fast parameters of class, but few Americans were poor to the point of extinction. With the birth of industrialization, the first working-class women to enter the factory system in significant numbers did so primarily for economic improvement and returned to agricultural society when they had accumulated comfortable nest-eggs. While many new immigrants had little in the way of financial resources, their entry into working-class occupations and lifestyles usually meant an effort to rise rather than a struggle to remain alive. In more recent times, working-class people draw sharp distinctions between themselves and those below the poverty level, resenting the welfare population strongly. Therefore, while working-class women have often earned or tried to get along on low incomes, they have not been "poor" in the sense of having the very lowest income or none at all. Historically, working-class women have struggled to remain above poverty.

The search for a definition of the American working-class woman is often further confused at the opposite end of the working-class economic spectrum—the middle class. The mobile society of colonial America had a strong identification with what Richard Hofstadter and others have called "the middling sort." Similarly, when the first large numbers of women went into the New England mills, they did so from a kind of rural middle-class heritage to which they returned on leaving their factory employment. Immigrants from many cultures quickly assimilated the middle-class goals of the burgeoning American society of the nineteenth century and sought at least the obvious aspects of middle-class status long before they achieved its underlying securities. This trend became even more pronounced with increasing technological developments, the growth of conspicuous consumption, and the economic self-satisfaction of the nation in the twentieth century. Therefore, while working-class women in reality fall between poverty and the middle class, their aspirations frequently lead them to identify with middle-class values. The term "lower middle class" often overlaps with this intermediate condition.

If these are the things which working-class women are not, then who are they and who have they been? Clearly, membership in the working-class is more than a matter of dollar income. It also involves attitudes, cultural assumptions, and a category broadly labeled "socioeconomic." Moreover, working-class women are not simply members of the working classes. They are "also" women, and as such they share certain distinguishing marks of gender in addition to national, racial, and ethnic concepts and characteristics of society and class. Yet here again, the problem of defining working-class women in America returns to the peculiar situation of their having so rarely defined themselves. Although some individuals have drawn attention to the lives and conditions of working-class women in the past, on the whole, most working-class women have been discouraged from developing attitudes on anything, and especially on themselves. Therefore, the historical definition of a white working-class woman in America has, until very recently, simply been that of a woman temporarily not yet in the middle class. Consequently, working-class women have not had an immediately apparent or consistent ideology or sense of social, political, economic, or cultural cohesiveness. This volume, therefore, has developed from a search for a consciously and unconsciously hidden minority in American history—white working-class women.

Working-class women are, of course, not limited to whites, and it can be argued effectively that a significant dimension to the study of working-class women will be added when other scholars investigate beyond the limitation of race. The subject, however, is vast; the material is often obscured; and the job of the researcher is monumental in so new a field. The decision to concentrate this study on white working-class women, therefore, was practical rather than conceptual. Although much of the recent work on working-class women has centered on "ethnics," especially those defined by European immigrant heritages, the objective of this volume is not the establishment of racial distinctions in investigating the history of white and nonwhite working-class women in America. Rather, this book is intended as an early entry into a comparatively new field, offered with the hope that it will encourage others to broaden the definitions and examine some of the premises advanced here in the light of additional research.

At the same time, one cannot help but sympathize with historians embarking on the pursuit of working-class women throughout American history. Evidence is available to some extent, but not readily and often not through the "usual" means of research. White working-class women in America have often been too busy living their history to record their own observations on it, and many of them have not seen any value in such an enterprise. Official preservers of records have also failed to see the worth of information on working-class women, so that such materials have often received less attention than those relating to more prominent or public topics. Hence, the available evidence is heavily weighted toward such overt activities as occupations or unionization and often includes little satisfying data on private lives and attitudes. The search for information takes the historian of working-class women to fewer of the diaries and journals which may offer insight to the political or diplomatic historian. And at the same time, sources which provide information for the social historian have often been oriented in other directions than toward working-class women. In some cases, judgments must be extrapolated from more general information on women, in others from materials on working-class men, and in still others from trade union and labor histories. Efforts to construct a treatment of America's white working-class women from secondary sources at this point in scholarly time will encounter enormous gaps and frequent frustrations.

Fascinating pieces of information lie hidden, however. In manuscript sources, for example, little direct testimony by working-class women themselves remains, but collections on social feminists, trade unionists, reformers, settlement houses, and others often contain vignettes and observations on the working-class from the perspective of middle- and upper-class concerned citizens. New techniques are also helping the investigator. For the last few generations, oral history—interviews with surviving working-class women— can fill in gaps in the archival record. And the detailed work of young scholars in particular is producing an encouraging growth in the dissertation literature investigating specific aspects of the lives and careers of white working-class women throughout American history.

While no work of scholarship is performed alone or without support, a topic such as this one requires particular help from other scholars, librarians, archivists, and friends. The synthesis and conclusions of this study are my own responsibility, but many others have contributed both personally and professionally to improving this volume. I cannot begin to thank them all adequately or to express the depth of my gratitude. But I do hope to acknowledge their kindness, generosity, talents, and skills.

Research on working-class women involves probing into many collections of information where working-class women may hide but have not yet been discovered. In this task of digging, I have been assisted by the library and archival staffs of the following institutions: Advisory Committee on the Economic Role of Women, Executive Office of the President, Council of Economic Advisers; American Association of University Women; American Jewish Archives; American Jewish Committee, Institute on Human Relations; American Jewish Historical Society; Archives of Labor History and Urban Affairs, Walter P. Reuther Library, Wayne State University; The Arthur and Elizabeth Schlesinger Library on the History of Women in America, Radcliffe College; Association for Childhood Education International; Biblioteca Femina, Northwestern University Library; The Catholic University; Center for Women Policy Studies; Chicago Historical Society; Columbia University; Citizens'

Advisory Council on the Status of Women; Galatea Collection, Boston Public Library; Georgetown University; Illinois Historical Survey, University of Illinois, Urbana; League of Women Voters of the United States; Library of Congress; Merrimack Valley Textile Museum; Michigan Historical Collections, Bentley Historical Library, University of Michigan; National Archives, Industrial and Social Branch; National Center for Urban Ethnic Affairs; New York Public Library; New York State Department of Labor Library; New York State School of Industrial and Labor Relations, Martin P. Catherwood Library, Cornell University; the Newberry Library; Project on the Status and Education of Women; Rape Crisis Center, Washington, D. C.; Resource Center on Sex Roles in Education, National Foundation for the Improvement of Education; Roosevelt University; Sophia Smith Collection, Smith College; Tamiment Library, New York University; United Nations Centre for Social Development and Humanitarian Affairs, Branch for the Promotion of Equality of Men and Women; The University of Chicago; University of Illinois at Chicago Circle; University of Rochester Library; University of Virginia; Virginia Commonwealth University; Virginia State Library; and the Women's Rights Project, American Civil Liberties Union. Two persons deserve special gratitude for their exceptional professional efficiency—Dione Miles, Reference Archivist at the Archives of Labor History and Urban Affairs at Wayne State University, and Janet McNeil, Director of Collections Development at the James Branch Cabell Library of Virginia Commonwealth University.

Several mentors, colleagues, and friends—most falling into all three categories—have read the manuscript and improved it both substantively and stylistically. While they may not share all of my conclusions, I would like to express my appreciation to Stuart Bruchey of Columbia University, Martha E. May of SUNY-Binghamton, and Thelma S. Biddle and Melvin I. Urofsky of Virginia Commonwealth University, as well as to the editors of this series, David E. Harrell, Jr., and Warren Kimball, for their constructive suggestions on the manuscript and their warm support while it was being developed. In addition, a number of friends provided both common sense and life-saving distractions during the research and writing; my special thanks to Bob and Bella Davis, Taylor Nathaniel Davis, Susan Grandis, Karen Roemer Paxton, Leslie O'Malley Finke, Nancy Wright, and Dorsey Bushnell.

In particular, I must thank my family for sharing their lives with me and with thousands of working-class women over hundreds of years of American history, for having luncheon with the Rosies and Florences, dinner with the Women's Trade Union League, and unquiet afternoons with the inmates of sweatshops and ghettos. My mother, Dorothy Ogden Estabrook, is as loyal a critic as she is a perfect typist. And my husband, E. Craig Kennedy, Jr., has been a bastion of logical good sense in the face of my insights and ravings. To them both, my love and gratitude.

Finally, to twelve years of students in New York, Pennsylvania, and Virginia, this volume is only a small expression of my thanks for the stimulation of the classroom and for the delights of sharing learning.

Part One: "She Must Be Married, Because She Don't Work": 1600-1900

1. Women, Girls, and Ladies in Early America

FROM THE FOUNDING of the first settlements in British North America early in the 1600s until the United States was well established in the early 1800s, the roles of women and distinctions among women evolved gradually and without much conscious attention. To look for working-class women in the colonies and the new nation is to look at most or almost none of the females in those societies. At first, no women. Then women for stability. Then women for prosperity. Then women for decoration. Then women for morality. Finally, kinds, castes, and classes of women. But in each case, women were given a set of rules to make them maximally beneficial to their new society. Women received instructions which eventually crystalized into proper norms for female life and behavior. Within this growing, changing, defining period of American history, therefore, rest many of the underlying assumptions about who women are, how they should behave, and how and why they differ from one another. If working-class women are difficult to single out in the very beginnings of the American experience, by the Age of Jackson not only are they evident but they already have a peculiar set of problems resting both on their femininity and their membership in the working classes.

America was not discovered for women. When Europeans set out to gather the riches of the New World, most governments and corporate developers assigned the task to "adventurers," men who would risk the hazards of the sea voyage and perils of the unknown land to seek fortunes for themselves and their sponsors. This acquisition of wealth would be so easy, they assumed, that permanent migration would not be necessary.

3

In the British-claimed territories along the Atlantic coast, however, these illusions hardly survived the first winter. Neglecting even minimal precautions of food and shelter, the Jamestown colony lost all but thirty-eight of its first white inhabitants before supply ships arrived and Captain John Smith assumed firm control in 1608. Leaders of the London Company soon realized that profits would not come from quick riches, gold nuggets picked from the ground, but from a stable life for farming families, a view reinforced by the "starving time" of 1610, during which Jamestown lost half of its replenished population. But resettlement on more favorable sites, individual rather than communal land-holding, and the successful cultivation and marketing of tobacco set the Virginia colony on the path toward long-term, large-scale agriculture.

This adjustment from rapid exploitation to more stabilized development meant many changes for the English colonies —renegotiated charters, headright and freehold land systems, self-government, and struggles for political power— but it also meant a new emphasis on orderly life, a condition which seemed to call for the presence of women. Of course, females had been in the colonies since the arrival of the second supply ship in 1608, when Thomas Forest brought his wife, Lucy, and her fourteen-year-old maidservant, Anne Buras. And the first colonial wedding took place that same year when laborer John Layton took a fourteen-year-old bride, perhaps the same Anne. Several dozen female names appear on passenger lists before 1616. Yet women were not part of the planning of Virginia until 1619, when the company had reached its decision on long-term settlement by male and female colonists. In May 1620 ninety potential wives (costing 150 pounds of tobacco each) arrived for the tenantry. Fifty more followed in the next two years, chosen with "extraordinary diligence" for their excellent reputations in their own communities.[1] Those who ventured further north also understood the significance of community in 1620. Eighteen wives, three of them pregnant, and eleven girls sailed on the Pilgrim ship *Mayflower.* Ten years later, Puritans also migrated as families.

Whether they journeyed in search of economic or religious opportunity, a majority of these settlers came from the yeomanry—small farmers, often crushed by the enclosure movement, seeking lands of their own. Others were laborers, even less well off in England but with similar ambitions for America. Their concern for the land, together with the lack of ready money, made wives and families particularly important to the New World farmers. In 1619 the Virginia House of Burgesses declared, "in a newe plantation it is not knowne whether man or woman be the most necessary"; and the assembly allotted husbands equal land shares for their wives.[2]

Women, therefore, brought social, moral, and economic value to their marriages—and seventeenth-century English and American communities took for granted that they would marry. Western civilization accepted male dominance and provided few legitimate outlets for unattached females. Daughters would grow up to become wives and then mothers, under the sanctions of their societies, their states, and their religious convictions. "He for God only, she for God in him," said John Milton in *Paradise Lost.*

The scarcity of wives, however, increased women's value in colonial America. Men sharply outnumbered women; only one in three immigrants to Virginia was female. An agricultural society placed a premium on productive wives, but many women did not survive frequent childbearing under primitive conditions, while others succumbed to disease and the harsh environment. Marriage and remarriage, therefore, offered opportunities to most females. One man proposed to a widow two days after the death of her first husband but was refused pending the birth of a posthumous child; he eventually sued the widow (unsuccessfully) for breach of promise when she married the administrator of her late husband's estate. Neither beauty nor wealth counted so heavily as virtue in rendering seventeenth-century women marriageable. A Swiss in South Carolina wrote to his brother: ". . . poor females who are of scanty means should come to America if they are virtuous and sensible." And a Maryland gallant reported a high marriage rate even for servants in this land of opportunity, saying, ". . . had they not come to such a Market with their Virginity, [they] might have kept it them until it had been mouldy."[3]

The Englishwoman in colonial America shared her husband's commitment to hard work and the belief that success (often taken as a sign of spiritual favor) could best be achieved by the collective labor of the family. William Bradford praised the first Pilgrim women for going "willingly into the fields" to set corn, taking their infants with them.[4] As the communities developed and cabins replaced sod huts, women worked in the house and yard, laboring in a family economy which produced most of its own food, clothing, and shelter. They worked beside men or at complementary tasks which supported the family's survival.

In public life, men dominated colonial society. Under Common Law, a married woman suffered "civil death," taking on the social status of her mate. The husband "headed" the household, only males being eligible to become "freemen." Moreover, contemporary culture retained near-primitive suspicions of women's power to corrupt, and clergymen reinforced these beliefs by dwelling on Eve's responsibility for man's fall from grace. Weak women were expected to depend on physically and morally superior males who owned property, participated in public affairs, and made essential decisions for those for whom they had responsibility—women, children, servants, and slaves.

Practice moderated some of these patriarchal institutions,

however. If centuries of "civilization" supported male superiority in England and Europe, primitive conditions in
America made for greater sexual as well as economic mobility, and a rough egalitarianism better served the needs of
frontier communities to survive and prosper. Moreover, in
the seventeenth century American society was more functional, less complex than it would later become; therefore,
women acquired status according to their contributions—
whether in work or in children. While colonial life remained
hard, women in America probably had better health, more
favorable living conditions, higher status, and greater opportunity to improve their lot than did those who remained in
Europe. American women married earlier, were less restricted by dowries, and often had legal protection for themselves and their children in antenuptial contracts. After the
early years, Virginia women of all stations ordered clothes
from England, with ordinary people copying the manners of
the colony's social leaders. Seventeenth-century Salem, Massachusetts, wives and mothers had a major control over inherited land. Courts in Plymouth Colony occasionally
permitted women to petition and make contracts, in 1663
awarding a widow a greater share of her husband's estate
than his will specified. Women obtained liquor licenses and
authorizations to conduct taverns or inns, often without the
mention of a husband at all. And in parts of New England,
men as well as women were obliged to comply with marital
sexual duties; a divorce was granted to a wife in 1686 because
the husband was "always unable to perform the act of generation."[5]

These exceptions only underscore the growing complexi-
ties of women's position in America in the seventeenth century. The Common Law gave women many duties but few
rights. In general, married women could not ordinarily sign
contracts, had no legal title to their own earnings or property,
and could not even claim their children in cases of legal

separation. Few communities actually permitted women to hold land, especially in the latter part of the century. And toward the end of the 1600s, the hysteria over witchcraft in Massachusetts, Virginia, and other colonies lashed out at many more female than male victims.[6]

But these property-related issues had little effect on one large group of women colonists—indentured servants. Men and women who could not afford to pay their passage to the New World took advantage of the need for labor in the colonies and signed indentures or certificates of bondage whereby they agreed to work for periods of from three to ten years in exchange for transportation to America and the hope of access to property after their term of service. Some came voluntarily, spurred by poverty; others were transported as kidnap victims by organizations which picked them up from London streets; many were sold by their jailers or elected servitude rather than prison. Thus, their previous condition—destitution or crime or social caste—was at first masked behind the demand for workers in the colonies and later melded into the great variety of the free population. Often referred to as "slaves," these servants gave over complete control of themselves to their new masters and mistresses for the term of the indenture. They usually received poor, if any, pay, were frequently treated harshly, and had neither privacy nor self-determination. On the other hand, they traded a limited term of restriction for dreams of success later, when they would be free. Many received a subsidy of land or tools at the end of the indenture period. They had redress to the courts in cases of excessive brutality. And colonial lifestyles left little room for privacy or nonconformity even among the free and affluent.

Yet women servants fared worse than men. Female convicts received longer or more severe sentences for the same crimes, and males brought 40 to 50 percent higher prices as servants. Even among free women, indigent widows were bound out or sold in some New England towns, and New Jersey required poor women to perform public work in the 1670s. Similarly, when apprenticeships became another source of labor, girls did not receive the thorough training given to boys even when their contracts specified that they be taught spinning and sewing. After performing domestic tasks until they came of age, apprenticed girls could not even say that they had learned a skill or trade during their years of bondage.[7]

During the first century of American colonial development, women had value and status usually in proportion to their functional contributions to the household and community. Work was expected of both men and women at most economic levels, with the society not yet secure or successful enough to concern itself with such luxuries as feminine beauty, charm, fashion, or frivolity. Men dominated women, who were expected to be attached to some male, usually by marriage. Yet, in practice, some women enjoyed fewer restrictions. For both men and women, whether farmers or artisans or shopkeepers, most activities of life and work took place in and around the homestead, making for greater closeness and less isolation within families and communities. Women engaged in a variety of tasks, including those they shared with men or inherited as widows. And women undoubtedly had greater opportunities for advancement in the colonies than at home.

In the eighteenth century, the British North American colonies began to assume a relative stability and prosperity, which altered colonial expectations and included changes in the situation of women. During the seventeenth century, working-class women had remained almost indistinguishable from all but the most prosperous planters' and merchants' ladies. Mistress and maidservant frequently shared the same tasks, and the maid might one day marry her master's brother. Or a young Dutch woman of a merchant household in New York might bind herself out as a domestic worker. Thus, persons moved rather freely into and out of working-class conditions; the nature of preindustrial society as well as this mobility factor hardly justified the use of the term "working-class" at all, although living situations of the poor or servants were generally less attractive than those on the rise. Some of these conditions persisted into the 1700s, but others altered. According to the Maryland census of 1755, approximately 9 percent of the adult white female population were servants or convicts, but free white adult males only outnumbered their female counterparts by 500—a distinct change in the scarcity of women. Forbidden to marry without their owners' consent, female servants still endured sexual exploitation by their masters; not only might they suffer rape, but should they conceive, they had to repay their masters for loss of their services during childbirth. As Benjamin Franklin advised in *Poor Richard's Almanac* in 1736, "Let they maidservant be faithful, strong and homely."[8]

But, unlike earlier colonial women, a wife need not be homely, particularly if her man were now rich enough to dispense with her labor. As Southern planters acquired vast fields and many slaves to work in them, skin color began to indicate caste among free white women: planters' females were protected from the sun, in contrast to "poor white" women, whose men still required their work in the fields. A rising urban middle class to the north began to imitate English styles, discovered etiquette and fashion, and evaded issues of women's humanity by stressing wifely and maternal duties, polarizing motherhood from sexuality.[9] Growing affluence for some portions of society meant domestic service as a form of employment for the lower classes, although women received only half the earnings of male servants, and mistresses still risked losing their domestics to marriage and the frontier. Employers advertised in newspapers: "Wanted. Two White Servant Maids, to serve in a small Family; the one for a Nurse-maid, to take Care of a Child or two; the other to Cook and do the other necessary Work about the House; They must be well recommended and engage to stay a Twelve-Month at least in the Family."[10]

Other occupations, including working-class jobs, opened in the eighteenth century, at the same time the sale of labor for wages increased. Women often found their lack of technical skill and knowledge a handicap in the early days of machine production. As in the seventeenth century, girls received little industrial education and their apprenticeships did not prepare them for trades.[11] Skilled factory work, therefore, usually went to men, who left their homes to earn wages, marking the first departures from the family production system, which remained in agriculture. An industrial class picture was beginning to emerge in America.

These social and economic adjustments also had a political side as the British North American colonies became Americanized. For several generations, England, engaged elsewhere, had largely ignored details of local government, exchange, and cultural development in America. But the reassertion of control in the 1760s met with colonial resistance, from men publicly and from women in less overtly political ways. Gentlemen passed resolutions of protest, boycotted British goods, and left to women the consumers' problems of finding substitutes for the banned tea or negotiating with merchants who hoarded sugar and coffee. Women often organized themselves as Daughters of Liberty and established antitea leagues, using such substitutes as sage and birch brew. Others publicly pledged to buy only domestic products, refusing to wear clothes imported from Britain, and making a point of displaying red-white-and-blue on their clothing. Abigail Adams informed her absent husband that a hundred women had set upon "one eminent, wealthy, stingy merchant (who is a bachelor)," taken his warehouse keys, and removed the coffee for which he was charging an exorbitant six shillings per pound, but Abigail added that she, for one, refused to believe that "he had personal chastisement among them."[12]

When protests gave way to war, women often made it possible for men to go out and fight. Taking up men's jobs (as widows had been doing for a century), providing homespun clothing for soldiers and civilians, raising funds to outfit men in the field, making bullets and arms, women supported the war effort in about the same proportions as men. Those of the middle and upper classes generally remained at home during the war (having a home in which to remain) and assumed responsibility for operating the farm or plantation or shop or business. A few prominent women, like Martha Washington, visited the armies, bringing comfort and Virginia hams to their officer husbands and using their organizational skills to set up camp hospitals and social services.

But the women most immediately involved in the war of the American Revolution were the women who themselves went to war—having nowhere else to go. Poor, illiterate marginal farmers or laborers had no safe home establishment which could support their wives and children in their absence, yet army service could mean economic opportunity, particularly if soldiers received land at the conclusion of the war. They saw little choice but to join the army and take their families along. Traditionally, the British forces had taken the presence of dependents for granted, allocating a certain number of "alleged wives" to each regiment and providing them with rations, a privilege not extended to women picked up on the march. Although American armies refused formal recognition to camp followers, officers often tolerated them in practice. Women generally received half the rations given to men, children a quarter. One Virginia captain ordered three women travelling with his company to work for their food; he divided his men, assigning a third to each woman for the washing of their clothes. Ordinarily, however, the women did not perform cooking, mending, or washing chores for the men; rather, men and women saw to their own domestic needs. And the women got along as best they could, often stealing or stripping the dead in order to survive and provide for their children. George Washington regarded the camp followers as a nuisance and an embarrassment; he issued twenty-five orders regarding them, including several forbidding their riding on army wagons and at least one urging that they be hired as nurses at Valley Forge in 1778. When camp followers actually fought with the armies, they usually served with the artillery because the infantry presented too many technical problems. The romantic tale of Molly Pitcher, carrying water to her husband and assuming his place at the cannon when he fell, belongs more accurately to an authentic woman gunner, Margaret Cochran Corbin, a camp follower who swore and drank like any soldier and probably died of syphilis.[13] A few women passed as men to serve in the armies; Deborah Sampson escaped from an abusive indenture in Massachusetts to live as "Robert Shirtliffe" until a serious wound led to her discovery. But Anna Maria Lane from New Hampshire enlisted with her husband and served in the Virginia cavalry without disguising her sex.[14]

The women who followed their men to war and the women who remained at home while their men fought supported the radical concept of a nation based on democracy, but few saw any significant personal gain in this changing system. Abigail Adams might warn her husband against male tyranny and threaten feminine rebellion if the makers of the new country did not "remember the ladies." Hannah Lee Corbin could complain that she suffered "taxation without representation" when she could not vote for tax commissioners who set rates on property she owned.[15] But most women never even raised such questions. Still involved in a preindustrial society in which they worked beside men and participated in production of goods, still sharing the workplace in the home, women felt that their work had value and earned them respect. If they desired a special role in the new nation, they could find it as "republican mothers" or "mothers of civilization." Under these titles, women could use their influence in the family to teach civic virtue to their children. Women could stand for morality, moderation, and social order at the time of nation-making and expansion of the country and the society. And while women occupied themselves with such worthy endeavors, they would stop asking questions or demanding more personal or political freedom.[16]

If public moralists worried that poorer women might be idle while republican mothers spread civic virtue, new American industrialization offered a solution. In 1791, in his "Report on Manufactures," Secretary of the Treasury Alexander Hamilton argued that "women and children are rendered more useful . . . by manufacturing establishments than they would otherwise be," as was the experience of English cotton manufacture in the preceding twenty years. Moreover, Hamilton reassured farmers who feared that manufacturing would cut into the male labor supply, "the husbandman himself experiences a new source of profit and support from the increased industry of his wife and daughters." The factory would offer "occasional and extra employment to industrious individuals and families" during times when they would otherwise be idle.

Manufacturing would also provide incomes for the indigent or the economically pressed. Colonial America had not developed public institutions to care for the destitute. Poor widows were sold as bond servants; orphans were apprenticed. The scarcity of labor seemed to mean jobs for all who wanted them; and religion, society, and culture glorified work. By the end of the eighteenth century, however, many communities complained of growing numbers of dependent poor. In particular, widows became more conspicuous, and seaport communities lamented unwed mothers abandoned by sailors. Land became scarce in the older, established areas, driving some to seek homesteads in the West and others to reduce the size of their families. But other communities experienced rapid urbanization, technological change, and population increases after 1790, raising questions of employment for these masses in the villages-become-cities. Finally, curtailment of family size and the departure of men from the home workplace into the wage system left some women with less to do at home at the same time that the factory took over some of their home-manufacture production.[17]

Before American women could enter manufacturing on any large scale, however, industry had to experience technological changes which increased the demand for semiskilled and unskilled workers. America had been dominated by skilled craftsmen, and since women had little access to the necessary training, even through apprenticeship, more manufacturing was done by men. Between 1790 and the War of 1812, manufacturers established and perfected the spinning system, and a few more women took their place at the primitive looms and other machines. After 1814, however, the introduction of the power loom not only opened the modern factory system but also provided, indeed required, employment of the semiskilled or unskilled workers—ordinarily women or children—thereby freeing men to advance into more highly skilled and better paying occupations.[18]

These beginnings of the Industrial Revolution brought differences between men and women workers, and between women and "ladies." Men left the home to work for wages; women either remained at home doing unpaid domestic work or also had their labor translated into a wage scale. Women continued to breed, engage in domestic manufacture, raise and socialize children, and maintain their families, but they performed these tasks in greater isolation from their husbands. And the term "work" came to mean labor in the marketplace for pay rather than the earlier organic unity of the family producing unit. Moreover, while marriage and motherhood remained the natural expectation for a female in industrial society, fatherhood would be a desirable option for a man only after his success in labor or business secured the financial future for his family. As affluence and industrialization produced a middle class in America, the work ethic increasingly concentrated on men.[19]

Working-class people may have shared such aspirations, but they would never have married or had children if they waited for the male to acquire a sufficient measure of success to enable him, alone, to support the family establishment by his wages. In contrast to the colonial period, when a penniless servant girl might take advantage of the scarcity of women to marry (and even marry upwards) without dowry, by the early nineteenth century, maidens without marriage-portions were well advised to acquire them in factory or domestic or teaching work, particularly if they dreamed of establishing households meeting middle-class standards of propriety. Wage scales made it impossible for most working-class families to survive on a single income; therefore, sons and daughters worked outside the home while wives either went out to work or supplemented family income within the household. These changes meant a different lifestyle: no longer did life revolve around the home; no longer did men and women engage in complementary tasks which reinforced family solidarity. The isolation of home and workplace had begun.

Yet industrialization also offered some opportunities for women, especially those of the lower classes. By working in a factory, a woman could earn wages which might be used to gain power or privileges at home, most effectively through the threat of withdrawal of work or income. The working woman might also escape some social pressures, move away from the closed-community supervision of neighbors, or even leave her parents' home and decide for herself how her wages would be spent. Wages and savings also gave these young women something comparable to a dowry in seeking a marriage partner.[20]

Overall, however, the greatest impact of industrialization upon women lay in increasing divisions among women by class. Working-class women were introduced to a confused set of aspirations: "mother of civilization" gave way to "lady" as the accepted role for " true" women in the first half of the nineteenth century. Now that middle- and upper-class men could afford to keep their women at home, usually with cheap domestic servants to take on household duties, society reaffirmed the home as woman's proper sphere. Simultaneously, licensing in many professions blocked entry of women into businesses in which they had formerly engaged, reinforcing the woman in the home by leaving her no place else to go. Magazines, books, and religious literature (which the mistress of the house now had learning and leisure time enough to read) preached the four cardinal female virtues of piety, purity, submissiveness, and domesticity.[21] Middle-class standards of propriety and morality extended to "groups previously prone to disorder"; premarital pregnancies, for example, dropped from a peak 30 percent in the second half of the eighteenth century to about 10 percent by mid-nineteenth century, partly because of religious enthusiasm, which "provided an outlet for female needs" and preached sexual restraint.[22] Relieved of household drudgery, even emancipated from the care of young children, given standards of behavior by her churches and favorite authors, sustained by the financial success of father or husband, the nineteenth-century "lady" became an adornment to her man's success, a symbol of his prosperity, an ornament kept at a safe distance from the sordid workplace. Moreover, since this Jacksonian era was clearly the time of the rising middle class, these people and their ideas had a disproportionate impact. If the militant middle-class "lady" was aping the manners of the more affluent upper-class woman, she also created the belief that this was, in fact, the correct way to behave, the ideal personage to be. And women of the working class agreed.

Despite some workingmen's organizations and a few examples of labor-class militancy, the working classes failed to develop either solidarity or a strong self-image in the first half of the nineteenth century. Many early women workers came from yeoman farmer stock and entered the factories temporarily before marrying back into the yeomanry. These women did not see themselves as part of an industrial proletariat, and for many their involvement with the factory system meant only a choice of employment, not a rejection of middle-class lifestyle. Even the rural and urban poor, surrounded by stories of economic success and easily accessible frontier land, did not see their working-class status as permanent. They, too, could regard paid work for women outside the home as a transitory state, to be abandoned as soon as possible for marriage and the domestic ideal of idleness. They served as mill "girls" until they became married "ladies." Therefore, while industrialization widened the gulf between middle-class and working-class women, the same phenomenon did not sharpen class perceptions; by presenting ladyhood as the goal for all women, society insured the commitment of working-class women (and men) to the struggle for upward mobility.[23]

By the Age of Jackson, with the start of industrialization, America showed the beginnings of a working class. If the status and role of working-class women had been blurred in the colonial period by an agricultural lifestyle and the emergence of a new society and nation, the first quarter of the nineteenth century witnessed a somewhat clearer perception of hierarchies among women. But the cultural emergence of the middle-class woman occurred earlier and more rapidly than that of the working-class woman. Therefore, by the time America actually had working-class women, the society also had fixed ideas about what women should be or become. And working-class women would, for many generations, expect to become something which they were not.

2. Temporary
Working-Class Women

JUST AS FEW settlers who came to the British North American colonies in the early 1600s expected to remain in America, few of the first women who entered the primitive factories of New England expected to spend the rest of their lives in the mills. These first factory girls represented a transition from family production and hand work to large-scale industrialization. And at the same time, they established a set of attitudes about American working women.

Before industrialization, families had manufactured household and personal articles in addition to their agricultural production. Each unit tried to supply its own food, clothing, shelter, and domestic comforts, often employing the labor of all members of the family. Farmers timed such activities to complement outdoor work, usually making cloth or baskets or other goods during periods when the weather prevented work in the fields. By the eighteenth century, however, a combination of specialization and technological advance had begun to alter family production. In textile production, for example, after 1733 mechanical improvements enabled one man using a flying shuttle to weave faster than on the earlier looms, which had required the labor of two persons; additional female spinners came in to supply him with yarn. The "spinning jenny" brought more technological change in the late 1780s. Beverly, Massachusetts, claimed the first spinning mill in 1787, and Philadelphia boasted a jenny of eighty spindles the following year, even before Samuel Slater constructed his famous carding and spinning plant in Pawtucket, Rhode Island, using Richard Arkwright's water-powered spinning frame.[1]

Although textile manufacture generally remained in the handicraft stage in the home throughout the seventeenth

and much of the eighteenth centuries, the colonials promoted manufacture. Colonial assemblies in Massachusetts,
Connecticut, and Virginia encouraged the production of
linen and cotton wool, and by the early 1700s the Southern
colonies were producing sizable amounts of good quality
linen. Communities viewed the promotion of manufactures
as a form of poor relief; Boston had spinning schools for
indigent women and children in the 1720s and again in 1770.
In 1753 the Society for Encouraging Industry and Employing
the Poor celebrated its second anniversary with three hundred young women operating spinning wheels on Boston
Common. Philadelphia, which had an association employing more than a hundred spinners and weavers as early as
1764, used patriotic arguments to promote American manufactures in 1775; the United Company of Philadelphia offered
"spinning and other work" to four hundred women "who
would otherwise have been destitute," a charitable act of
self-interest repeated in 1788 by the Pennsylvania Society for
the Encouragement of Manufactures and the Useful Arts.
New York promoted linen; Georgia, silk. The women thus
employed generally did custom work, usually still in their
own homes. Most women spun or knitted by hand at home;
only a few assisted men in the shops.[2]

Early factories did not yet contain the entire cloth-making
process; cotton thread and woolen yarn, produced in the
spinning mills, were still sent to neighboring towns to be
woven at home. Men continued to weave, but increasing
numbers of women joined them. One company gave a third
of its weaving to women, while almost all the weavers attached to a New Hampshire cotton mill before the War of 1812
were female. At the same time, a few men took up machine
spinning, but the early textile industry primarily came to
employ women and children. When Secretary of the Treasury Albert Gallatin gathered information on eighty-seven
mills in 1810, he found they employed five hundred men and

seven times as many women and children. And six years later, the House of Representatives learned that ten thousand men, sixty-six thousand women and female children, and twenty-four thousand boys worked in the cotton cloth industry.[3]

An essential revolution took place in textile manufacturing in 1814 with the introduction of the first power loom at Waltham, Massachusetts. These improved machines would require only semiskilled or unskilled operators, who need not be paid the high wages of trained craftsmen. Moreover, Eli Whitney's earlier conception of interchangeable machine parts made the new equipment easier to build and maintain. Use of power-driven looms as well as the jennies brought the entire textile production process into the factory.[4] And a combination of patriotic impulse and the need for goods during the War of 1812 encouraged the development of American factory production to reduce dependency on imported items.

But early mill owners found factory labor both scarce and expensive. The population of the United States remained small, and cheap frontier land kept much of the available labor force in farming, which had been the primary American occupation for two centuries. Following the English example, Samuel Slater and other manufacturers in Rhode Island, Connecticut, and southern Massachusetts used the "family system" of employment. In the two decades after 1816, the *Massachusetts Spy* published calls for workers in seventeen towns near Worcester, generally for "families of five or six children each." Respondents were frequently illiterate, poor, marginal farmers with many children. Large numbers of workers in the family mills were children—45 percent in Massachusetts and 55 percent in Rhode Island in 1820. More than one observer described this family labor force as "often very ignorant, and too often vicious." Clearly, New England manufacturers would prefer a more docile group of employees.[5]

Entrepreneurs in Waltham solved the need for operatives in another way. The new, more complete, power-driven factory system ideally suited the needs of textile manufacturers like Francis Cabot Lowell, if they could find appropriate workers. While travelling in Europe for his health and business in 1810 and 1811, Lowell had visited the cotton manufactories of Lancashire and came under the influence of Robert Dale Owen's utopian living experiment at New Lanark. Lowell returned to the United States in 1812, as war broke out, with plans for an ideal mill and manufacturing community, one which would avoid the labor difficulties he had observed in England. With his brother-in-law and another investor, Lowell secured a charter for the Boston Manufacturing Company in 1813, selected a site in Waltham with both water power and canal transportation to the coast, capitalized the operation at $300,000, and began manufacture of cotton, woolen, and linen cloth—using women workers.[6]

More than twenty years earlier, Alexander Hamilton had reassured the nation's farmers that manufacturing would not threaten America's commitment to the land because female workers could be used rather than diverting men and boys into the factory. Throughout the eighteenth century many communities had promoted the employment of poor, abandoned, or widowed women in various manufacturing ventures. Departure of many men for attractive Western lands left a surplus of unmarried young women in the East, especially in New England. Moreover, the new machines no longer required male strength or skilled training. Women were considered more dextrous than men, hence better suited to delicate finger-movement tasks. Society assumed women could withstand the tedium of factory life better than men. And since women had traditionally worked in unskilled areas, their wage rates remained comparatively low. Finally, if the women workers could be selected from the old Yankee yeoman stock, their breeding and training would probably make them docile workers, grateful for the opportunity to leave the drudgery of the farm for the chance to earn wages before returning home to marry. Here, among the daughters of New England, were Lowell's dependable, steady, semiskilled, and inexpensive workers. As the Friends of Domestic Industry pointed out, "Daughters are now emphatically a blessing to the farmer."[7]

Of course, manufacturers had to recruit this new labor supply. Some built their factories in areas with many surrounding farms, thereby calling on the farmers' daughters (and, in slack agricultural seasons, their wives as well). Others, who employed workers whose homes were at a distance, hoped that the operatives would bring back friends when they returned from vacations. But by the early 1820s, a number of Massachusetts companies commissioned agents to travel as far as Vermont and New Hampshire to find workers. The agents spoke of adventure in the mill towns, easy and neat working conditions, leisure time for literary and cultural pursuits, and the purchase of silk dresses with factory wages. The girls were not poor in the first place, but many were bored with country life and anticipated greater opportunities for sociability, education, or independence in the cities. They also hoped for a temporary career at high wages. "Gain, and not bread, is the object of their pursuit," said one recruiting agent, who argued that "their sole object in leaving home and coming here from places so remote, and entering upon an entirely new course of life, is to make more money by their exertions than they can in any other employment. . . . Few intend to make this their permanent residence, or to devote their lives, or even a great portion of it, to the business of manufacturing." Unlike the urban poor or indigent widows for whom charitable societies had sought manufacturing employment in the previous century, these Yankee farm girls neither came from the city working classes nor intended to remain in them permanently. In a very real sense, America's first large group of working-class women were only casual visitors to that status.[8]

Factory employment still carried a stigma in agrarian America, and Yankee farmers, who had heard of British slums and degradation in factory towns, would hardly permit their daughters to go into an unprotected environment, even for good wages. Aware of this concern, manufacturers in Waltham shielded the early mill girls in carefully regulated company boarding houses under the supervision of highly respectable matrons. Since many of the first mills were constructed on sites which lacked adequate housing to begin with, the boarding houses solved both the dwelling and the morality questions, while they also gave the owners a large measure of control over their employees' nonworking hours. At Lowell and other towns which copied the "Waltham System" of boardinghouses, operatives were obliged to tell factory managers where they were living, and boardinghouse keepers, often employed or licensed by the mill owners, had to report on the names, employment, and moral and religious conduct of their residents. None but company employees could live in the boardinghouses, and the keepers were usually married women or widows with young children working in the mills. Company rules varied, but all regulated boardinghouse life in some way. Lowell doors were locked at ten o'clock in the evening; Hamilton Company employees could not entertain company "at unseasonable hours"; boarders and their families were advised to be vaccinated against disease; and most companies required regular attendance at religious worship. For the privilege of boarding, Lowell mill girls paid $1.25 per week (out of wages rarely as high as $3.00) until 1836, when a 25¢ increase was shared equally by the company and the workers; depression caused a reduction back to $1.25 in the early 1840s, but prices rose thereafter until Lowell operatives were paying $2.25 and the company an addition 50¢ toward board in the 1860s. By the

1840s some boarders complained of crowded, stuffy bedrooms, occupied by four to six girls, but in the earlier days,
when matrons competed for residents, those who worked
longest at the mill had special rooms and matrons boasted of
low rents and fine food.[9]

The boardinghouses helped many new operatives adjust to
factory life. One of the most famous of the mill girls, Harriet
Hanson, recalled the "very curious sight" of the arrival of
new country girls "dressed in various and outlandish fash-
ions, with their arms brimful of bandboxes containing all
their worldly goods." The new arrivals wore cards giving
their names—names as singular as their appearance—
Samantha, Triphena, Plumy, Kezia, Aseneth, Elgardy, Leafy,
Ruhamah, Lovey, Almaretta, Sarepta, and Florilla. They
spoke a dialect of broken English and Scottish inflected with
the nasal Yankee twang. And their sorrowful manner indicated terrible homesickness. But socialization in the mills
and boardinghouses quickly provided companionship and
education in more sophisticated town ways, and mill girls
were said to dress so tastefully that observers in church could
not distinguish them from the daughters of the town's first
citizens. Harriet Hanson also spoke of an "*esprit de corps*
among these households; any advantage secured by one of
the number was usually shared by others belonging to her set
or group." The girls shared their books, letters from home,
and literary compositions. The same solidarity carried over
into the mills, where two or three girls would tend extra
looms or frames to save the pay of a companion absent for
half a day.[10]

Education and literary endeavors ranked high among the
things for which the mill communities received praise. Unlike workers in the family mills, the girls entering the boardinghouse factories usually had some prior education; an
investigation in 1844 found only ten or twelve illiterates
among four hundred operatives at Lowell, and those were

foreign born. Some operatives worked only in the winter busy season in order to teach in country schools or attend normal schools in the summers. Many girls attended school in the evenings or formed their own "Improvement Circles." Factory girls pasted poetry or Biblical passages over their looms to be memorized.[11] This apparently pleasant and contented pursuit of learning reached a high point in the 1840s with the publication, by the girls themselves, of *The Lowell Offering.*

According to its editor, Harriet Farley, the *Offering* was intended to "adorn a tale" rather than to "point a moral." It became a vehicle for the essays, stories, letters, poems, music, and fantasies of the operatives. Stories of sugar-making expeditions, Oriental princesses, shipwrecks, and dying parents appeared beside poems of nature, friendship, and dreams of rich marriages. The *Offering* and similar journals, like the *Operatives Magazine,* fit well into the sentimental literature of their day. Moreover, few periodicals at that time were composed and edited by women. Contributions to the *Offering,* said Harriet Hanson, added to a girl's desirability as a wife. "No doubt these young men thought that, if a young woman had the writing talent, rare in those days, she naturally would have other rare talents towards the making of a good wife," she reasoned, although Victorians feared that literary endeavors could produce mental and uterine damage.[12]

The *Offering* provided the mill girls with an outlet for their own realities and fancies; many of their contributions dealt with nature or New England life, but a considerable number of fictional accounts spoke of their reasons for being in the mills. The "Susan Miller" story is typical. According to its author, the death of her drunkard father left Susan's family not only without support but also heavily in debt; the farm was mortgaged, and the family even owed the local dressmaker for their mourning clothes. As the oldest child,

Susan tried to comfort her shocked mother and, declaring herself "young and strong," assumed care of the family. Her own hopes for marriage had been blighted when her suitor lost interest while she had been confined at home during her father's final struggle with delerium tremens, and he offered no assistance now. First arranging with their principal creditor not to evict the family from their farm while she earned enough to settle the mortgage, Susan decided to go to Lowell to find work, dismissing warnings of that town's wickedness and corruption with a simple faith in her own virtue. After instructing her younger sister in the household duties which would insure their mother's comfort, Susan left for Lowell. On the first day, she found mill work exhausting, the women cold and heartless, and her boardinghouse room strange and lacking in comforts. But each day brought greater pleasure, she said, as she adjusted to her new life, found her wages high, and took comfort in the knowledge that her income went for a "noble cause." Each quarter she sent a payment to the creditor. After two years, a sister joined her, as did others later, although she opposed their coming too early so that their minds and bodies might be strengthened by country life. She regarded her life as happy, spoke glowingly of strong friendships in the factory and the comforts of her church, rejoiced in occasional visits home, and remained in Lowell a year after the debt had been paid, when she returned to her mother and younger brothers and sister, announcing her expectation that she would become an old maid.[13] Similar stories glorified hard work for noble purposes.

The *Lowell Offering* never pretended to advocate reform, and its editors vigorously avoided either class or labor crusades. The magazine grew out of the girls' own improvement societies under the sponsorship of the local Universalist minister. From the beginning, Harriet Farley and her assistant, Harriot Curtis, believed that the journal should defend the respectability and culture of the operatives by displaying their charming, virtuous, and inspirational compositions. For the same reasons, editorials supported and defended factory life, reasoning that any exposure of deteriorating conditions might reflect badly on the characters of the mill girls rather than on the owners. In 1845, when significant labor unrest struck Lowell, and female labor reform associations arose to demand improvements in wages and working conditions, working-class and reform critics attacked the *Lowell Offering* as an organ of the corporation, engaged in deliberately misleading efforts to gloss over the harsh realities of factory and boardinghouse existence. Harriet Farley vigorously denied charges that she was "a vile tool for aristocratic tyrants" and said that the perilous financial conditions of the journal proved the withdrawal of the owners' support. Whatever evils might be connected to the factory system would not be remedied by denunciations in the *Offering,* she argued, although she granted that "it is much easier to instill a feeling of self-respect, of desire for excellence, among the well-paid, than an ill-paid class of operatives," and she occasionally gave information about working hours and conditions. But she found the situation at Lowell no more confining and dull than "the lot of most New England females." Despite her protestations, the magazine, already in financial difficulty, did not survive long after the attacks, although Harriet Farley did establish and edit a successor journal, the *New England Offering,* from 1847 to 1850.[14]

Throughout the lifetime of the *Lowell Offering,* and even from the beginning of the establishment of the boarding-house mills, New England society showed great concern for the respectability and character of the mill girls. One of the frequently cited reasons for the construction of the boarding-houses revolved around the protection of virtue, and many observers, both European and American, in the 1820s and 1830s praised the respectability of young women living under the Waltham system. Even President Andrew Jackson declared himself favorably impressed. By the late 1830s, however, after sporadic labor protests, the *Boston Daily Times* began to question "the scale of civilization, health, morals, and intellectuality" of the Lowell mill workers, printing stories that mill girls went to "infamous places of resort" after dances and "were not returned to their homes until daylight," or publishing a physician's indiscreet remarks about his treatment of girls for venereal diseases and claims that New York and Boston prostitutes sought millwork when they became diseased.[15] Almost immediately, the *Lowell Courier* rushed to the defense in editorials as well as a series of articles by Dr. Elisha Bartlett, later issued as a pamphlet under the title "A Vindication of the Character and Condition of the Females Employed in the Lowell Mills against the Charges contained in the Boston Times and Boston Quarterly Review." After some unkind observations about the editor of the *Review* and assertions of his own independence, Dr. Bartlett responded to the substance of the criticism, defending both the conditions of the boardinghouses and the requirement by some corporations for residence. Speaking of health, he claimed a very low death rate for operatives, praised their diet, and argued that 80 percent of the girls thought themselves as healthy as or healthier than they were before they entered the mills. As for the attacks on morality, Dr. Bartlett first registered shock and then praised the girls' intelligence, educational level, religious participation, and savings accounts, as well as the supervision by boardinghouse matrons and mill overseers, whose "censorship is despotic," concluding that any moral lapse would lead to dismissal. He compared the Lowell girls favorably in all respects to seamstresses in large coastal cities and to the factory population of Portsmouth.[16] Two years later the debate resumed when an unnamed "Citizen of Lowell" wrote a reply in the *Vox Populi,* reprinted as a pamphlet called "Corporations and Operatives: Being an Exposition of the Condition of Factory Operatives, and a Review of the 'Vindication,' by Elisha Bartlett, M.D." This critic vilified the *Courier* as a paid tool of the factory owners, attacked Bartlett's selective statistics and his comparison with the decaying town of Portsmouth, and argued hotly about wages and working conditions.[17] But as late as 1850, in a book of advice to "young ladies who are dependent on their own exertions," Rev. James Porter continued to praise the character of the mill girls, again citing the boardinghouses' and operatives' support of the churches in his argument that the factory business was honorable and that vocation should not be a criterion for respectability.[18]

While many of the mill girls may have appreciated these chivalrous defenses, a significant number could, and did, speak for themselves, offering a considerable body of literature describing their lives, expectations, conduct, and reasons for working. Although some critics have charged that these more prosperous, middle-class factory girls offer a distorted view of their experiences in working-class life,[19] writers like Harriet Farley or Lucy Larcom or Harriet Hanson never pretended to be speaking for an industrial proletariat, and their testimony usually dealt with the early days when the Waltham System still depended on the daughters of Yankee farmers as a labor supply, rather than the 1840s and 1850s, when the factory population had changed.

Perhaps the best known of the articulate mill girls, Lucy Larcom, came from a Huguenot family in Beverly, Massachusetts. When Lucy's captain father died, leaving a large family of children from two marriages, the widowed mother went to Lowell as matron of a boardinghouse. Mrs. Larcom tried to keep her children in school—Lucy had begun at age two—but financial difficulties forced her to agree to send her daughters into the mills. Lucy, then eleven or twelve, later recalled, "I thought it would be a pleasure to feel that I was not a trouble or burden or expense to anybody." She found the work easy, with intervals when she could play, but her family became dependent on her weekly income of a dollar and she could not be spared to attend high school, although she was academically prepared. Instead, she sought outlets through writing, publishing pieces in the *Lowell Offering.* But Lucy had few illusions: "We did not call ourselves ladies," she said almost fifty years later; "we did not forget that we were working girls, wearing coarse aprons suitable to our work, and that there was some danger of our becoming drudges." On the other hand, ten years in the Lowell mills taught Lucy Larcom both that "the world's workers ... are more honorable company than its idlers," and that coarse work had value, as great as refined employment, "for occupations, like bodies, receive their value from the soul that animates them." Yet Lucy, too, made a point of asserting the moral worth of the mill girls and the concern of owners like Francis Cabot Lowell that the mill community be kept "free from all that could be harmful to personal character." Mill girls, she said, read good books, primarily a Bible brought from home, but also essays, stories, and verse, and they formed their own Improvement Circles, attended lyceum lectures, wrote for the *Lowell Offering,* and spoke of the influence of nearby utopian communities such as Brook Farm. Lucy graduated from Lowell's mills to teach school and attend college. Eventually she returned to Beverly to teach literature, write prize-winning poetry, instruct at Wheaton Seminary, where she founded the college newspaper, and contribute both prose and poetry to a variety of journals, often on the subject of her early life in the mills.[20]

Lucy's contemporary Harriet Hanson achieved similar fame as a writer. Her family also moved to Lowell after the father's death, and her mother kept a boardinghouse. Harriet became a bobbin doffer at age ten, engaged in her first labor protest the next year, contributed sporadically to the *Lowell Offering,* and married William Stevens Robinson, abolitionist editor of the *Lowell Courier,* in 1848. During the 1850s and Civil War years, Harriet supported her husband's antislavery activities and political career and, after his death, worked for woman suffrage. But in the 1880s and 1890s, she recalled her factory career in a number of publications, some sharing Lucy Larcom's conservative and romantic reminiscences of the Lowell community—the respectable mill girls and their noble motives for working: "the most prevailing incentive to our labor was to secure the means of education for some *male* member of the family." But others complained of the low caste of factory girls and the cruel treatment of overseers, to whom the worker "was but a brute, a slave, to be beaten, pinched, and pushed around."[21]

About ten years older than Lucy Larcom and Harriet Hanson, Harriet Farley came to the mills from New Hampshire, where her father served as a Congregational minister and schoolmaster. She had already contributed to her family's support for about ten years by teaching and various home manufactures such as shoe-binding and plaiting straw for hats. The move to Lowell in 1837 represented a new independence for Harriet, who found particular satisfaction in the Improvement Circle there. Her defense of mill owners against the attacks of Orestes Brownson brought her to the attention of the sponsor of the *Lowell Offering,* and Harriet exchanged mill work for the editorship of that journal in 1842. More conservative than the younger Lucy Larcom and Harriet Hanson, Harriet Farley wrote polite, sentimental, or defensive editorials upholding the virtue and especially the intelligence of the mill girls, while she published their own pieces of a similar tone. When the *Lowell Offering* failed to survive the attacks of labor militants in 1845, she wrote for other women's periodicals, including *Godey's Lady's Book.*

Eventually, she married an inventor and retired from literary work at his insistence, although she wrote again after his death.[22]

In contrast, Harriet Farley's assistant editor of the *Lowell Offering,* Harriot F. Curtis, was of less reserved character. Harriet Hanson described her mind as "intensely masculine," and she sharply resented the limitations her contemporaries placed on women. Already known as a novelist before she joined the *Offering,* she acted as its business manager and travelling agent for three years, making the magazine self-supporting. Leaving that job to care for her blind, aged mother and later an invalid niece, she had little success in finding gainful employment, refused the "solution" of marriage, and continued writing novels while supporting such causes as abolition and "equal pay for equal labor."[23]

Most of the mill girls came from similar backgrounds; a number achieved later distinction. Laura Currier, one of four sisters in the mills, went on to establish the library in Haverhill, New Hampshire. Eliza Jane Cate wrote eight books. Margaret Foley became a sculptor and cameo-cutter. Lydia S. Hall did missionary work among the Choctaw Indians, survived the rigors of "Bleeding Kansas," and served as "acting U.S. Treasurer in the absence of a male chief." And Clementine Averill won brief fame in 1850 for a vigorous defense of operatives against the attacks of an Alabama senator who had tried to argue that Southern slaves were better off than Northern factory workers.[24]

Of the other thousands, almost nothing is known of their personal feelings beyond what was recorded by their more articulate coworkers, although it is possible to discover their hours, wages, and conditions of work. In the 1820s manufacturing employees in Massachusetts generally worked twelve or thirteen hours per day except on Sundays, although a few places recorded hours as long as fifteen or sixteen. By the 1830s the summer workday lasted from 5:00 A.M. until sundown, and in the winter the day began "as soon as the hands can see to advantage," continuing until 7:00 or 7:30 P.M. Similar estimates of eleven to thirteen hours, depending on the month, prevailed in the 1840s. But operatives increasingly complained that the work day was extended from five to thirty minutes by overseers changing clocks or delaying bells. Hours varied according to task, with spinners and weavers often working longer than warpers, whose work required them to stand. But some girls chose long hours, since they were usually paid by the piece and desired to earn as much as possible.[25]

Not all operatives worked the full year or remained employed permanently. "Those of the mill girls who had homes," said Harriet Hanson, "generally worked from eight to ten months in the year; the rest of the time was spent with parents or friends." Some taught school in the summer. And a Massachusetts law forbade the employment of anyone under fifteen years of age for more than nine months per year, the rest of the time to be spent at school. At the same time, girls might move to another mill or leave the industry; an 1845 study found 25 percent of the girls in eight Lowell mills had been there less than a year, 50 percent less than three years, and only 5 percent more than ten years.[26] From the beginning of the Waltham System, the Yankee mill girls had regarded their factory years as temporary, usually until they returned home to marry. They came to the mills in search of financial gain rather than a new career and lifestyle.

The mill girls, therefore, placed considerable emphasis on their high factory wages, since they could not earn as much in any other occupation. Before the factory system came to New England, a woman might earn between $2 and $3 per month in addition to her board, usually at domestic or farm work or in teaching. But early prejudices against the factory required owners to offer more favorable rates in order to lure the farm girls to the mills. As early as 1812, women cotton spinners in southern Massachusetts earned between $2.33 and $2.75 a week, of which they paid board and washing bills of $1.08 to $1.16. By the late 1830s, Lowell mills paid women between $1.00 and $3.00 a week in addition to board; similar averages were reported in New York, New Hampshire, Vermont, Maine, Connecticut, Rhode Island, New Jersey, Pennsylvania, Delaware, Maryland, and Virginia, although wages were higher in New England than in the South. Unlike the family mills of Rhode Island, owners of the boardinghouse mills did not build company stores; nor did they pay in script. Lowell operatives received cash wages each month and could save or spend their income where they chose. Throughout the 1830s and 1840s, manufacturers reduced the piece rates, but by tending more looms and using improved machinery, the girls could generally maintain the same weekly income. Harriet Hanson claimed that overseers accepted the girls' own tallies of the number of pieces produced and that they were paid for overtime, but the machines usually carried measuring clocks as well.[27]

If the early mill girls found the comparatively high wages they had sought in the factory towns, the sense of independence, which also lured them there, remained subject to many restrictions. Whether to assert control over the new factory force or to redeem promises of their continued respectability, many owners using the Waltham System required that the operatives live in company-owned boardinghouses, where the printed regulations included the hanging up of bonnet and shawl, the seating at table by length of service in the mill, the prohibition of "unnecessary dirt ... such as apple cores or peels, or nut shells," and the requirement that each boarder retire to bed when the doors were locked at ten o'clock. Many companies refused employment to "any one who is habitually absent from public worship on the Sabbath," although only one corporation specified the church its employees must attend. Within the factories, some overseers locked operatives in during working hours (leading to several disasters when fire broke out). A Dover, New Hampshire, company forbade "spiritous liquor, smoking, or any kind of amusement" on its premises, and all manufacturers discharged employees for immoral conduct. Operatives needed their overseers' permission to be absent from work and received it only in serious cases and when other workers could be found to do the job. Moreover, millhands might be subject to many more rules than appeared in print, and owners enforced the regulations so unevenly as to give no clear guidelines of what workers might expect in practice, beyond the requirement that they satisfy their overseers and supervisors. One rule in particular changed in purpose and enforcement over time—the obligation that new employees remain in the mill a full year. When homesick girls left the early mills after only a few weeks, or rival firms hired away skilled workers just as they had completed their training, owners instituted the one-year agreement to insure a dependable labor force. But as turnouts, strikes, and labor discontent interrupted production in the 1830s and 1840s, manufacturers used this regulation to rid themselves of agitators and strikers, introducing a virtual "blacklist" to keep operatives at their jobs.[28]

By the late 1820s, cotton mill workers did occasionally walk out of their factories in protest against some change in wages, hours, or working conditions. Men and women protested lower wages and longer hours as early as 1824 in Pawtucket, Rhode Island, and in July 1828 young boys and girls in Patterson, New Jersey, struck successfully against a change in their dinner hour from twelve to one o'clock. But the first significant strike of female factory workers occurred at Dover, New Hampshire, in December 1828, when three or four hundred girls and women marched in procession out of the factory in reaction to seven "obnoxious regulations," including requirements that persons entering the yard or leaving work have the agent's or overseer's permission, a 12½¢ fine for arriving after the bell, prohibition of talking at work except on business, and operatives' obligation to apply for permission to leave their employment. Press reaction to the walkout ranged from horror to hilarity; one journal said that the strike showed "the Yankee sex in a new and unexpected light" and wondered whether the governor would have to "call out the militia to prevent a gynecocracy," while others ignored the strike itself but quoted the placard inscriptions and antiemployer poetry carried by the workers on their public march. Soon after the incident, Dover manufacturers required employees to sign the usual agreements, with the addition of a pledge to accept wages set by the employer and not to "be engaged in any combination whereby the work may be impeded or the company's interest in any way injured." But in 1834 eight hundred Dover women again struck against a wage reduction, although this time they rejected street parades for a meeting in the courthouse, at which they passed resolutions against reduced wages and against the owners' efforts to starve the strikers into submission, and called on editors to oppose "the system of slavery attempted to be established in our manufacturing establishments." Again, conservatives argued that the women should be grateful to be employed at all, and the operatives returned to work unsatisfied.[29]

Even Lowell, where the Waltham System appeared at its most harmonious, experienced walkouts in 1834 and 1836. When Lowell manufacturers announced a 15 percent decrease in wages effective 1 March 1834, a change the *Lowell Journal* called a "small reduction," the girls held a number of meetings. The young woman who presided lost her position in the mill, and when she received her final wages, she waved her bonnet in the air as a signal to the nearly eight hundred women workers to leave the factory and march through the town. A strike leader delivered a passionate oration on the rights of women and the evils of the "monied aristocracy." Within three days, newspapers reported two thousand strikers and spoke of the women issuing a proclamation for union solidarity and restoration of the wage rates. But gradually, girls drifted back into the mills, or others from surrounding areas came to take their places. And the press criticized the strikers who, even at reduced rates, would be earning more than women could get at other occupations in New England. Two years later, another strike protested an increase in the price of board which meant 12½¢ less spendable pay for the girls. The corporations now faced a dilemma involving two groups of their female constituents. Boardinghouses were leased to matrons on the understanding that they would charge no more than $1.25 per week, but housekeepers had to pay increasing prices for produce and claimed that they could no longer house and feed mill girls at this rate, while the operatives earned $2.50 per week. Accordingly, about twenty-five hundred mill girls formed the Factory Girls Association, agreed to deal with the owners only through the union, and indulged in speeches comparing the manufacturers' actions to those which had led to the American Revolution. Despite their strong resolve the protestors were back at work within a month, "fairly starved out," according to one newspaper. Similar strikes, with the same results, took place at Patterson, New Jersey, and several places in Pennsylvania in the 1830s.[30]

On the surface, these worker protests seemed to involve simple issues of reduction in wages or increase in the number of machines operatives had to tend, but the underlying questions were much more complex. Textile mills depended on investors for their capital, investors who demanded a high rate of return on their money. Throughout the 1820s and into the 1830s, most mills paid well; the Boston Manufacturing Company returned investors' original money within four years, and other mills paid out dividends of 5½ to 14 percent

throughout the prosperous 1830s and even into the early
1840s, despite a general economic decline. But poor management and increases in the price of raw cotton cut into profits,
and agents had to find means to maintain investors' profits.
Technological improvements provided a partial answer
since they made possible increased production. In a process
known as the "speed-up," operatives tended more and faster
machines while receiving lower piece rates for each item
produced. In effect, however, operatives' net wages remained
about the same because the new machines produced cloth
more rapidly and took on some of the tasks previously done
by hand. Even with the speed-up, the work was not strenuous, although it became much more monotonous than it had
been when the factories opened twenty years earlier. To the
mill girls, the issue was not technological improvements,
which left their total wages about the same, but rather reduction in the rates, which seemed to force them to work
harder. To complete the circle, striking mill girls withdrew
their savings from Lowell banks, leading to complaints by
the owners that the capital base for the mills was now even
more restricted.

At the same time, factory work lost some of its relative
attractiveness. Wages in other occupations, such as teaching,
rose; mill work was no longer the highest paid respectable
occupation for women in New England. And the combination of the speed-up and the increasing monotony of their
work led operatives to notice the dismal atmosphere of their
employment—the thick stone walls, small windows, gloomy
lighting, lack of fresh air, incessant machine noises, flying
lint, and stinking whale-oil lamps. (And if these conditions
prevailed in the large boardinghouse mills of the Waltham
System, which were constantly subject to public observation,
the less publicized family mills were probably even worse.)

Even when business conditions improved in the 1840s,
wage reductions continued or piece rates moved up and

down in relation to the speed of the machines and the number of looms tended by each worker. Sometimes, operatives who wanted to maintain income levels or earn more actually requested the speed-up, but ordinarily they merely resented wage reductions and resorted to sporadic strikes.

Some of these walkouts indicate temporary labor organizations, but usually the strikes failed because operatives could not muster more than brief displays of picturesque resistance, often under a patriotic theme, and were poorly equipped to survive without their mill wages, especially when they lived in mill-controlled boardinghouses. Lacking organization, leadership, financial support, and techniques to make use of their numbers, the operatives actually engaged in demonstrations rather than effective strikes. Most operatives, including many early protestors, preferred to trust their employers rather than seek assistance from "outsiders" such as government, but employers imposed contracts which included dismissal and blacklisting for strikers. The public disapproved of striking women or laughed at them, despite their appeals to democracy, republicanism, and the ideals of the American Revolution. Male trade unionists supported women only when they were well-established in skilled sectors of the trade, such as New York bookbinders. New England textile men passed sympathetic resolutions when mill girls protested for their rights, but the National Trades Union, meeting in 1836, expressed concern at "the injurious tendencies the introduction of the female system has upon the male operatives." And women themselves looked to the ideal of True Womanhood—woman's place in the middle-class home—rather than to public activity, especially labor agitation.[31]

Although many of the early labor walkouts involved wages or regulations, by the 1840s protests increasingly concentrated on the length of the workday. Requests for shorter working hours began as early as 1825 and the issue resurfaced throughout the 1830s, when workers wanted fewer hours but rejected any plan to reduce wages accordingly. As the abolitionist movement gained publicity, workers began to speak of "wage slavery." And as middle-class concepts of womanhood spread, workers used the argument that civic virtue would decline if future mothers had no time for "moral, religious, and intellectual culture." At the same time, local unions and individual reformers started to coordinate their efforts into workingmen's associations, several of which included women.

While earlier turnouts seem to have been spontaneous and sporadic responses to particular incidents or grievances, the ten-hour struggle of the 1840s represented more organized, sustained activity. In Western Pennsylvania, for example, factory women demanded higher wages and the end of the store-order system at the beginning of the 1840s; by 1843 they again turned out to object to longer hours without a raise in pay; and the following year they protested another pay cut. But in 1845 they shifted from wages to hours, and although their strike did not win the ten-hour day they wanted, they did elicit a promise from employers that they might continue the ten-hour agitation and that Pittsburgh owners would institute the ten-hour day when it was adopted elsewhere. Realizing the importance of united efforts, therefore, the Pennsylvania women sought cooperation in New England, especially in Lowell and Manchester, where cotton-mill operatives had established labor organizations.[32]

Agitation for higher wages and shorter hours in Lowell led to the founding of the Lowell Female Labor Reform Association in January 1845, under the leadership of Sarah G. Bagley. A veteran of ten years' employment as a piece weaver in two Lowell mills, Bagley gradually became disillusioned with factory life and throughout the early 1840s encouraged a number of protests against conditions. When the Massachusetts legislature of 1844 established a special commission to investigate American labor conditions, she organized more than four hundred members into the Female Labor Reform Association to speak to the lawmakers on behalf of the operatives and, if that strategy failed, to appeal to the public for support of workers' rights. Hearings began in February 1845, with Sarah Bagley and other articulate women workers offering testimony regarding their wages, hours, health, and working conditions. Only a few years earlier, society had been shocked when women spoke out in public on behalf of the slave; nineteenth-century ideals of womanhood praised modesty and reticence over publicity and argumentation. But the Lowell girls had already established something of a bluestocking reputation, and they now argued that their intellectual achievements were jeopardized by factory conditions which left them little energy or time for their former well-known literary and cultural pursuits.

Although their main objective was a ten-hour day, the mill girls testified about many other aspects of their working and living situations. Wages now averaged $2 per week in addition to board. Workers complained that a speed-up usually accompanied each pay cut. Food and lodging had deteriorated in the boardinghouses, with girls sleeping six in a room, two in a bed. In winter, factory air remained foul from hundreds of whale-oil lamps, lighted because operatives began work before daybreak; dozens of women became ill from the fumes. One woman declared that she had lost one year's work in seven because of illness.

The legislators listed carefully to this evidence and were so impressed by the intelligence, virtue, and articulateness of the witnesses, and by their efforts in securing a thousand signatures to their petition for reform—as well as by the charming flower beds the owners planted around the factories and boardinghouses—that they concluded that "labor is on an equality with capital and indeed controls it." Such strong-minded operatives could clearly take care of themselves, the legislators decided; they did not need the interference of the state.[33]

Meanwhile, Sarah Bagley and her colleagues tried to rally popular opinion to their cause. When the *Lowell Offering* refused to become an instrument for reform, Bagley denounced its editor as "a mouthpiece of the corporations" and led such attacks on the periodical that it ceased publication within a year. Articles rejected by the *Offering* were distributed as pamphlets, and when a workingman's paper, the *Voice of Industry,* moved to Lowell, it became a major outlet for the ten-hour reformers.[34]

The Lowell Female Labor Reform Association also affiliated with the New England Workingmen's Association and used its conventions to expose grievances. Largely because of the presence of the women's groups, the association altered its constitution and changed its name to the New England Labor Reform League. This body passed resolutions against blacklisting for labor activities and in support of both the character and the objectives of the mill girls. Sarah Bagley and her associates also encouraged the formation of similar female labor reform associations in other communities such as Dover in New Hampshire, Fall River in Massachusetts, and New York City. In these places as well, the groups sought favorable press coverage and outlets for the ten-hour argument. They expanded to include women in other occupations —tailoresses, seamstresses, shirt makers, bookbinders, cap makers, straw workers, and others—uniting them under the Biblical argument that "the laborer is worthy of his hire." Social leaders sometimes supported these groups, offering financial aid and moral endorsements, including letters to newspapers defending the conduct of the working women at their meetings.[35]

These groups also employed more sophisticated means of securing their goals. In the past, grievances had led to near-spontaneous walkouts which lasted no more than a few days because the strikers lacked financial support other than their wages; they were doubly caught since rents to the company-controlled boardinghouses were part of those wages. Moreover, participation in a turnout could mean dismissal with loss of wages already owed and might lead to the blacklist, which would prevent employment in other factories. But the constitution of the Lowell Female Labor Association pledged members to "disapprove of all hostile measures, strikes, and turn-outs until all pacific measures proved abortive." The union addressed the legislature by petition and testimony rather than strikes, which would have evoked public hostility. Workers sought favorable public attention by presenting ten-hour orations at "social gatherings." When a large Lowell corporation announced a simultaneous speed-up and reduction in the piece rates, operatives held a meeting rather than a turnout, and nearly every woman worker pledged not to accept the increased load until she also received additional pay; the company cancelled the speed-up. Finally, in 1847, the Lowell group reorganized itself into the Lowell Female Industrial Reform and Mutual Aid Society, with initiation fees, dues, and fines for nonattendance to raise money for a sick fund, as well as broad commitments to "the mental, moral and physical improvement of this sex."[36] Although the new association reaffirmed its commitment to unionism, Sarah Bagley and the earlier militants faded from the organization, perhaps because the reformers had accomplished their original purpose—the ten-hour law.

"All Hail New Hampshire!" said the *Voice of Industry* on 9 July 1847, "the Ten Hour Bill passed the House by one hundred and forty-four majority!" Pennsylvania followed in 1848, New Jersey in 1851, although these successes included provisions whereby employers could offer their operatives "special contracts" giving them the option of working more than ten hours—which in practice became a choice between a longer work day and no work at all. New York editor Horace Greeley and other critics had some hard words for this "egregious flummery."[37]

Reform agitation, with its small and partial successes and more frequent failures, showed clearly that mill conditions had deteriorated by the 1840s and that the Yankee girls found factory life significantly less attractive than they had twenty and thirty years earlier. When Francis Cabot Lowell and similar men established their model factory communities, farmers' daughters were drawn by opportunities for independence and adventure, as well as more interesting work at higher wages than they could find as dairymaids or schoolteachers at home or as seamstresses or straw braiders in other towns. Boardinghouse life complemented relationships which arose in mills, and as late as the 1830s many of these corporations represented attractive young feminine enclaves. In July 1836, for example, the Hamilton Manufacturing Company had a work force 74 percent female, 96 percent native-born, 80 percent between fifteen and thirty years old, and 75 percent living in boardinghouses. The sense of community ran strong, with considerable peer encouragement (and pressure) for cooperation both in cultural activities and in labor protests; 95 percent of the women who struck the Hamilton mill in October 1836 lived in boardinghouses, as did three-quarters of the signers of the ten-hour petition in 1845.[38]

But by the 1840s many Yankee mill girls found more to protest and less to praise in their factories. Why journey to Lowell to share a bedroom with five other girls? Why work seventy-two and more hours per week for $2, when schoolteachers' wages were increasing? Why try to bargain with unreceptive mill owners over piece wages and speed-ups? Why compete for deteriorating wages with an immigrant population to whom such low pay actually meant an improvement over their European poverty? And why fight against growing sentiment for the protection of native-born ladies, when they might marry local young men who could take advantage of cheap land or increasing opportunities for both rural and urban nonindustrial employment?[39] For a while, Yankee and immigrant worked side by side, with no apparent disagreements or change in the work quality or behavior of the workers. But gradually the mills and mill communities changed. Lowell, for example, grew from seventeen to thirty-three thousand between 1830 and 1850, and its employed population increased from sixty-one hundred to eleven thousand four hundred in the same years. And while the Hamilton Company hired only 4 percent foreign-born workers in 1836, it employed 62 percent non-natives in 1860, with the Irish alone constituting 47 percent of the total work force. In some cases, the older type of factory worker left the mills because she refused to compete with cheaper, immigrant labor. But more often, New England girls simply found the factories less attractive and abandoned them, leaving empty places into which Irish and other immigrants flowed.[40]

The Yankee girls went home—but they had never intended to become permanent members of the working classes in any case. Their presence in the factories simply marked a transition stage, a period which established the presence of women in manufacturing employment. At the same time, they created historical grounds for the assumption that women who worked did so from choice rather than necessity and that they would remain on the job only until they could find something else they would prefer to do.

3. Immigrant Women from Several Cultures

IN THE FIRST days of industrialization, most American manufacturers preferred to hire native labor, even offering attractive wages to secure what they regarded as a more docile and dependable work force. But within a generation, the population of cotton textile mills and other industries had become more markedly ethnic, and family employment replaced the experiments of the Waltham System. First the Irish and then other European immigrants entered the factories, accepting wages which were better than they had found in the old country but lower than native-born workers demanded. This new population experienced a series of adjustments to America; some assimilated outright into the new host culture while others retained portions of the cultural and intellectual baggage brought from Europe. For the women in particular, transition from Europe to America marked not only changes in geography and lifestyle, but also adjustments in terms of the technological developments taking place within industrialized America.

A gradual change began in the mid-1830s and accelerated throughout the 1840s. Irish women first entered the New England textile factories as waste pickers and scrub women, and the Yankee girls found their speech and dress as curious as the earlier mill girls had found the manners of the newer country girls. By the 1840s a combination of potato famines and rent problems drove many Irish from their homeland. Increasing numbers sought factory employment in America. Other groups from the Continent came in search of land or work or political refuge, especially after 1848, and the ethnic composition of the American working classes began to show their impact as early as the 1850s. By then, industry was well established, a labor supply no longer so scarce, and manufac-

turers sought cheaper workers. Moreover, continued technological improvements of the machines meant less skill
required of those who tended them; thus, employment opportunities increased for untrained women and children at the
same time that native-born females withdrew from the factories in search of better wages or more "proper" and "wom-
anly" occupations.

Just as they had sent out agents to gather farm girls for
factory work, manufacturers now encouraged European immigration. Half the Lowell operatives were Irish in the
1850s, and overseers from Lowell, New Bedford, Salem, and
other communities imported families from Canada and Europe to work in their mills. Within ten years, the Lawrence
factories employed American, English, Irish, Scottish, German, Italian, French, Canadian, and Portuguese operatives,
and employment records of at least one Massachusetts factory contain significant numbers of Lebanese and other Middle Eastern names.[1]

Throughout much of the nineteenth century, these ethnic
groups remained more aware of their differences than of
their common condition as a working class, and American-
born workers nourished nativist prejudices against immigrants, particularly the unskilled women workers. Despite
brief periods of cooperation, any development of working-
class consciousness or solidarity would be delayed by old-
country rivalries and the increasing subdivision of labor
according to skill and sex. In Philadelphia, for example, artisans formed a Merchants' Union of Trade Associations in the
late 1820s but felt no identity of interest with unskilled laborers who were drawn increasingly from immigrant and
female groups. Or, where urban industrialization affected
basic crafts, as in Newark, New Jersey, while adult males
continued to dominate both in craft work and in household
organization, each craft split into hostile ethnic and religious groups. Both bourgeoisie and workers began to live in

neighborhoods segregated by wealth. Occupations of women also varied by ethnic groups: English, Irish, German, and Scandinavian immigrant women who spoke or learned English gravitated toward domestic service as the century continued, while Italian, Russian, Polish, and Slavic girls worked in manufacturing. And while immigrant women, even wives, worked for pay in greater proportions than white native-born women, these immigrant families still hoped to achieve sufficient economic security and American success levels to be able to keep at least their married women at home, in imitation of the native-born middle class.[2]

The experiences of these immigrant women in America frequently depended as much on their European origins and the social and cultural ideas they and their group brought with them as they did on conditions prevailing in the United States in the era of their arrival.

Unlike a number of other groups, the Irish came to America to stay. Driven out by crop failures and rents, accustomed to working and earning as families, concerned with earning for survival rather than asserting their character and intellectual achievements, the Irish represented the first large non-English and non-native addition to the American working classes. While single persons might take up domestic or farm labor, many families sought work in New England textile mills, precisely because that industrial system could now take maximum advantage of the work skills of the entire family.

By the 1840s Irish women had graduated from scrubwomen to operatives, performing the full range of factory tasks in increasing proportions. Only 37.5 percent of spinners were Irish women in 1850, but that group grew to 76.7 percent in 1865. Weavers showed a more dramatic shift, from 18.2 to 66.6 percent in the same years. But wages did not rise significantly. Spinners earned an average of $11.33 per month in 1850 and $14.07 in 1865; weavers went from $13.70 to $19.26.

Only dressers, where the Irish first increased threefold and then dropped by half, earned a dramatic $23.62 in 1865 in contrast to $13.02 in 1850; but only 18.2 percent of dressers were Irish women. And even these wage figures are distorted, since Irish workers were clustered at the lower end of the wage scales, earning less than the averages. Because of the low wages, the Irish sent their children into the factories, and technology accommodated them. Machine improvements and automation obliged workers to tend more and faster machines, but the same factors made those jobs less complex and opened them to unskilled labor. A hierarchy of work assignments based on skill intensified old sex distinctions in jobs; trained men had access to skilled and supervisory positions with higher wages and status, while women and children received no industrial education and were relegated to lower pay scales of secondary or supplementary workers. High turnover rates, especially for women, seemed to indicate that immigrant women, like the earlier Yankee mill girls, also regarded factory work as transitory; almost two-thirds of female workers stayed in Lowell mills less than four years in the mid-1840s, with periods of absence, and in 1855 only 7 percent of the women had been present for five years. In particular, women left paid work upon marriage, although some were taking factory piecework into their homes in the 1860s.[3]

Yankee girls often worked from choice rather than for survival, although many of them eventually contributed to their families' well-being; the Irish worked as families out of necessity, to meet current needs. In a New England town in the 1860s, a family with three children required about $500 to live for one year, yet the father typically earned only about $270 in the mill. This family, therefore, needed the wages of the woman and children, but since the Irish wife-mother increasingly remained at home, the earning burden shifted to the children. In contrast to Ireland, where the father could hire out his family's labor as a unit for a price paid to him, New England manufacturers paid each worker separately according to task, and even the practice of handing over wages of an entire family to its male head quickly broke down in favor of separate payments. Not only did the father lose the prestige of handling the family's income, but in some recorded cases, the children contributed up to 72 percent of the group's earnings. Adult sons and daughters remained in the factory at the sacrifice both of their independence and of their standard of living. Previously imperious fathers became frustrated when unmarried sons and daughters in their mid-twenties refused to be bullied in homes where they were making the major financial contributions. Some men left. Because of death, injury, or desertion of fathers, 44 percent of Lowell's worker households were headed by women in the 1860s, making these mothers even more dependent on the mill wages of their children, especially their adult daughters. Studies often showed young women in their mid-twenties remaining unmarried, working as mill girls to help support older brothers who stayed idle at home. The Irish, both in textile towns and larger cities, showed no reluctance to permit unmarried women to work outside the home when their income would help the family economy.[4]

While married Irish women sought the appearance of remaining in the household, many had to contribute to family income. In New York City in the 1850s, for example, when rent took half of a poor man's wages and food and fuel prices rose by nearly a third in 1854, a family of four needed $11 a week to survive. But common laborers and factory workers averaged less than $5 weekly; depressions in 1854 and 1857 meant wage cuts; and most workers faced seasonal layoffs. Nearly half of the Irish families in the Sixth Ward (an area stretching from Broadway to the Bowery and including the Five Points slum) had at least one additional family member at work, usually the wives. Of the 4,200 Irish women aged fifteen to forty-nine in the area, 44 percent were gainfully employed, and while the proportions decreased with age, still 35 percent of women over forty worked for pay. Young, unmarried women usually found employment as domestics or in service as hotel maids, waitresses, cooks, or personal servants. Older women worked as housekeepers or laundresses. More than a third of Irish girls also worked in the sewing trades as dressmakers, seamstresses, tailoresses, cap and vest makers, milliners, or artificial flower makers—usually at piece rates under which a seamstress might, with hard work, finish three shirts a day and make about 50¢ per week, although some seamstresses earned as much as $91 in a year. In other manufacturing industries, such as upholstering or printing or bookbinding or cigar making or box making, women occupied the least skilled positions and received between a third and a half of men's wages for work that depended on stamina and manual dexterity. Some older women kept stores, working from 4:00 A.M., when they bought goods from farmers, until they closed the shops at 10:00 P.M. Their weekly profits might be as high as $4.

Age and marital status usually determined the kinds of work Irish women performed in their neighborhood. Most workers outside the home were young, single, and without obligations which required their presence in the household during the day. But married women, in order to maintain a reasonably stable family life, chose occupations which permitted them to continue to function as housewives and mothers. Although census takers did not record keeping boarders as gainful employment, about a quarter of these women supplemented income by this means, which was considered an extension of women's traditional housework. A smaller percentage added to their husbands' earnings by other occupations, especially in the sewing trades. Tailors and their wives often worked together at home, sometimes with the children.

Widows or other women heads of households particularly suffered from limited opportunities to do work where they could also supervise their children. A childless widow might join another household or go into domestic service, but 47 percent of widowed mothers had to send their children out to work. Nevertheless, they struggled to sustain their strong family ties, showing that the "uprooting" of emigration and the "alienation" of urban living may have changed lifestyles but did not alter Irish family relations. Factors which might have caused disintegration actually led to greater dependencies. Survival and prosperity for Irish immigrants, therefore, meant the survival and mobility of the family.[5]

On the whole, the Irish repeated patterns set by the Yankees, whom they replaced at the lower occupational levels and then followed upward. Originally greeted with considerable hostility in the 1840s, the Irish came to dominate unskilled factory work in the 1850s; by the 1880s the men at least had made inroads into the more skilled machinists' fields.[6] Copying the American example, Irish married women left the industrial work force as quickly as possible to take up less visible means of earning within the home. Emancipation from the mills did not mean departure from the working class for these women, however, since income levels remained low, even with several family members working. Irish women could not spend a few years within the industrial system and then leap to more prestigious social status. But that improved condition became their goal—this group, too, chose to regard its membership in the proletariat as a passing phase, to be escaped as soon as possible. Adopting the values and aspirations of the native-born population, Irish-Americans, with few exceptions, plodded diligently in the direction of the middle class.

The "older immigration" of the mid-nineteenth century, of which the Irish, English, French, Germans, and Scandinavians were a part, gave way in later years to increasing numbers of immigrants from southern and eastern Europe; many more Italians, for example, came after the 1870s. Earlier Italian immigrants often went to South America, but between 1876 and 1926, nearly nine million came to the United States, mainly from central or southern Italy. Unattached males predominated. Working as sharecroppers, farm laborers, building tradesmen, and other artisans, they sought American fortunes to take home to Italy, where they might buy land and social status; more than 60 percent of Italian immigrants to the United States did not stay.

When Italian women came to this country, nearly all of them accompanied family groups or were travelling to join a husband or father who had emigrated earlier. Still governed by a strict patriarchal culture, the southern Italians believed that family work and family property belonged to the family group rather than to the individual, and many Italian immigrants tried to reproduce peasant customs in their new nonagricultural situations. Men controlled families and households; women cooperated in assuming subordinate positions and bolstering male prestige. Maleness often meant doing something women could not do, and for this reason, Italian immigrant women frequently denied that they "worked." Men worked; women remained home.[7]

Italian women who "did not work" contributed significantly to family income. A study of Italian families in New York City early in the twentieth century showed that in almost every case the father was regarded as head of the household, although he brought in income to only 383 of the 544 houses. Large families, averaging 6.2 persons, required more than a single wage-earner in any case. Over a thousand women in these households worked for pay; 87.4 percent of those with outside jobs were single and two-thirds were under twenty-one. Nine out of ten of these women lived with their families, and 86 percent turned in their pay envelopes unopened to the household manager; fewer than 10 percent retained small sums for clothing, carfare, and lunches. "These facts are all the more striking," commented the investigator, "because it is not unusual to find families in which the sons were not giving a cent to the support of the home." Since half of these women had contributed to their own support in Italy, and some of the northern women had even worked in factories, few unmarried daughters questioned working in America. But once married, they retired into the household. Mothers often served as janitors for the buildings in which their families lived, either for pay or for reduced rents. More than a third of these women did piecework at home or took in lodgers or both. The woman who "did not work," therefore, had only to keep her tenement house in order, look after her children, embroider or finish garments twelve hours a day, and reinforce the authority of her husband or eldest son. In return, she lived in a protected environment, in which she rarely left the house except in the company of a male relative and took satisfaction in despising an American industrial process which would have given her higher pay for shorter hours. "They only do cheap work in this country," one woman declared. "In Italy it would take six months to do a pillow and here it must be done in three or four hours. Cheap work!"[8]

When Italians are compared with other immigrants, the close integration of the Italian woman's family and work functions, as well as her deference to men, is even more striking. Southern Italians living in Buffalo, New York, at the turn of the century strongly favored conservative forms of female employment, usually at home or in workrooms where they would be under the supervision of relatives. When economic necessity required another income, male children were taken out of school and sent into factories so that women could remain sheltered at home. Since male authority in Italy had not depended on constant earning, seasonal work or unemployment in Buffalo did not undermine masculine dominance, and Italian women seem to have neither received nor sought increased influence within the household when they brought in earnings. In contrast, Polish women worked as domestics or in factories and gained a bargaining power within their families in accordance with their financial contribution; the same distinction holds true for Polish, Jewish, and Lithuanian girls in Chicago in those years.[9]

Rosa Cavalleri was one of many Italian working-class women who did what was necessary in order to survive— dutifully acknowledging an occasional "miracle"—and did not waste precious time and energy philosophizing about it. Born in northern Italy, abandoned at an orphanage, Rosa grew up in the silkmaking district, where people combined agricultural and industrial work. Rosa's life revolved around men more than she might have wanted. In early adolescence, she married Santino, an older workman whom she disliked but whom her foster mother admired for the 2,000 lira he had earned in America. A mother herself at fifteen, she reluctantly left her baby with relatives to join her husband in a Missouri mining town. "You will get smart in America," her friends said, "and in America you will not be so poor." On the trans-Atlantic passage, she prayed unsuccessfully that she would be rejected at the Castle Garden immigration reception center so she would not have to see Santino, but she also found warm travelling companions like Francesca, who was less concerned that she was going to marry a man she had never seen than that he was a Tuscan rather than a Lombard. Rosa enjoyed the trip, especially since "there was no one to scold" when she danced with strange men, even Poles and Jews, because, "when I was dancing I forgot for a little while that I was the wife of Santino going to him in America." After a number of adventures, including the loss of money stolen by a well-dressed compatriot and the proud refusal of food offered by Americans on the cross-country train trip, Rosa joined Santino in Missouri, where she kept house, cooked for many Italian miners, had another baby, sent for her boy in Italy, and endured Santino's jealous threats and murderous rages. Finally, after two nights of remaining awake to watch Santino stand over her with a knife, she took the children and her saved pennies and fled to Chicago, to relatives of the man Santino suspected as her lover.

"I always was praying," Rosa said, and she prayed herself through the next twenty years. She washed shirts for plasterers and stonemasons at 80¢ a week until she found a job scrubbing floors at a restaurant. Both her husband and her apparent suitor followed her to Chicago, the husband to charge her in court with abandonment and adultery, the other man, Gionin, to marry her and give her three more children. During the depression of the 1890s, when Gionin worked at a sawmill in Wisconsin only to have his cousin borrow and never return his $30 savings, Rosa prayed often for bread for her children and found work scrubbing an occasional saloon for 50¢. City food distribution also helped; after waiting as much as half the day in winter snow and windstorms, "we used to get for one week a piece of salt pork and some dried peas and the loaf of bread and some coffee or some tea." But Rosa was afraid to return to the bread line after policemen kept order by hitting the waiting women on the head with their clubs. Her six-year-old son hauled coal and wood to earn a nickel a week, the price of a good soup bone. But Rosa prayed for bread and "the Virgin made a miracle": a dancer paid Rosa a meal and a dollar a week to clean her house and wash her silk underwear. And when Gionin, conscience-stricken over their civil marriage, abandoned her and the five children, she prayed again, and the priest convinced Gionin that leaving them to starve would be a worse sin. Occasionally, Rosa indulged in some good-natured complaining, wondering "why everybody in

Chicago didn't die" from the garbage, lamenting the lack of pleasures for "us poor women" while the men got drunk or played games with wooden balls in the alley or tossed about Italian cheeses when the alley was too dirty. Eventually, she learned enough English "to go by the priest in the Irish church and confess myself and make the priest understand what was a sin." But she was so tired from scrubbing and washing that she fell asleep in her woman's club writing class "and never learned to do the writing in English." Finally, she moved into the neighborhood of the Chicago Commons settlement house where she cleaned, substituted for the cook, and told stories of her life—first to the other cleaning women, then to the residents, and finally at large meetings where she shared the platform with "a big *somebody*" from Washington. Rosa Cavalleri, "Mrs. C.," remained at the settlement until her death in 1943, almost sixty years after she came to the United States.[10] Above all else, Rosa and women like her found ways to survive in America, small "miracles" which did not radically disrupt the social and psychological system they brought with them.

Other groups of women struggled to keep only parts of their former lives and viewed the United States more as a chance for change; many Jewish immigrant women held this hope. Eastern European Jews would later speak with a bittersweet nostalgia for the *shtetl*—their ghetto communities separated by laws, police restrictions, and often physical barriers from the towns of Gentiles. Home might have been a one-room thatched cottage or a city apartment; families were large, frequently with half- or step- sisters and brothers, and sometimes as much as twenty years between the eldest and youngest child. Infant mortality was common. Education was mainly the concern of boys; girls learned only enough to run a household and perform religious duties. Traditions and ritual observances permeated the culture. But arbitrary changes in authority, compulsory army service for young men, legal limitations on how Jews might earn a living, and increasing pogroms on top of the decay of Czarist Russia left little stability and less security in life. A little girl recalled her instinctive secrecy when she found a cache of underground books and pamphlets in the attic, and her tutor's caution, inspired by fear of the *okrana* (secret police), when children asked seemingly innocent political questions. Another testified that although her father should have been exempted from military service as the only son, he was drafted anyway to fill the village's quota and escaped service only when her angry, desperate, pregnant mother made the day-long trip "to the city where this powerful functionary had his seat" to plead for her husband's release. To a child, a new pair of shoes "with little brass hooks on them" meant happiness and pride; to mothers, surviving another week on three rubles was a victory. But often people would recall, "I don't remember being happy or unhappy. I just lived and so did my parents."[11]

Some wanted more than staying alive; many dreamed of America. "We came to get away from the pogroms," said one; another described barricading windows at night. Some fled military conscription while others spoke of escaping from government repression of freedom of expression. Eastern Europeans knew of *Kesselgarten* (Castle Garden) and continued to use the term even after Ellis Island became the principal immigrant reception center. Names like George Washington, Abraham Lincoln, and Thomas Edison (whose picture appeared on the boxes in which record cylinders arrived from relatives in America) were familiar, as were the writings of Mark Twain and Jack London. Most of all, the United States was both "a free world" and "a land of gold." One immigrant believed that "in America, it rained money every two weeks." Another at least expected that "everyone can earn a living there," especially when a storekeeper's son returned after a few months in New York "with a black derby hat and gold teeth, the first we have ever seen." Those who opposed emigration did so on religious grounds; "I thought of the United States," one said, "as a place where even the bricks were unkosher."[12]

Nevertheless, many families decided to make the journey: 411,650 Jews came between 1885 and 1898, another 1,382,500 by 1914. Often the father went first, to find work and a place to live, leaving the mother, who had frequently been a principal breadwinner anyway, in charge of the children until he sent passage money. But it took trouble, time, and considerable money to leave. Not only was it necessary to purchase a passport, but officials expected bribes for issuing one, and the fees also included hiring a guide to get across the border. Sometimes several families appeared on the same passport. Those who could not afford the documents left illegally, and guides would smuggle families or runaway soldiers into the next country, for a price. Eventually, the immigrant would reach a port of embarkation such as Hamburg and then endure steerage, seasickness, crowds, lack of privacy—as one woman recalled, "Oy, was that an ocean cruise!" At least one family was lucky: when a child came down with measles, the mother and the other children joined him in luxurious quarantine in a stateroom.[13] Until 1891, immigrants entered the United States with comparative ease; quotas, visas, and affadavits would not be introduced until the twentieth century. But the first restriction laws in 1891 prohibited paupers; immigrants had to produce evidence of employment, support, or "show money" to convince officials that they would not become public burdens. Until 1910, when the Department of Commerce and Labor ruled against "assisted immigrants," private organizations such as the Hebrew Sheltering and Immigrant Aid Society (HIAS) met ships, loaned "show money," provided overnight lodging, and put immigrants on trains to their next location.

During their first days, immigrants combined amazement

with instant Americanization. Reminiscences are crowded with open-mouthed gaping at electric lights, laundry on pulley lines, streetcars, fire engines, plush train seats (for everyone, not just first class!), bananas, ice cream, lemons "as big as grapefruit." Relatives whisked "greenhorns" off to Turkish baths to wash away Europe and travel and bought them new "American" clothes. Fathers proudly introduced their families to walk-up, cold-water, tenement flats with tiny windowless bedrooms, a single stove for heating and cooking, and backyard latrines; relatives could sleep on the sofa or on folding cots. "It seemed quite advanced compared with our home in Khelm," said one young girl, who also remarked about her first Passover in America: "there was a sense of safety and hope that we had never felt in Poland."[14]

That child's security lasted about two years—until her father died of influenza, leaving three young children and a pregnant widow. But even where no family tragedy struck, many newcomers found that they had to seek work immediately in order to survive. Teen-age sisters, in Chicago from Czechoslovakia in the late 1870s, sought menial work after their family was robbed of its savings. A merchant's daughter, brought over by her "rich" brother, an auctioneer on the Coney Island boardwalk, had to work as a servant until she learned to operate a sewing machine and could join her sister in a Philadelphia factory.[15] The pregnant widow kept her family together with help from the United Hebrew Charities until the latest baby was born. But since she was then tied down with nursing, she took in sewing, rented the bedroom to a boarder, tended a cousin's soda fountain, and placed her two sons in a Hebrew orphanage where they could get an education. When the baby was weaned, she left her with a relative, put the older girl into the orphanage, and took a job in a fur factory. Within a year, she was still lining capes but had both daughters with her; in two more years, she had lost her job, returned to taking in sewing, and sent the elder daughter, now thirteen, out to work. The United Hebrew Charities found the girl a job running errands in a department store, working sixty-four hours a week for $2.16 (the sixteen cents was for keeping her apron laundered and she saved the money by doing it herself). An error in a customer's change cost her that job, but the agency placed her again, at $2.25 per week, selling women's muslin underwear, babies' dresses, coats and caps, and shirtwaists. After three years, her salary had risen to $2.75. Against her mother's wishes, the young woman decided that factory work would be more profitable. After buying her own sewing machine for $30, furnishing her own threads, and serving an unpaid trial period, she went to work sewing linings in caps and earned $6 her first week. Not only did her mother disapprove of the factory as less genteel than the store, but she was shocked when her "dutiful daughter" refused to hand over her entire pay, retaining a dollar for lunches, needles, and thread. Later, the girl kept more money for materials for the clothes her mother made; she could not afford a dressmaker and had to put up with the humiliation of her mother's efforts, on which "something always went wrong."[16]

Paid work was not new to Jewish women; in fact, the continuity of employment may have eased their initial adjustment to America. Many Eastern European Jewish women had been the sole supporters of their families while their husbands studied Torah; in America, the honor of "holding the book" often put wives to work while husbands attended secular schools. Even in families where the men were not scholars, earning a living had been sexless in the *shtetl,* although patriarchal traditions placed men at the heads of households.[17]

Immigrant Jewish women continued to contribute to family support. A third of the Jewish households in Philadelphia included a female wage-earner; 73 percent of unmarried women were part of the labor force, and 7 percent of married women worked outside their homes. Many women were full partners in small businesses, spending almost as much time as the men in the stores, although men were increasingly described in America as "working" while women were "minding the store." Some women, bringing more merchant experience than their husbands, took the initiative in opening businesses. Others took up pushcart operations, a career which quickly formed its own hierarchy, with the greatest status held by women who owned their carts and had a regular location and clientele. All this they managed in addition to retaining full responsibilities for the household and family. First generation immigrant married women with children also earned at home by keeping lodgers, looking after children of mothers who worked in stores and factories, laundering, sewing, or doing a variety of piecework.[18]

Many Jewish women worked in the needle trades, at home or in sweatshops or factories. They may have had experience in this field abroad, or, if they did not, others had warned them to claim that they could operate a sewing machine so they would be allowed into the country by immigration authorities. In the early twentieth century, the needle trades became 65 percent Jewish; young, unmarried women generally worked in the shops, wives in their homes. Some women, usually the displaced or widowed, became *schnorrers* (professional beggars) and were so adept at the art of soliciting contributions that they rented children (25¢ a day for a baby) as props to increase almsgiving. A few, lured by dance hall pimps or depressed by factory life or unemployment, turned to prostitution, although their numbers were kept down by strong community pressures; parents sat *shiva* for fallen daughters, regarding them as dead, and various Hebrew benevolent and relief societies tried to stand in the way of complete destitution.[19]

For the most part, working-class Jewish immigrant women coped with daily problems by transferring those old-country skills and social patterns which would be useful while taking advantage of American opportunities. They bargained with peddlars to stretch hard-earned dollars, made small amounts of food feed large families, remade clothes, used coats as blankets and chairs as beds, and, when necessary, fought for their rights. When kosher butchers gave in to wholesalers and raised the price of meat to 17 or 18¢ a pound, Orthodox Jewish women on New York's Lower East Side first protested that they could not afford to keep kosher households at the new rates and demanded that a rabbi set reasonable prices. After the butchers ignored their protests, they established the Ladies Anti-Beef Trust Association, arranged a boycott which spread to Brooklyn, Boston, and Newark, and then, under the leadership of a woman butcher, invaded the shops, doused the meat with kerosene, and set fire to it. Arrested and charged with riot, four "ringleaders of the mob" appeared in court, where they were fined. When the judge asked Rebecca Ablowitz why she had taken part in the violence, she told him, "We don't riot. But if all we did was to weep at home, nobody would notice it; so we have to do something to help ourselves."[20]

In order to help themselves, Jewish women also sought education. One of the great dreams of *shtetl* girls was the opportunity in America for girls as well as boys to go to school. While families rarely encouraged young women to go beyond minimal education, foreign-born Jewish women made up the second largest group in the evening schools of New York City in 1910 and 1911, where they learned English, acquired vocational skills like dressmaking to prepare for the job market, or later studied stenography and bookkeeping to move into better jobs.[21] Married women had less chance to continue their education, and many husbands forbade it. One woman, signing herself "The Discontented Wife," wrote to the editor of the Yiddish language daily newspaper to ask whether she had the right to go to night school. Admitting that she was dissatisfied "to be just a wife and mother," she took care to add that she had not neglected her children and her house, but she resented the behavior of her husband, who claimed to favor the emancipation of women but intentionally kept her waiting at the door when she returned from classes and left her short of household money so that she would have to do the laundry herself if she had so much time for "foolishness" like going to school. The editor replied that the man should not want to keep his wife enslaved if he believed in women's emancipation, and the wife had the right to go to school two evenings a week.[22]

Other Jewish women also experienced problems of adjusting and conflicts with traditional patterns of behavior. Novelist Anzia Yezierska, who spoke candidly of the loneliness, poverty, and desires of immigrant Jews, achieved fame and wealth by her writing but constantly struggled against her father's contempt for her literary work and attacks on her for not marrying.[23] Women wrote pathetic appeals to the "Bintel Brief" column in the *Jewish Daily Forward,* complaining of desertions, bigamous husbands, sexual exploitation by relatives or shop foremen, or their own guilt for desires to remarry or marry a non-Jew. Others spoke bitterly of supporting husbands through school only to be discarded as unfit to be married to educated, professional men. And some denounced men who resisted Americanization, which would mean a better income for their families.[24] They suffered the burdens of both American and Jewish expectations. In many Eastern European Jewish immigrant families, power in the household flowed toward these women, while external society pressured them toward docility. Some reacted with "legendary selflessness" but occasionally became transformed into "the brassy-voiced, smothering, and shrewish mama upon whom generations of unsettled sons would blame everything from intellectual sterility to sexual incompetence."[25] Some critics accused them of betraying the aspirations which had sustained them in the *shtetl*, the dreams that in America they could be freer about marriage, education, jobs, and even involvement in political causes. But torn between these hopes and traditional patriarchal aspects of *shtetl* culture, reinforced by desires for middle-class status in America, they compromised. Although the first generation continued to work in about the same proportions as *shtetl* women, they married as avidly as Italians or Irish or Poles, few elected single life or unconventional lifestyles, and most became devoted to upward mobility.[26] In the end, because Eastern European Jews came to America in family groups, with urban skills and the intention to remain, they experienced greater cross-class mobility than other ethnic groups who came with similar burdens of an alien language and traditions.[27]

The experiences and adaptations of these various groups of immigrant women were, in part, shaped by the traditions that they brought from Europe—strong sense of family, practical adaptability to social and economic realities, and varying attitudes on the roles of women within their individual cultures. Moreover, the very experience of immigration had a particular selection effect; as Mary Antin, an immigrant from Russia, said, "What we get in steerage is not the refuse, but the sinew and bone of all the nations."[28] Driven by necessity but demonstrating the stamina, the courage, and the imagination to undertake the rigors of immigrant life, these women were the strong, the tenacious, the adaptable who found ways to come, to stay, to take advantage of American opportunities while America made use of them.

4. Industrialization and Organization

THE SECOND HALF of the nineteenth century witnessed the uncomfortable entry of women into particular strata of the American industrial system, their accommodation to the new work role as well as to societal expectations, and tenuous efforts to organize for improvement of the conditions they found there. Despite great progress in manufacturing, technological advances, and territorial expansion, this era of prosperity and opportunity was more the "Gilded Age," as Mark Twain labeled it, than any Golden Era, especially for working-class women. Population growth, nationwide integration of the economy, and the rush toward self-interest led to impersonality and anonymity for all but the most successful. A social version of the doctrine of "survival of the fittest" identified virtue with wealth and material success. And distinctions between upper- and middle-class "ladies" and working-class "girls" sharpened with the triumph of Victorian manners and the permanence of the factory system.

For a time, it seemed that working-class women might develop their own set of responses to their new industrial condition. Marked numbers of these women understood the dilemma of surviving on tiny incomes: in 1868 a corset stitcher earned $1 per dozen, a sewer of straw hats received 4¢ per bonnet, and a lace collar maker got 22¢ a dozen, generally earning about $4 per week.[1] Living in crowded tenements, enduring pregnancies they could not prevent, struggling to find means to supplement factory wages, and hoping that at least their children might share some of the promises of the American dream, working-class women placed their first priority on survival. For most, that meant conformity with the rules made by the successful, adaptation to the occupations and lifestyles dictated by the factory sys-

68

tem. But for others, it began to mean the beginnings of organized efforts on their own behalf. Through trade unions, cooperatives, strikes, and occasionally feminism, they searched for different kinds of solutions to their economic and social problems.

The War Between the States, like the American Revolution, altered the lives of women of all classes, but working-class women had fewer choices in the ways in which they would be affected. Both Northern and Southern women managed businesses, farms, and plantations while men went to fight; they also helped meet the needs of military and civilian populations engaged in total warfare. Southern women in particular, with only limited local industrialization, revived home production processes not used since colonial days to compensate for the loss of imported goods cut off by the Yankee blockade. Women made clothing, worked in munitions factories, advanced in teaching and nursing, moved into federal government offices for the first time, learned skilled trades such as printing, and a few even became teamsters or steamboat captains. Nearly four hundred women masqueraded as men to serve in the ranks of both armies. Many turned camp follower, some to join husbands as cooks or washerwomen, others in less "wifely" capacities (the euphemism "hooker" originated from the large number of prostitutes who followed one army so devotedly that they were named for its general—"Joe Hooker's Girls").[2]

For the working-class woman, in marginal economic circumstances, the war meant few opportunities and many problems. Rich men might buy their way out of the military draft; a poor man could earn as much as three hundred dollars for his family by taking another's place, and some unscrupulous substitutes sold and resold their services. Poor men, of course, could not afford to pay someone else to go. As the war continued, the draft spread, and new immigrant men volunteered to prove their patriotism, increasing numbers of women were left without a male breadwinner, a condition all too frequently made permanent by death or disabling wounds. By the end of the 1860s, in Boston alone, an estimated twenty-five thousand women had joined the working force because of the war, many as seamstresses. At the same time, while wartime industries and the expansion of the factory system opened jobs to women, a large number of cotton factories closed and dismissed their operatives. Many of these workers also glutted the sewing trades, where the subcontract system for army uniforms paid pitifully small wages: women who sewed gray woolen shirts for Union soldiers received a dollar a dozen from contractors who then sold the same work to the army for $1.75 a dozen. And at the end of the war, after so many wives and widows had been driven into the factories, soldiers returned to claim their jobs.[3]

The pattern of the war years continued. Throughout the nineteenth century, increasing numbers of women sought work. In 1870 a total of 1.8 million American women were gainfully employed, 2.6 million in 1880, 4 million in 1890, and 5.3 million in 1900. The proportion of female breadwinners grew from 14.8 percent to 18.3 percent in the same period. Women could be found in nearly two hundred occupations. And the female manufacturing population expanded from 225 thousand in 1850 to more than twice that number in 1880 and nearly double that again in 1900. By 1882 the United States government had taken sufficient notice of working women to conduct the first census about them, interviewing 14,918 women in twenty-two cities. Typically, white women worked outside their homes before marriage and then disappeared from the gainful employment statistics; in 1890, 70.5 percent of all working women reported were single, 12.9 percent married, 15.7 percent widowed, and 0.9 percent divorced. The vast majority of these women worked from necessity rather than choice; an 1887 study by the United States Bureau of Labor, involving seventeen thousand working girls, showed that on the average, they came from families of five persons, three of whom were employed.[4]

Women had first entered manufacturing in large numbers through the textile industry, and their numbers grew as machine developments continued to reduce the level of skill needed to operate the factories—from nearly 87 thousand in 1850 to over 126 thousand in 1870 and more than 258 thousand in 1890. When women possessed skills, they earned well; a group of Scottish immigrant women who came to a Holyoke, Massachusetts, mill in 1853 as skilled weavers were all able to pay off the debts of their passage within four months and saved between 25 and 50 percent of their $16 to $21 monthly salary.[5] But increasingly, work in skilled areas, such as dressing rooms, went to men, and while women composed more than half the textile work force in 1850, their proportion had dropped to 40.6 percent in 1900, with the greatest concentrations in the least skilled and lowest paid occupations. After the Civil War, for example, with the beginnings of industrialization in the New South, many women and children found work in the Southeastern textile mills; 46.5 percent of operatives in 161 Southern mills were adult females in 1880. But the innovation of the automated loom and a growing technological polarity, which called for both highly skilled and very unskilled labor, caused an employment shift of both sex and age. Jobs demanding skill or strength were given to adult men, while boys and girls or very low-paid women worked as machine tenders.[6]

At the same time, working-class ethnicity began to change in the textile industry. The Irish dominated lower-level mill work before the Civil War, but they moved into more skilled tasks or out of the industry by the 1880s, when increasing numbers of French Canadians entered the factories of New England and New York. Many of these families lived on the brink of poverty, depending on child labor to stay out of debt. Yet, despite hazardous working conditions, company paternalism, cramped housing, and technological dependency, both Irish and French Canadians kept their families together, developed ethnic community networks, and achieved some sense of security and social status. For example, by the 1870s, Irish workers in Cohoes, New York, began to buy property. French-Canadian operatives in the Manchester, New Hampshire, area used family networks to recruit workers, and in some cases even controlled labor turnover and the kinds of tasks in which relatives would be placed. In these factories, marriage and child-bearing no longer took working-class women out of the mills; despite religious pressures to marry, stay home, and not limit families, many daughters postponed or avoided marriage, and married women stayed in the mills. Many only took time off to bear children; most continued working until the children were old enough to earn; and significant numbers remained employed "temporarily" all their lives. But while sons would be encouraged to strive for better positions, even moving from factory to factory by way of the kinship network to obtain higher status and wages, daughters frequently stayed in the same jobs to stabilize family income and insure a reintroduction for the men when they chose to return to a former mill.[7]

In other industries as well as textiles, machine manufacture and the division of labor affected women's involvement; in the manufacture of boots and shoes, for example, women entered, left, and reentered work because of technological adjustments. Early in the nineteenth century, as the shoe-making or cordwaining trade became industrialized, women stitched and bound the uppers in their own homes while men worked in small shops. Between 1855 and 1865, however, the sewing machine revolutionized the industry. Since the machines were heavy and hard to operate, women lost their positions as stitchers and binders; although they made up

nearly a third of boot and shoe employees in 1850, they constituted only about 14 percent of the industry twenty years later.
But as water and steam power replaced brute strength in the
operation of machines and tasks were further subdivided,
women returned to the industry, this time to the factories,
and by 1900 they held a larger proportion of jobs in the industry than they had half a century earlier.[8]

Some industries, such as cigar making, developed in ways
which increased not only the number of women employed,
but also their share in the trade. Fewer than two thousand
women worked in the tobacco industry in 1850, and they constituted about 14 percent of the labor force, but by 1900 more
than 53 thousand women made up 37.5 percent of tobacco
workers—and not all of them were clustered in the cheaper
work areas. Early in the nineteenth century, Connecticut
farmers' wives and daughters converted most of the state's
tobacco production into cigars, which they used as barter
currency at local stores, often paying for the family's entire
annual supply of groceries and dry goods. But their work was
crude and compared badly with factory-made cigars. The
first Connecticut cigar factory in 1810 hired only women, but
they made up only a third of workers in that area by 1856
because the trade had become highly skilled and immigrant
men were able to create more competitive handmade products. Cuban men and later Germans brought the skills to
make the highly favored Spanish and German cigars. In 1869,
however, skilled Bohemian immigrant women began to take
over a larger share of the industry. These workers took cigar
making back into the home as a tenement industry, primarily in New York. The women owned their own wooden molds
and tools, lived and worked in rented rooms usually owned
by their employers, and sent money back to Bohemia to pay
their farmer husbands' passage to America. When the men
arrived, their wives taught them the less skilled aspects of
the trade. By the late 1880s mechanization also gave employ-

ment to women, who were often brought in to tend machines during strikes. In Philadelphia in 1888, for example, 73.1 percent of employees in machine factories were women, and females made up 36.1 percent of handcraft operations.[9]

Technology and the division of labor, then, generally created employment opportunities to which women could respond. More than 115 thousand women worked in clothing trades in 1850; that number grew to almost 327 thousand in 1890 and over 401 thousand by 1900. In food-related production, the numbers jumped dramatically from under a thousand at mid-century to more than 64 thousand by 1900. Paper and printing employment increased ten times in the same years. The 43 women potters of 1850 grew to 4,481 by the end of the century. And even between 1880 and 1900, women electrical workers increased from a mere 72 to more than 6 thousand. These newer kinds of work tended to draw women away from more traditional jobs such as domestic employment; while the number of female servants doubled in the last thirty years of the nineteenth century, their proportion of the servant trade dropped from 41.8 to 35 percent, and the percentage of working women engaged as domestics declined from 58 to 39 percent.[10]

Of course, the nature of women's work generally depended on opportunities available in their local communities. Pittsburgh, for example, was a heavy manufacturing town with no light industrial jobs for women; therefore, they turned to domestic service, sewing, teaching, or prostitution to contribute to family income. Most members of the working classes lacked stable incomes and few could afford such luxuries as sewers, indoor water, gas heating, or washing machines, which would have lightened the women's work load. In addition, the iron, steel, and glass mills meant dangerous work for men, which often left widows who were dependent on charity or the labor of their children.[11]

Life was neither picturesque nor romantic for such women. In a brutally realistic novel set in her native West Virginia in 1861, Rebecca Harding Davis, a middle-class author, told of "Life in the Iron Mills," letting much of the story emerge through the immigrant mother. Weary from her own day in the cotton mill, the woman takes supper (including part of her own food) to her son on the night shift in the iron mill. Numb with fatigue, she collapses on a bundle of rags in the corner, where she is discovered by visitors to the factory, who observe her hunched ugliness and compare it with curiosity to a dramatic and beautiful sculpture of a woman, crafted by her son out of waste materials. The mother overhears the visitors' comments about her boy's apparent aspiration to higher things and their patronizing observation that he is limited and condemned by a lack of money. Soon after, she steals for him and fights his agony over whether to be honest or to keep the money and start a new life. But he is arrested for the crime and dies in jail of lung disease at the age of nineteen.[12]

The story of women's earnings is no less depressing. While daily wages and annual income in manufacturing increased by about 50 percent overall between 1860 and 1890, adult males generally received 75 percent more than adult females, although there were great variations among occupations. In the boot and shoe trade, women earned 60 percent of men's average daily wages, while in box manufacturing, they got only 29 percent. In hourly wage rates, the figures varied from a low of women earning 28 percent of what men received in printing, to a high of 83 percent in woolen mills and dyeing and finishing. Much of the range can be explained by the concentration of women in less skilled tasks within each trade. In identical occupations and establishments, women sometimes earned more than men; female cloth-room hands in cotton goods factories in 1860 earned 122 percent of the rates paid to men, but women slipped to 66 percent by 1890. Conversely, women woolen weavers were earning 78 percent of men's wages in 1860 but rose to 96 percent thirty years later. But dollar amounts were pathetically low. At a rate of 4 to 6¢ each, flannel shirts brought sewing women in Philadelphia weekly wages of $2.16 to $4.32 in 1863; at the same time, New York City umbrella sewers earned $3.00 a week.[13]

Even somewhat higher wages later in the century failed to support an independent or comfortable life. An 1884 study of twenty thousand working girls in Boston revealed average weekly earnings of only $6.35—when they worked. But only 26 percent were employed the entire year, and the rest lost more than twelve weeks employment annually; the actual average weekly wage, therefore, fell to $4.91. By the 1880s and 1890s, room and board cost more than $3.00 a week, and care and replacement of clothing would require another $1.50. Moreover, many of these girls had responsibilities to their families; most lived with parents or relatives and remained unmarried into their mid-twenties.[14]

Investigators and reformers worried that such minimal wages would force young women to seek immoral alternatives. The Boston report indignantly challenged anyone to equate the city's "honest, industrious and virtuous" working girls with prostitutes, praising instead their "heroic struggle against many obstacles, and in the face of peculiar temptations." Others argued against the prejudices attached to women's wage labor and urged higher wages, both because the workers deserved equitable pay and to preserve them from lapses of morality.[15]

But American corporations in the late nineteenth century had little time for such concerns. No longer were mills owned and controlled by men who designed model factory communities. Incorporation, public sale of stocks, separation of ownership from control, use of hired managers, and an increase in the supply of labor left employers unconcerned with the welfare or morals of workers who could be replaced easily. In particular, women had very tenuous ties to their jobs since most were untrained, unskilled, and represented no investment by their employers. Violation of a petty rule, slightly imperfect work, or refusal to yield to an overseer's advances could result in loss of job. Moreover, many women worked in seasonal trades with several slack months of unemployment each year.

Conditions became spectacularly bad under the "sweating system." By the 1880s many parts of clothing manufacture had been taken over by contract work. In "inside" shops, usually attached to a selling house, the whole garment would be completed within the factory. But in "outside" shops, cut garments would be sent out to be assembled and stitched, returning to the factory for examination. Middlemen or contractors usually handled the transfer and return of goods between manufacturers and workers, making their profits by selling the finished garments for more than they paid the seamstresses. Some contractors operated their own factories, usually tenement rooms where several workers sewed long hours in unsanitary conditions for small and shrinking wages. Others, especially in New York City's heavily Jewish Tenth Ward district, permitted the workers to turn their homes into shops. A kitchen or bedroom became a workroom during the long day; tenement flats often had only one or two rooms and a single window; piles of garments served as beds for children. The work week in "inside" shops averaged about eighty-four hours, but "outside" and "home" workers frequently worked fifteen or sixteen hours a day, and some all night as well in the busy seasons. Pieceworkers earned between 15 and 25¢ for stitching an entire cloak, a task which took three and a half hours. Sweatshop workers might make as much as $15 a week, until price cuts reduced their income for the same work to $6 and $7 by 1885. An income of $12 to $15 was possible only by laboring fourteen hours a day and required the aid of other family members.[16]

Women endured these conditions because they had few choices. Untrained, unskilled, trapped into poverty and family responsibilities, many elected merely to survive against seemingly unendurable outside forces. Tied to children whom they could neither afford nor abandon, sometimes supporting a drunken or maimed husband, often with younger brothers and sisters to protect, few could risk the loss of a job by protesting against low wages, long hours, cuts in the piecework rates, or hazards to health and safety in the factories. Even fewer could afford to risk being blacklisted for joining a labor union, which would mean no employment anywhere in the industry. Mothers had no time to attend organizational meetings and no money to spare for union dues. Victorian modesty opposed the inclusion of women in men's working-class assemblies. A society which, at all levels, considered women temporary, secondary, and supplementary earners would hardly encourage them to defy discrimination or oppression.

Although women workers were less fully and less continuously organized than men in the nineteenth century, some did seek to improve their conditions either individually or collectively. And where women did organize, their militancy often exceeded that of men. Sewing women, for example, had been publicizing poor wages and unsanitary conditions since 1825. New York City tailoresses began to hold meetings in that year and by 1831 sought newspaper coverage of their arguments that females were generally oppressed. Soon after, the United Tailoresses' Society fostered a strike of sixteen hundred women for at least four weeks on behalf of an established list of prices for their sewing work; they negotiated with officers of the employers' group, but the results are unrecorded. The seamstresses then organized themselves as a benevolent society and received both praise and aid from leading citizens. Similarly, in the 1830s tailoresses in Baltimore and Philadelphia organized, passed resolutions demanding increased rates, and made good their threat of a strike when their demands were not met. Journeymen tailors in Baltimore supported the women, and the Philadelphians received help from Matthew Carey in their complaints to the Secretary of War regarding low prices paid for stitching army clothing. The seamstresses and their advisers understood the importance of publicity; in 1835 the Female Improvement Society of the City and County of Philadelphia (tailoresses, folders, milliners, corsetmakers, seamstresses, binders, stockmakers, and cloakmakers) established a price scale, which they published in newspapers with lists of employers who did and did not pay those rates. They asked $2.00, rather than the $1.75 offered by the clothiers, for a single-breasted hunting coat with flaps, and an additional 12¢ for each extra outside breast pocket. Employers wanted to pay 25¢ for duck pantaloons; the tailoresses demanded 37¢. Both sides agreed on 18¢ for "drawers of all descriptions." The list included more than two dozen major articles, each with separate rates according to fabric, decoration, extra pockets, and the like.[17]

Through the middle of the century, however, sewing women never united on the best means to achieve their demands. On the other hand, the United Tailoresses Society of the 1830s became a kind of labor union, stressing problems of class and sex oppression, cooperating only with feminist workers, and using the technique of withholding work to force concessions. In contrast, the Shirt Sewers' Cooperative union of the 1850s depended on male reformers who established a storefront producers' cooperative and appealed to public sympathy through a press campaign. Later, the Sewingwomen's Protective and Benevolent Union combined a mutual aid society with trade unionism and sought the support of male unionists. During the Civil War, sewing women in Cincinnati appealed to President Lincoln to abolish the subcontract system, which took 40 percent of their income. And after the war, seamstresses in New York, Buffalo, Detroit, Boston, and Baltimore formed a variety of unions, protective associations, and protest organizations to seek redress of low wages, bad living conditions, immigrant competition, mechanization, and the division of labor. Whatever their tactics or objectives, however, none of these groups lasted more than a year or two, and few could show any concrete gains.[18]

Textile workers, on the other hand, organized less frequently but could claim some successes. The last stand of the farmers' daughters in 1845 on behalf of the ten-hour day may have been counted a failure in the short run, but by 1847 New Hampshire had passed a ten-hour law, to be followed by Pennsylvania in 1848 and New Jersey in 1851. In the 1850s and 1860s, as native New England girls withdrew from the mills and gave their places to immigrants with more modest standards of living, few protests were made. But in 1860 at Dover, New Hampshire, eight hundred workers struck against a wage reduction. Sympathizers, "young ladies of high culture and independent social position," brought funds to aid the factory women; nevertheless, the strike failed. Six years later, at Fall River, women refused to join male weavers in accepting a 10 percent cut; instead, they formed their own association, struck three mills, persuaded the men to walk out, halted thirty-five hundred looms for nearly three months, and won.[19]

Successful strike activity was not necessarily the test of effective organization. At a local level working-class women such as the laundresses and collar workers of Troy, New York, established some strong unions. Laundry women in the early 1860s earned $2 to $3 per week for twelve- to fourteen-hour days standing over washtubs and ironing tables in oppressive heat. Diligent union work over the next several years raised their earnings to $8 to $14 per week, although hours and conditions remained unchanged. When the four hundred Troy laundresses demanded further increases in 1869, however, employers united to crush the union, even advertising a new paper collar to threaten the strikers. Led by the union president, the women then established a cooperative Union Linen Collar and Cuff Manufactory and for a few weeks successfully marketed their output through a New York merchant. The cooperative eventually failed, but the union itself had lasted more than twice as long as other women's union efforts and had, in passing, become sufficiently prosperous to send large donations to striking iron moulders and bricklayers.[20]

Working-class women also furthered their needs through other organizations and methods. San Francisco laundresses publicized their concerns about Chinese competition, while New York saleswomen opposed the employment of Massachusetts and Pennsylvania girls. In Hazelton, Pennsylvania, a boardinghouse keeper organized an "Amazon army" of miners' wives to drive off scab workers. And female cap makers in New York won the support of a wealthy German employer who had attended a union meeting by defending him from the men's personal attacks. Women joined leagues in favor of the eight-hour workday, and a Boston observer commented that they seemed as deeply interested as the men, "although they do not talk so much upon the floor." In Massachusetts and New York, women formed statewide organizations, uniting a number of local unions such as cap makers, laundresses, compositors, and shoemakers "to procure diminution of the hours of labor in the factories, to ameliorate the condition of working women generally, and to take steps to form protective organizations of all trades." Of the thirty national trade unions existing in the 1860s, however, only two, the printers and cigar makers, were open to women, and even in these cases, debate continued among the men over whether they should cooperate with women, many of whom had first entered the trades as strikebreakers.[21]

Only women shoe workers gained sufficient strength to form their own national union. Lynn, Massachusetts, had been the center of shoe manufacturing since the eighteenth century, and nearly every woman in the town did piecework in her own home by 1833, when a thousand women shoe binders formed the Female Society of Lynn and Vicinity for the Protection and Promotion of Female Industry. Since workers set their own hours and working conditions at home, early demands centered on pay rates for finished goods. Profits had increased, and most employers agreed to the women's price list. While the local officers of this early union were women, men represented the group in dealing with the other workers' organizations. Although the Lynn society lasted little more than a year, similar organizations formed in Lynn, New York, and Philadelphia in the 1830s and 1840s to establish price scales and help members to find work. By the 1850s the trade had shifted to factories, and wages had dropped considerably, especially in the wake of the Panic of 1857. During the winter of 1860 five thousand women in Lynn and nearby towns made a spectacular demonstration, with a parade and mass meeting calling for an end to their "slavery" and improvement of working conditions. Their strike forced the manufacturers to compromise and resulted in the formation of a shoemakers' union, the Knights of St. Crispin. Women shoe workers formed the Daughters of St. Crispin, the only national women's trades union in the United States, with chapters throughout Massachusetts, Maine, and New York, and as far away as Chicago, San Francisco, and cities in Canada. Resolutions at the annual convention demanded "the same rate of compensation for equal skill displayed, or the same hours of toil, as is paid other laborers in the same branches of business." The Daughters of St. Crispin remained active nationally for about four years, longer in local groups. But the depression following the panic of 1873 led to the union's gradual disappearance, although two hundred Lynn women tried to revive it in 1876. Thereafter, women stitchers generally seemed to fall into the pattern of being young, temporary workers, living with their families, unorganized, weak, low-paid, and ignored by labor organizers. Moreover, in order to prevent strikes, employers extracted an ironclad contract under which they held back 20 percent of a worker's wages until securing a deposit of $50, which the worker would forfeit if she left her employment without two weeks' notice. Despite such repressive tactics, some women responded militantly. Women shoe workers in Haverhill, Massachusetts, in 1895, apparently more independent than others, joined Jewish and Armenian men in forfeiting their deposit to go out on strike, and they proved their militancy by remaining out and parading in the snow to publicize their grievances.[22]

Meanwhile, one faction of the women's rights movement took up the cause of working-class women. As early as 1850, active feminists such as Lucretia Mott and Elizabeth Oakes Smith supported a cooperative sewing shop established by Philadelphia seamstresses. And middle- and upper-class women had often come to the equal rights and suffrage questions by way of charitable or abolitionist work. As post–Civil War settlements made it clear that the vote would go to black men but not to women of any race, however, the suffrage movement split for a time on objectives and tactics. One group chose to work specifically for the vote, avoiding any other issues, especially those which might antagonize potential conservative supporters of that narrowly defined cause. The other group, led by Elizabeth Cady Stanton and Susan B. Anthony in New York, defined its feminism more broadly and included the causes of working and non-middle-class women. Elizabeth Stanton had been one of the sponsors of the Seneca Falls convention of 1848, at which American women first issued a declaration of their rights; she had also written widely on women's issues and joined her husband in his abolitionist work. Susan Anthony, also from an abolitionist background, had worked with Stanton for suffrage since 1850. In 1868 they established *The Revolution,* a women's newspaper which took up an extensive range of issues of the day, including pleas for the training and equitable pay of working women as well as arguments for the organization of women workers.

Suffragists and labor organizers came together at the offices of *The Revolution* in 1868 to form the Working Women's Association of New York. The founders hoped to unite all organizations concerned with the improvement of women's condition. Similar protective associations had been tried in Chicago, St. Louis, Indianapolis, Boston, Philadelphia, and New York throughout the 1860s, often as attempts to overcome the poor pay of women during the war, obtain work for the unemployed, or prevent actual starvation. Civic leaders and businessmen often supported these enterprises. A New York group claimed to have found work for more than three thousand young women between 1865 and 1868 but could place only about a fifth of the job-seekers of 1869. The Working Women's Association, however, concentrated primarily on suffrage and trade unionism rather than employment— and eventually failed because its members could not agree on the relationship between the two themes. Stanton and Anthony argued that women would never be free to engage in work or careers or battle for improved working and earning conditions until they possessed the ballot as a weapon; for them, suffrage held the solution to many social and economic demands which working women would make. To Augusta Lewis of the typographers' union and other trade unionists, however, "business purposes" came first; once labor and economic consciousness was established, they reasoned, then women could be educated on the benefits of the vote. To their credit, the editors of *The Revolution* reported arguments on both sides of the issue, and the association struggled on for about two years trying to resolve the questions of priorities and tactics.[23]

While the debate continued within the Working Women's Association, the same women, both reformers and unionists, established ties with the National Labor Union, the major central organizing force for workers between 1866 and 1872. The National Labor Union encouraged unionization of women, admitted women to full membership, and welcomed women delegates to its annual congresses. William H. Sylvis, head of the organization, personally supported suffrage and even wrote for *The Revolution*. But on feminist issues, Sylvis was ahead of his colleagues. The NLU never endorsed the vote for women and actually viewed labor organization among women only as a means to the improvement of men's condition to the point where women could eventually return to the home. Anthony was seated as a delegate to the 1868 convention because she represented the Working Women's Association, and other women who stood for similar protective organizations were also present as delegates. But Stanton, representing the Women's Suffrage Association, could only take her seat after the convention resolved that her admission should not be regarded as an endorsement of votes for women. However, that convention did pass resolutions supporting female workers, including condemnation of "low wages, long hours, and damaging service," a call for the eight-hour day in women's work, and a demand for state and national legislation "securing equal salaries for equal work" in government employment. The following year, however, the convention refused to admit Anthony, claiming that she did not represent a genuine labor organization. In fact, male typesetters blocked acceptance of her credentials because she and Stanton had encouraged young women to become strikebreakers at low wages in order to learn the skills of the printing trade. By 1869 Anthony and Stanton had suffered the sacrifice of women's rights to male negro rights in the Fourteenth Amendment and were reluctant to see women's issues subordinated to worker solidarity while men continued to dominate the trades. Having been denied admission on such grounds, the suffrage leaders now viewed trade unions as enemies of the suffrage and correctly saw that the skilled unionist would carry the NLU into opposition to women's rights.[24]

Even when the issue was unionization rather than feminism, as in the typographers' union, women workers had found recognition difficult. Although women had actually practiced the trade since the eighteenth century and the text of the Declaration of Independence had been printed by a woman, male typesetters opposed the hiring of females throughout the first half of the nineteenth century. Young women first obtained such employment in New York City in 1853 when the publisher and editor of the *Day Book* took on forty girls to be trained during a strike. The following year at its convention in Buffalo, the National Typographical Union condemned "this injurious innovation" and asserted that it would be detrimental to the morals and sensibilities of modest young women who might have to set type for "medical and other scientific works." But the national group left the actual decision of female employment to the locals. Editors like Horace Greeley endorsed the employment of female compositors, arguing that women would not take men's wages since they would undoubtedly leave to marry. But outside of New York, printers' unions excluded women, and the Boston local debated in 1865 whether to expel any member who worked in an office which employed female compositors. By the late 1860s, however, the women's rights movement had become more articulate, and Susan B. Anthony urged women to take advantage of strikes to learn the typesetting trade. Simultaneously, six women in New York, under the leadership of Augusta Lewis, organized themselves to seek better pay and conditions; on 8 October 1868 they formed Women's Typographical Union No. 1 and soon increased their membership to forty. Within six months, they won a wage increase; and early in 1869 the women supported a strike by male compositors. At the annual convention of the National Typographical Union in Albany that summer, the powerful New York men's local, No. 6, endorsed the women's petition for a charter, and the national body agreed to recognize women printers who organized themselves into groups of seven or more and who agreed to the same price scales as male locals in their area. The next year the International Union elected Augusta Lewis its corresponding secretary, and two years later she reported on conditions of both men and women in the trade. Although membership dwindled until Women's Typographical Union No. 1 dissolved in 1878, women printers would be admitted to mixed locals in the 1890s, receiving the same pay as men.[25]

In contrast to the resistance to women shown by many unions, the Knights of Labor eventually sponsored and encouraged the organization of women. Begun in 1869 as a secret society of Philadelphia garment workers, the Knights became the nation's first large-scale national labor federation; rather than establishing locals with members from separate crafts, the organization set up a network of local, district, and general assemblies representing many trades—specifically excepting lawyers, bankers, professional gamblers, stockbrokers, and dealers in intoxicating drink. But the original constitution made no provision for women. Perhaps the founders worried that unskilled women tenders of the new machines would undercut men's wage standards, or shared a Victorian male belief that women should be excluded from serious issues. By 1879, however, a socialist Knight, Phillip Van Patten, asked the General Assembly to permit women to form their own local assemblies; although a decision was postponed at that time, another man organized the first women's local, a group of shoe workers in Philadelphia, in 1881. Faced with that reality, the 1882 annual meeting permitted initiation of females of at least sixteen years of age. Mrs. Terence Powderly, wife of the Grand Master Workman, was the first woman enrolled, and the Philadelphia local became the first women's assembly. Throughout the early 1880s, the Knights remained ambivalent toward "lady Knights"; while they encouraged women to unionize and push for better wages, they continued to believe that women's proper sphere was in the home and that a victory for the Knights, in the form of decent wages for men, would eliminate the need for women to perform wage labor. In 1885, however, women members made their presence felt, and the organization appointed a committee to gather information on women's work. The following year female delegates to the annual convention formed themselves into a permanent lobby to investigate conditions of women's labor and agitate for equal pay for equal work.

Plans for this lobby included the appointment of Leonora Barry as paid general investigator. An Irish immigrant widow with three small children, Mrs. Barry had left dressmaking because of failing eyesight. Turning to work in a hosiery mill, she was horrified by working conditions and the insults young women workers suffered. Therefore, she joined the Knights of Labor and within two years led her local as master workman. As investigator of industrial conditions affecting women and children in 1887, 1888, and 1889, she conducted the first systematic and documented inquiry by a labor organization. Simultaneously, she organized women's assemblies and cooperative factories, established a working women's benefit fund, promoted industrial schools, and worked for passage of a factory inspection law in Pennsylvania. Her own life and work revealed many of the limitations of women's labor in the late nineteenth century. Barry abandoned her factory visits when she learned that women workers lost their jobs for taking her through the mills. She refused to lobby legislators for the Pennsylvania act because it would be "unladylike." And when she married again in 1890, she retired from her investigations because she believed that women should not work outside the home unless driven to it by economic necessity. Although Barry, in her letter of resignation, encouraged the union to continue the work of the women's section, the Knights themselves soon faced a general decline. Terence Powderly correctly compared Barry's marriage to death—the death of the women's department, which was dissolved at the 1890 convention when the single woman delegate refused to take on the job of investigator. While local groups remained active into the early twentieth century, women's involvement in a national trade union movement would be suspended for many years.[26]

Instead, the vast majority of America's working-class women in the late nineteenth century accommodated themselves to the heavy burden of social and economic realities. They took what jobs they could get, often grateful for the technological changes which had put employment within their reach. When possible, they abandoned the labor market in a formal sense upon marriage, retreating into the home in imitation of middle class practices. But the necessity to contribute to family incomes even after marriage forced them to find surreptitious means of earning. Pride of economic survival warred with shame of married women's employment.

For the unmarried working-class woman or the woman who stayed out in the work force, lack of training and skills kept her in low-paying jobs with no opportunities for advancement. Cut off from independent action, few saw the benefits of collective activity, and most agreed with the general social judgment that public organizations were no place for women. If they failed to escape from the factory system through marriage, they would remain disgruntled but docile workers.

For the few, however, impossible working conditions or their own ambitions drove them into activities to help themselves or into alliances with those who promised some sort of improvement. Employment agencies, trade unions, cooperative marketing groups, benefit societies all attracted some adherents, even if only for a short time. Sympathetic feminists briefly extended their concerns beyond the issue of suffrage to espouse the causes of women workers. In some cases, the women organized themselves; in others, they joined with existing unions when the male members would permit their participation. But the essential problem which the working-class woman failed to address in the late nineteenth century, the problem which ultimately caused the decline of each of these organizations and activities, was the reconciliation of the woman as woman with the woman as worker. In a society which increasingly drew sexual distinctions in its personal and public realms, it almost seemed as if the working-class women would have to make a choice—to be women or to be workers. For the time being, at least, they could not be both, at least not comfortably or profitably.

Part Two: "I Can't Live on Hopes and Virtue": 1900-40

5. Working-Class Women Become Working Women

HAVING ACHIEVED industrialization and great-nation status, the United States was ready to come into the "modern" world. As the country entered the twentieth century, population had grown to seventy-six million, with men still outnumbering women by two million; a girl child born in 1900 could expect to live until 1948. While most Americans remained in rural areas, industrialization was luring more workers to the city. These late Victorians exalted their own prosperity, virtue, and moral superiority. Women were extolled as feminine, motherly upholders of public and private morality. The home was sacred. Middle-class values seemed safely entrenched.[1]

Patterns set by working-class women throughout the 1800s were apparently to continue: single women left the spotlight of the work force upon marriage; if they had to supplement the family income, they hid their activities from the public eye, aping the manners of middle-class women who did not have to earn after marriage. At the same time, growing numbers of women entered the paid labor force, usually at its lowest levels, and more of them remained there than ever before. More than five million women over ten years of age were reported as gainfully employed in 1900; they represented 21.2 percent of all women and 18.3 percent of all workers. Of these, single women outnumbered married women by more than seven to one, and over a third of unmarried women worked. Working women were most likely to be found in service jobs; 64 percent of female employment fell under domestic or other service categories. Another significant group, almost a quarter, were factory operatives, and large segments continued to work as dressmakers and laundresses. Only small fractions had jobs as professionals, proprietors, or managers. And while a growing number began to enter white collar, clerical, and sales occupations, the working woman of 1900 was most commonly a working-class woman, employed out of necessity at unskilled or semi-skilled tasks. Moreover, these women clustered into dispro-portionately "female" occupations at a rate three and a half times as high as the percentage of women in the total labor force. The average worker of 1900 spent fifty-nine hours per week on the job at 21.6¢ per hour for an average weekly in-come of $12.74, but the situation of skilled working men in-flated those figures; typically, women worked longer and earned less. Therefore, if the average worker could buy a pound of butter or ten pounds of flour with 1.2 hours of labor, or a dozen eggs for an hour's work, the working-class women faced a much less favorable exchange rate. She undoubtedly had to spend more than the average third of her income for food, fifth on housing, and eighth on clothing—leaving her little or nothing for savings, medical care, or recrea-tion.[2]

Middle-class moralizers pointed out that the world of work was fundamentally incompatible with femininity. Working, especially under factory conditions, damaged a woman's health, unbalanced her temperament, undermined distinc-tions between men and women, and led to weaknesses which could interfere with motherhood. Since immigrants were led to believe that "it was a crime to be a greenhorn" and were often influenced by their exposure to middle-class living while they worked as servants, the idea that work unsexed women spread beyond the polite journals of the bourgeoisie. Public schools, especially in adult education, reinforced ideas of a domestic role for women, as did many other agen-cies of Americanization which tried to teach health, moral-ity, thrift, and conformity. A visiting nurse, for example, complained about a Polish mother who "refused to nurse her baby because she wants to work in the mill."[3]

Yet wages remained too low for an individual to become economically self-sufficient, and working-class families could not survive on the income of a single breadwinner. The father remained the primary earner, but his income would be supplemented by older sons, older daughters, younger sons, and younger daughters, as necessary, with the mother usually the last to take on wage labor outside the home. A thirteen-year-old girl told a New York investigating committee that she had not been to school in this country, forgot how to spell "cat," received $2 per week for sixty hours in a necktie factory, had an older sister employed and a sick father; her mother, she said, "ain't working because I am working, but before, when I didn't work, she worked."[4]

If married women worked outside the home, it was not by choice. Widowhood or the need to support a disabled husband drove more of these women into the work force. Nearly 1 percent of railway trainmen died each year at the turn of the century, 1 percent of coal miners every two years. One husband in five did not see age forty-five. And industrial accidents disabled fifteen thousand men in Illinois alone between 1907 and 1912. Of 140 women surveyed by the United States Bureau of Labor Statistics in 1908, 94 were widowed, deserted, or married to accident victims. The various charity organizations of New York studied 985 widows in 1910 and found that 84 percent of them worked, usually as cleaners in offices or other places or as janitresses. Married women also went out to work when their husbands faced unemployment, such as during the depression following the panic of 1893. More than half the principal breadwinners of a large sampling of working-class families were out of work in 1901. The demand for servants made it possible for women to find employment as laundresses, cleaners, or domestics in private homes while their husbands were forced out of factory jobs by economic conditions or seasonal unemployment.[5]

Like the working-class women of the late nineteenth century, however, married women still tried to find ways to earn without leaving their households. Many took in lodgers. Immigrant men often came to America before their families, and rural young men and women frequently needed rooms near their new city jobs. By 1910 about 5 percent of the country's population boarded away from their relatives. A survey made in 1890 showed one household in five had boarders; a similar investigation in New York in 1907 found one out of two. And in some mill villages, taking lodgers was an industry in itself. In places where heavy industrial employment had no openings for women and where household life was subordinated to mill life, wives, especially among immigrant groups, supplemented family income by taking boarders, even though irregular factory hours disrupted any hope for an orderly household routine. Some families even had cooperative households, with relatives or neighbors sharing kitchen facilities.[6]

Home work also brought income through the labor of wives and children. In a typical case, where the father worked as a porter but could not earn enough to pay the $10 monthly rent on three rooms as well as feed and clothe the family, the grandmother, mother, and two older daughters made artifical flowers in a kitchen-workroom by the light of the single window in an adjoining room. The three-year-old divided the petals; her four-year-old sister separated the stems, dipping each into paste; and the mother and grandmother assembled the petals on the stems. At 10¢ a gross, they could earn about $1.20 a day by working from 8:00 or 9:00 in the morning until 7:00 or 8:00 at night. From April to October, of course, they earned nothing because that was the slack season in their trade. Although the wife, an Italian immigrant, had earned more and enjoyed her work more when she was in a candy factory before getting married, she refused to consider returning to that work: "We can't go out to work after we're married," she said.[7]

At the same time that they contributed to family income, working-class housewives retained full responsibility for the household's domestic tasks. Cooking, cleaning, sewing, and surviving continued to be women's work. The poor wives who lived in tenements and slums faced increasing pressures of hopelessness and ugliness while they made personal war on poverty, disease, dirt, and demoralization.

Living was usually crowded. In order to maximize profits on expensive urban real estate, landlords built tenements in "dumbbell" shape, with only an air shaft separating one building from the next. A thousand persons might thus live on one acre. Refuse collected in the shaft, and one observer told of stench so vile and air so foul "that the occupants do not employ the windows as a means of getting air." Residents shared what toilet facilities existed; fewer than 2 percent of New York City tenement occupants had private toilets in the 1890s, while only about three hundred out of a quarter of a million slum dwellers in the same area ever had the opportunity to use a bathtub. Water often had to be carried from a hydrant on the street. Privacy was a luxury too ridiculous to be considered. Indulging in a walk through the neighborhood often meant yet another trip down and up five and more flights of stairs, already trodden several times a day for water, fuel, and food supplies. Working-class budgets had little enough room for filling starches and practically none for meat or fresh vegetables; a bit of pork rind or side meat might flavor a soup or stew. Working-class housewives squeezed all they could from pay envelopes and remained ever conscious of the threat of yet worse times during the slack season. As one observer testified, "tenement house life destroys a certain delicacy of feeling."[8]

Even as they struggled with living and earning conditions, married working-class women in the early twentieth century suffered changes and limitations in the opportunities available to them at home. Fewer single young men and women lived away from their families; if they did leave home, they found lodging in organized homes or in separate apartments or shared quarters with coworkers rather than boarding with other families. Moreover, reformers pressed for laws forbidding home work because of sweatshop conditions. The home manufacture of clothing, tobacco products, foodstuffs, and similar goods faced increasing competition from better controlled and more efficient factories. Working-class women, therefore, might continue to serve as budget managers and domestic workers for their own families, but in growing numbers, because of shrinking opportunities within the home, they now had to combine these activities with outside paid employment, a condition especially difficult for mothers of young children. Some women could leave their youngsters with an aged or ill relative; many shifted the burden of mothering to the eldest daughter, who might be as young as seven. Or, as one woman said, "I give them their breakfast, put the meal on the table for them, lock the front door and the gate in the backyard, and go away."[9]

Some women, like Rose Haggerty, kept their families together at great personal cost. Daughter of a happy-go-lucky but seldom employed longshoreman, Rose grew up in a Cherry Street tenement in New York, and by age seven had already learned to protect her five younger brothers and sisters as best she could from the oppressive poverty, dirt, and drunkenness of their parents. By the time Rose was fourteen, her father and a brother had died, her mother was an invalid, and Rose was working ten hours a day in a paper bag factory to earn $2.50 a week to pay their $6.00 a month rent. With the aid of an old shoemaker, she bought a sewing machine and learned to stitch shirts at home, often spending fourteen hours a day at her machine. Skill and hard work brought her income to as high as $35.00 a month within two years, while her five-year-old sister kept house. The family became reasonably happy and conservatively comfortable until jobbers reduced by half the prices for shirts. Rose now received 4¢ a dozen to hem shirt flaps and could not afford enough food or heat for her family. Untrained for other work, she resisted suggestions that she put the children in an asylum and marry to attain some personal security. Finally, refused payment for her work when the foreman rejected one piece, Rose considered throwing herself in the river but was stopped by a sailor who promised her money to spend the night with him. In the morning, she took the money, refused his offer of marriage, and concluded that she had made a bargain with a new trade, one which would mean food and warmth for the children. Rose told an investigator that she did not expect to live long but hoped that the children would be "well along" when she left them. As for her choice, she said that she had lived twenty years poor, cheerful, and virtuous; now, she said, "let God Almighty judge who's to blame most—I that was driven, or them that drove me to the pass I'm in."[10]

Many working-class women resisted selling their virtue to survive but, increasingly, they sold their labor. By 1900 the working-class woman in America was becoming a working woman, and her labor was passing from home to factory. The introduction of machinery, artificial power, and division of tasks drew her into the industrial system. But her lack of skills, permanence, or organization made her vulnerable to prejudice and exploitation, often in the form of low wages, long hours, and bad conditions. Although her numbers and share of the work force had grown tremendously—it had more than tripled in the preceding thirty years—she was little better off than she had been in the 1820s.[11]

The typical working woman at the turn of the century was the young, single daughter of ambitious immigrants or native parents who were not yet safely entrenched in the middle class. She had minimal public education, no trade or craft training, and no intention of remaining at paid employment after her marriage. Even older married women workers still struggled to regard their employment as temporary or supplementary to the income of a husband-breadwinner. Yet many remained "temporary," secondary workers all their lives.

These women worked under deplorable conditions. Coming to their jobs without skills, they learned from another worker or their foreman. One English-speaking garment operative told of learning from a Polish tailor and a German seamstress who could not even communicate with one another. Another factory employee's apprenticeship ended after the foreman showed her how to thread the needle of her power sewing machine and pointed out the on-off switch. When new workers entered sweatshops, they frequently received no wages while learning the trade, and the unpaid training periods were sometimes extended long beyond the time when apprentices were producing finished goods. Immigrant women knew so little English that many never understood these arrangements. Others, ignorant of arithmetic and bookkeeping, were cheated of small amounts from each pay envelope or had wages held back for several weeks by employers who promised to pay "next time." For these reasons, managers found it profitable to hire greenhorns and often preferred women to men workers. Hiring bosses sought only someone who could perform a simple, repetitive task quickly and accurately. And these insecure employees so desperately needed their jobs that they would not risk losing even poor wages with complaints about the noise, dirt, smells, heat, humidity, overcrowding, dim light, unhealthy processes, dangerous machinery, or employers' violation of the law.[12]

Few restrictions limited the absolute power of management. A boss could fine a girl half a day's pay if she wasted a dime's worth of material. Employers could require church attendance of workers or tell Jewish employees, "If you don't show up on Saturday, don't show up on Monday." When saleswomen in stores occasionally used seats provided for them by law, floor-walkers would order them to do something which required standing. Foremen could pinch or fondle girls without their having any redress, and inspectors could promise fewer rejections of work in exchange for sexual favors. Few could afford to refuse—and then the women were blamed as enticers.[13]

Hours varied but were usually long. A grocery clerk reported working eleven hours every day except Saturdays and the eves of holidays, when she worked fourteen. A drugstore employee arrived at 7:00 A.M. and remained until 11:00 P.M. Women in transportation in New York spent between nine and fourteen hours at work every day. And busy seasons meant additional evening and weekend work, which had to be accepted in order to keep the job. If they worked hard and long during the regular season, these women might face as much as five months' unemployment during the slack times in their trades. Other women worked at night, either in search of better pay or to free themselves for child care during the day. In one survey in New York, all the women night workers with families did their own housework and washing, prepared three meals a day, and averaged four and a half hours' sleep in twenty-four—sometimes at one-hour intervals, sometimes for an hour or two in the morning and again in the afternoon. "It's hard to work nights," one woman said, "but you got to live."[14]

For an average sixty-hour workweek, the American factory woman could expect between $5.00 and $6.00 per week. In the heavily industrialized Northeast, she might begin at $1.50 a week in her early teens or $3.00 a week if she were older. Wages were lower in the South, higher in the West. But few factory girls made more than $8.00, the usual pay for completely unskilled men.

Although many male workers saw women as competitors,

in fact, women usually performed work peripheral to the well-paid and highly skilled occupations dominated by men or were relegated to unskilled trades where wages were too low to attract men. But women were still regarded as working for "pin money," an argument which assumed that they would accept lower wages because they did not really need the income. Some women did work by choice, as supplementary or voluntary earners. But the vast majority of working-class women were employed out of necessity, often as breadwinners for their families. A combination of lack of skills, willingness to accept lower wages in order to be employed at all, the "pin money" theory, and hopes that their working days would be temporary depressed the wages of these women. Lacking vocational education, strength in trade unionism, or protective legislation, they had almost no means of improving their income. Moreover, they received these wage rates only while they worked; many women alternated between frenzied seasons of work and no work at all.[15]

In 1900 domestic service still employed more working-class women than any other occupation. Since the 1840s, the flood of immigrant women had taken advantage of the demand for domestic workers in boardinghouses, hotels, and private houses. As household help, nurses, maids, cooks, laundresses, and waitresses, they needed little advance training and could acquire the necessary skills after they were hired. The Irish had to overcome anti-Catholic prejudice, which led to job listings such as "Woman Wanted.—To do general housework. English, Scotch, Welsh, German, or any country or color except Irish." At first, many employers found Irish girls too self-assured, with an independence often mistaken for impertinence. But with the rising demand for servants, good workers had little real trouble finding jobs. By 1850, 80 percent of all domestics in New York were Irish and a quarter of all Irish immigrants were "in service," compared with only a tenth of Germans. A generation later, the census showed 1.2 million women working as housekeepers, charwomen, chambermaids, cooks, and other kinds of servants; half were second-generation Americans. Service as a career had certain limitations, however. While a servant in a private household escaped the dangers of factory life, she generally spent long hours with little personal freedom and worked as hard as her mistress required. A maid might work from 6:00 A.M. to 10:00 P.M. or later if the family entertained. She was allowed out one evening a week and every other Sunday afternoon and evening but was required to return at 10:00 P.M. She therefore worked over one hundred hours a week, and since most servants "lived in," she enjoyed neither independence nor privacy.[16]

Hotel workers were no better off. Nearly all were uneducated and foreign. Most had lodging included in their job benefits, but their rooms were often small, dark, and poorly ventilated, some containing only a bed and soap box with no room for a chair. Frequently two girls shared a bed. In a survey made in Chicago, chambermaids reported that they ate in a storeroom under the kitchen, opposite the boilers, in intense heat, and their meals consisted of "comebacks," the leavings from guests' plates. When hotels violated the ten-hour-workday law, managers warned employees never to speak of their work to investigators, on threat of dismissal. And even hotel housekeepers pointed out moral temptations. "The majority of girls who work in hotels go wrong sooner or later," said one; "No one cared," reported another. Guests corrupted chambermaids; waiters despoiled the kitchen help. And the girls faced the results alone; managers ignored or abetted the conduct of guests, and a sixteen-year-old bellboy was "allowed to disappear" while a fifteen-year-old Polish immigrant girl bore his child in Chicago's House of the Good Shepherd. But the greatest complaints came not from sexual exploitation but from hard work. "I am so tired from backache that I can't stand up straight," said one.[17]

Women in restaurants might work twelve hours a day and more than sixty hours a week, although the law called for nine-hour days and fifty-four-hour weeks. Most waitresses said they worked in restaurants because they could get their meals at work and save on expenses. A waitress needed no training and little skill if she possessed good looks; pretty girls often served men while homely girls were put to work in the room reserved for women customers. Since wages remained low and the pressures of continuous standing, walking, lifting, and nervous strain caused frequent physical collapse, many waitresses claimed that they desired to have "as good a time as possible while their youth and attractiveness last[ed]." Some girls supplemented their wages by accepting help from a "gentleman friend." Others complained of bad treatment: "People think they can say almost anything to a waitress."[18]

Although laundry work was declining as an occupation for women by the turn of the century, females remained the largest percentage of workers in commercial steam laundries as well as private hand laundries. In steam laundries, women worked more than sixty-four and sometimes as many as eighty hours a week, usually distributed over five days, for about $6.50 per week in wages. Hours and working conditions seemed capricious; sometimes managers gave supper money, sometimes not. Fingers could get caught in unguarded mangles or burned on the flame of collar-finishing machines. Girls could starch faster standing than sitting, so no chairs were available. And an industry crowded with inexperienced people made work highly competitive.[19]

While domestic work still held the lead in jobs for women in 1900, a smaller proportion of working-class women were seeking jobs as domestics or in other service occupations, primarily because they could now find work in manufacturing or retailing at higher wages and with greater personal freedom. Natives and second-generation immigrants tended to move toward the factories and shops, while few houseworkers had been born in this country. Higher wages, shorter hours, time off, and vacations attracted the better educated away from domestic and other service. But even more important to the women who migrated from housework to mill or store was the opportunity to control their own lives. "I will not be at everybody's beck and call," said one; and another: "I would not have a woman say '*my servant*,' referring to me."[20]

Within the manufacturing trades, women's involvement in clothing industries had grown rapidly by 1900. Mechanization and the division of labor transferred many formerly male tasks to women. But workers still faced the home work, subcontract, sweatshop, and piecework systems. Seamstresses still had to purchase their own sewing machines and pay for electricity and thread. And while women moved into the trade in large numbers, they did not generally rise into the more skilled, better paid, and supervisory positions. Among cloth hat and cap makers, for example, women constituted about 20 percent of the trade but were concentrated in lining-making and trimming, while men remained cutters, operators, and finishers—skilled work which meant higher wages. Even when men and women performed the same tasks, wage scales differed: a skilled man finishing women's jackets received a third more than a skilled woman doing the same work, and male ironers earned 25 percent more than females.[21]

Little order existed in clothing manufacture. Investigators could not discover a homogeneous age, a clear set of reasons for working, or information on industriousness or quality of work. In the millinery trade, which enjoyed comparatively high prestige among women's occupations, the labor supply was highly elastic, probably owing to a large number of amateur milliners who usually worked at home but might occasionally seek employment in a shop. This competition from the amateurs, as well as irregular seasons of employment, played havoc with wages, hours, and working conditions. Cleveland milliners earned as little as $3 and as much as $50 per week, according to their specialty (makers, trimmers, designers) and place of employment (retail shops, millinery departments in stores, or wholesale houses). In New York, more than two-thirds worked over fifty-one hours a week, when they worked. The fall busy season lasted from August through November, the spring rush from January to the middle of May, but girls might work as little as thirty-two weeks in a year.[22]

Women also sought work in other industries, finding the least resistance when their work did not compete with that of men. When women entered meat processing, men welcomed them so long as they went into departments already labeled "women's work," such as packing, where wages were low and employment irregular. But entry of women into "men's departments," such as sausage stuffing, was resisted on the premise that women were neither permanent nor serious workers and their presence would depress wages. The same reactions prevailed in canneries, where little girls scrubbed cans and women painted and labeled them. In the confectionery trade, men made candy; girls wrapped it. As food processing moved out of the home and became industrialized, men took the place of women as bakers, brewers, and makers of dairy products.[23]

Just as working-class women migrated from domestic to manufacturing employment at the turn of the century, the early flow of middle-class women into white-collar work also carried some working-class girls into offices and sales jobs. Women had been employed as copyists and clerks as early as the 1860s, and their numbers grew as corporate business expanded during the 1870s and 1880s. But the office remained primarily a male province until the 1890s, when a combination of the widespread use of mechanical writing machines and the relative cheapness of female labor brought more women into office work. Moreover, since one and a half times as many women as men graduated from high school by 1900, and women were generally excluded from the professions, many entered offices, frequently by way of business schools which trained them as stenographers, typists, clerks, copyists, and bookkeepers. At the turn of the century, women accounted for three-quarters of the stenographers and typists and a sixth of the nation's clerks. While most of the women who took up office work were already middle class, the higher wages and greater prestige of white-collar employment attracted increasing numbers of working-class girls. A factory operative could expect to earn between $1.50 and $8.00 per week, compared to $6.00 to $15.00 available to stenographers and typists.[24] Similarly, since women had proved "a great success" as telegraph operators, they were sought as telephone operators and dominated that occupation from its inception, outnumbering men by ratios of eighteen to one in 1902. Recruited like the Lowell mill girls for their breeding and respectability, the early telephone operators were carefully trained in techniques and acceptable responses to the public. By the early twentieth century, they were earning $15.00 a week starting salary.[25]

Although office and telephone work were open to only a few working-class women, more sought to rise by taking sales jobs, which required less skill, education, or training. As early as the 1860s, reformers had urged the employment of women in stores to relieve the glut of sewing women on the labor market. Since these women had no alternative means of income, many agreed to work long hours in poor conditions for low wages. Retail managers frequently "hired" a young girl without wages on the pretext of teaching her the business; after six months, she might receive an "increase" to $2 a week. Women reported working from 8:00 A.M. to 9:00 P.M. for $7 a week. And they were required to dress better than factory girls. In retail stores, as in offices, women rarely did the same work as men, and few ever rose into supervisory positions. Thus it was neither wages nor career opportunities which attracted working-class women to sales jobs. Rather, the superior refinement and prestige of white-collar over manual labor drew those who wished to rise out of the working-class but lacked the skills for office work.[26]

The working situation of working-class women, therefore, appeared to be changing at the turn of the century. While these women were more likely to seek paid employment outside the home, they were beginning to shift the kinds of jobs they took from domestic and service activities to manufacturing jobs. And a few participated in the movement into white-collar employment. These adjustments often reflected the search for better wages and occasionally for more prestigious means of making a living.

When working was translated into living, the picture for working-class women remained grim. An investigation of twenty-two thousand women workers aged fourteen to fifty in Pittsburgh in 1907 and 1908 showed that 60 percent earned less than $7 per week, the minimum recommended for "decent living." Women remained at the lowest levels of "casual laborers," described as "temporarily permanent." Since Pittsburgh had a limited number of industries which used women workers, further reducing their pay, and since women did not spend time in training or compete for more exacting and better paid positions, they remained in lower grade occupations. Fewer than 1 percent could be described as skilled; 1.9 percent were handicraft workers; 23.2 percent did hand work requiring machinery; 31.1 percent operated machines; 13.9 percent tended machines; 13.3 percent did wrapping and labeling; and 15.8 percent performed hand work requiring no dexterity. Workers were required to stand in cracker factories, laundries, cleaners, metal works, some pressrooms and mercantile houses, and factories making lamps, glass, mirrors, brooms, paper boxes, soap, and trunks. They endured industrial dusts in garment and mattress making and in mirror polishing, heat from the cracker ovens, steam and gas in laundries and in cleaning and dyeing. Tobacco workers showed a high percentage of tuberculosis. Although state law limited their labor to sixty hours per week, the provision allowing twelve hours per day and no fixed closing time made the law difficult to enforce. Seasonal overtime represented a special problem; paper-box makers, for example, were affected by the Christmas rush. Native-born women held the best positions; the worst went to the most recent immigrants, Italians and Slavs.[27]

Girls often seemed defensive about their employment and tended to support their critics' accusations that they were working for frivolous reasons rather than from necessity. Some claimed that they worked to be independent and to spend their money as they pleased. Upper-class observers deplored the extravagance of this "craving for many and varied dresses," and worried that the "desire to test the world" would break down moral reserve. Journals fed working girls on romantic and escapist stories, such as the intervention of wealthy women to alleviate ill health and hardships of poor-but-virtuous factory girls.[28] But harsh reality was closer to the story of Hazel Burkhart.

Hazel wanted to escape from the limitations of parents, home, and small-town life, so she followed her friend Minnie to the riches and splendors of the city. Tired of penny-pinching restrictions at home, enticed by Minnie's promise that "we can live awful nice by clubbin' together" on $6 a week each, and intrigued by the prospect of companionship with other young people—especially young men—Hazel ignored the cries of alarm raised by a local spinster who had, after all, never been to the city and had only read magazine articles about it. Hazel left home. Despite an uncomfortable first night sharing Minnie's thin mattress, Hazel began city life with a luxurious 15¢ breakfast, although Minnie warned, "we dassen't do this again—ever." Minnie advised against living in a dormitory because the matrons were usually poor relations of the home's rich sponsors, and because the rules generally meant "if you ever want to do anything, it must be wrong; if you hate it, it's sure to be what you ought to do." Similarly, she found no nice boardinghouses for $6 girls. But when Hazel obtained work in Minnie's factory office, the girls took a decent room at $10 a month, although it meant commuting forty minutes to work on the elevated car. By using the landlady's gas stove and bringing in rolls and eggs or apples, they could keep breakfast expenses at about 5¢ each; a lunch of coffee and pie cost about 10¢. Minnie resisted nagging hunger at dinner in order to save money for clothes, but Hazel indulged herself in an extra 5¢ worth of jelly-roll at lunch and spent an extravagant 20¢ on her dinner. Her attitude changed, however, when Minnie used her savings to buy "something dead swell," an addition of false hair which won her an invitation to a dance with a young man in their office. While Hazel now saved her meal money for hair, Minnie's beau created a problem; the landlady evicted the girls when she discovered the young man in their room. "The other tenants would be sure to make trouble," she said, "if they knew I let to girls that ain't partic'lar." Minnie and Hazel found another room, with a less concerned landlady, but Minnie lost her boyfriend anyway when he "got fresh" and she resisted. The girls moved again, to a $2-a-week room without heat or closet or bathroom. But they had decided to save on rent and food in order to buy clothes which would attract "a swell fellow" rather than "a cheap skate" who "wants to sit around in a parlor."

Every compromise now went toward new winter clothes. By doing their own laundry and skimping on food, by spending a nickel on the shows only twice a week, and by walking to save carfare, they still had only $3 a week for clothing. But a coworker revealed that clothes could be purchased on the installment plan, and Minnie—who thought herself a fool for not thinking of that sooner—took Hazel off for three ecstatic hours of selecting their winter wardrobes. Hazel regretfully rejected a velveteen suit and furs for plain cloth, but each girl spent over $40 and agreed to pay $2 a week so that the winter clothes would be theirs by April, when they would need spring clothes. But they could wear the finery while they paid for it, and its first outing won them invitations to supper and a show from "two of the best-looking fellows in the mailing cage." As Minnie said, "Them clothes has saved us some money a'ready—got us free dinners an' free shows." Since the boys earned only $12 a week, and the shows lasted only an hour, the young people often spent the remainder of the evening in the "family room" of a saloon, drinking beer and listening to the phonograph or piano player. Life was charming until the January slump, when both girls were laid off and could find no work until another seasonal rush would begin.

Life deteriorated. The young men bought them an occasional dinner. The landlady waited for the rent as long as her drunken husband would permit. The store's collection agent threatened them with state prison. Fatigue, hunger, and constant rejection of their pleas for work wore them down. Finally, one night after a dance, Minnie did not return until dawn, when she confessed to Hazel that she had given up. "I gotta eat, and I dassen't be particular how I do it," she said, "I gotta have a bed to sleep on, and I dassen't be particular who pays fer it—because *I can't.*" Her young man could not ask her to marry him on $12 a week, so they were "goin' to do the next best thing." Minnie told Hazel, "I can't live on hopes and virtue."

Hazel swore that she was not shocked and did not judge herself any better than Minnie. "You feel like it was worth that to live," she replied, "I don't. That's all." A minute later, two half-dressed tenants picked up Hazel's limp body from the dark hallway, four floors below.[29]

6. Self-Help without Self-Awareness

WORKING-CLASS WOMEN in the early twentieth century were more involved in the struggle to leave the working class than in the development of an awareness of themselves as part of it. American society still appeared sufficiently ambitious and mobile to draw attention to the successful middle class. While the American dream of the nineteenth century had centered around ownership of a small family farm, after 1900 objectives shifted to supervisory or white-collar jobs for men, mothers who did not go out to work, ownership of a modest house, and perhaps a move to the growing suburbs.

"The development of industry," said one educated woman, "has created a vast amount of new wealth, and women more than men have profited by the great increase in productivity." But in stressing the growing leisure and self-gratification offered to middle-class women through industrial income of middle-class men, that author tended to overlook the many women who worked within that industrialization. Studies in poor neighborhoods, such as New York's West Side, indicated that ambitious families desired the "mark of the middle class married woman," namely "not to work." And where women complained of the injustices of birth, which allowed some women to "waste in idleness and luxury" while the industrial system cost other women their health and character, the solution suggested was the extension of idleness and luxury to the working-class woman rather than any questioning of the factory system. Moreover, working-class girls resented slurs upon their characters simply because they performed manual labor, and they tried to assert their intelligence and purity in defense. But they admitted that even within their own ranks "the sewing girl thinks herself above the mill girl." When working-class people had a chance for some of the benefits of middle-class life, their modest gains obscured their own social realities. In what one historian has called the "embourgeoisement of the working class," factory and community often provided avenues of social fulfillment for working-class families, especially those headed by women—small affluence, ownership of property, lessening of if not escape from economic worries, and middle-class attitudes about security.[1]

Chances for the development of working-class consciousness suffered also from nationalist antagonisms within the working classes. Often, trades were segregated along ethnic lines. Among garment workers, for example, Jewish girls were usually employed in the shops, while Italian women worked as finishers at home. Moreover, old and new hatreds kept working women apart. Eastern European Jewish girls resented the presence of Polish coworkers at their union meetings, when the Poles acted as spies for employers who would dismiss union members. And Russian Jewish women who made artificial flowers despised Italian women for accepting lower pay for their work, thereby depressing wage rates; most of the Jewish girls were self-supporting, while the Italian women worked within a family earning structure in which their wages only supplemented others' income. "If they were more civilized," said one Jewish woman, "they wouldn't take such low pay. But they go without hats and gloves and umbrellas."[2]

Those working-class women who were not lured by middle-class standards or kept apart by internal disputes still had little time or energy to use on issues not directly related to survival. A Polish man lamented that no one pitied his pregnant wife, although she was too poor to buy shoes and wore his old ones. A respectable wife regretted that she had not sold her youth and good looks for "ease and comfort and a quick death." And a mother responded acidly to a question about her children's spiritual welfare with, "t'aint souls that count," but bodies to be driven "till they drop in their tracks."[3]

Groups which challenged the middle-class or capitalistic systems rarely appreciated women's roles. The International Workers of the World included women both in the ranks and as organizers and leaders. More than half of the twenty-three thousand participants in the textile workers' strike in Lawrence, Massachusetts, in 1912 were women and children who stayed away from their jobs for ten weeks to protest insufficient wages and a speed-up. Among the leaders at Lawrence, and again in the Paterson, New Jersey, silk strike a year later, was Elizabeth Gurley Flynn, who had made her first speech at age fifteen, left school two years later to devote all her time to labor organizing, joined "Big Bill" Haywood and others in forming the IWW, organized textile workers and miners, and was immortalized by Joe Hill's famous ballad "The Rebel Girl." But within the organization, she had to fight male opposition to women attending meetings and marching on picket lines while she herself faced threats of jail and bodily harm.[4]

Socialists welcomed women into the movement but never developed a feminist analysis or solutions which gave women more than subordinate roles. Although some early socialists of the 1820s had recognized the importance of women's equality to questions of wage-labor, they often became sidetracked into issues of free love or social child raising. By the 1870s Marxism rejected feminism, although some utopians in the Gilded Age proposed a synthesis of ethical socialism with genteel femininity, and women who sought social organization outside the ranks of suffrage and clubwomen's groups often followed their husbands toward socialism. By the turn of the century the Socialist Party of America seemed to offer some means for women to gain status within the movement. At first, women were organized only on the fringes in "Ladies Auxiliaries" or in self-education study clubs or in volunteer work. In 1908 the Socialist party established a Woman's National Committee to absorb the independent groups and recruit women members and organizers. At its peak, the party probably had between twelve and fifteen thousand women members, with many thousands more affiliated. But women failed to organize in sufficient numbers to gain parity with men; more women joined from outside than from within the working class; and men remained suspicious of women's activities as "middle-class" and "nonproletarian." Even women like Elizabeth Gurley Flynn were indifferent to the organization of women as women, and male leaders dismissed discussion of suffrage or feminism as trivial sex issues which distracted attention from more essential class questions. When the general movement began to fade after 1912, the party finances became strained. Women's functions were among the first to be abandoned; an independent women's movement could not be revived, and female socialism suffered a precipitate decline by 1920.[5]

Even women who themselves took a radical position on working-class issues never reconciled their feminism with their radicalism. Anarchist Emma Goldman, who conspired with Alexander Berkman to assassinate steel magnate Henry Clay Frick and served several jail sentences for her anarchist and pacifist activities, vacillated on whether to subordinate her concern for women to the cause of anarchism and repeatedly became disillusioned with her lovers and male colleagues when they rejected consideration of women as women.

Similarly, the famous "Mother" Jones was unsympathetic to a women's movement and even exploited miners' wives and children in her efforts to help the men. Mary Harris Jones, an Irish immigrant, daughter of a railroad laborer, was converted to trade unionism by her iron moulder husband before she lost him and their four children in a yellow fever epidemic. After working as a nurse and seamstress and losing all her possessions in the Chicago fire of 1871, she became an organizer for the Knights of Labor and gained fame during the violent railroad strikes of 1877. By 1900 she had formed a close connection with the coal miners and caused considerable problems for mine owners and public officials until her death in 1930 (allegedly at a hundred years of age). If she occasionally made daring speeches such as "God Almighty made a woman, and the Rockefeller gang of thieves made the ladies," and briefly cooperated with working women in textile mills and breweries, she remained ambivalent toward them, believing that all women—except herself—should remain at home and attend to domestic duties. She dismissed suffragists and the Women's Trade Union League as too middle class for her notice and subordinated all issues to the economic battle for men. Like other organizers such as Ella Bloor, she used the title "Mother" and accepted designations such as "angel of light" and "patron saint" of the coal miners. She preferred to work with men and regarded miners' wives as unwanted daughters-in-law who might occasionally be used for the good of "her boys." Whenever she organized women, she treated them as auxiliaries to their men, urging them to encourage husbands to "stand firm," to attack policemen guarding struck property, to create noise by singing to their babies in jail, to teach their children about economic conditions—all to advance the cause of the workingman. Mother Jones disliked women in general and saw no reason to support working-class women except by improving the wages and working conditions of their husbands.[6]

Trade unionism represented one avenue for the organization of employed working-class women. Self-help would be preferable to presumptuous "social work," said one advocate, who stressed the intangible educational and social benefits of unionization as well as opportunities to use the power gained through organization to obtain increased wages and improved shop conditions. The age of industrial warfare and crippling competition should give way to cooperation and systematic negotiations, argued others, who applauded humanitarian sentiments which pitied underpaid women workers but cited the concrete efforts of unionization—shorter hours, increased wages, reduction of piece work, sanitary conditions, child labor laws—to urge that working girls develop a collective consciousness for their own good. In appealing for membership, unionists warned the unorganized woman worker that she was a tragic underbidder in the labor market and her own worst competitor.[7]

But women did not join unions in great numbers. After the disruption of the Knights of Labor in the 1890s, women's membership actually decreased. In New York State, for example, 7,488 women constituted 4.5 percent of persons in labor organizations in 1894. Their numbers grew to 15,509 in 1902, but by 1908 only 10,698 women were in unions and made up only 2.9 percent of union members. On the average, less than 2 percent of all women wage earners belonged to unions in 1910, and slightly more than 5 percent of women in manufacturing jobs were unionized.[8]

Unionists found women difficult to organize. Low-paid, unskilled, marginal women workers could not afford to lose their jobs by antagonizing employers with their union membership. One trade union woman was fired when her non-union coworkers went out on strike against her advice, because the foreman thought she must have initiated their action. But employers' opposition to unions and discrimination against members had less impact than the attitudes and situations of the women themselves. In the first place, women workers were unaware of organizing traditions for women in or out of the workplace. Few factory girls had heard of the Lowell Female Labor Reform Association or the Daughters of St. Crispin or the Women's Typographical

Union No. 1. Moreover, outsiders usually claimed credit for efforts to improve women's working conditions; reformers, male unionists, and middle-class women's organizations sponsored reform legislation or publicity campaigns to obtain justice for the working girl. Women workers lacked group consciousness, clinging to nineteenth-century ideals of individualism and "freedom of contract," which separated workers from one another and undermined collective bargaining. In addition, they had little physical cohesiveness, since they were dispersed in a vast number of industrial establishments, which impeded organizers' efforts to come into contact with them.[9]

Perhaps the greatest obstacle to unionization lay in the working woman's refusal to see industrial labor as her life's work. Most wage-earning women not only were young but were looking forward to marriage, which would remove them from the work force to the home. As temporary employees, they could not recognize any long-term function for themselves as workers or union members and were reluctant to join an organization without prospects of immediate benefits. Organizers complained about brief, runaway enthusiasm and unrealistic objectives among women workers; a girl in charge of a strike at a Michigan corset factory romantically decided to lead a grand revolution and received thirty unromantic days in jail, and a Chicago waitress mistakenly expected workers to "rise up in protest against the whole situation" when they saw her defying an injunction against picketing. When young women were drawn into unions for some specific purpose or because of a particular grievance, they often drifted out of the organization once that point had been gained. Women would accept low wages and poor working conditions—again, because they expected to be leaving soon to marry. Or, they would move casually from shop to shop in search of more comfortable environments rather than struggle together to improve their present situations. Women could also put up with the physical and emotional pressures of piecework and speed-ups in the short run but did not expect to be able to endure such treatment throughout a long industrial career. Since they did not anticipate continued employment, they saw no reason to insure against it. The typical woman worker remained untrained, cheap, and easily replaceable from the pool of new immigrants or other unskilled women. In addition, middle-class affectations often kept working-class women away from labor unions. Critics charged that female industrial workers preferred to associate with women who did not work, that they hesitated to link themselves with "foreigners," especially Jews, and that they found it "unseemly" to attend meetings with men whom they had not met socially.[10]

Men also resisted the admission of women to trade unions or supported unequal treatment of male and female union members. Many men viewed women as a threatening underclass of workers who undermined men's wages, sacrificed their femininity, and jeopardized the sanctity of family life. From this perspective, women worked for "pin money," competed with men, accepted lower wages, and therefore either forced men out of their jobs or obliged them to work for less money. In fact, unskilled women posed no real threat to more highly trained men, and the only sound economic arguments which could blame women for the deterioration of men's wages were technological advances whereby skilled work could be taken over by machines tended by unskilled women, or women could be used as strikebreakers to force protesting men back to their jobs. But even these attacks proved thin. Technological advance usually carried skilled men upwards, making room for unskilled women at the bottom. And, except for the typographical trades in the nineteenth century, women rarely acted as strikebreakers even to learn a trade, because they would be dismissed as soon as the strike had been settled.[11]

Critics also argued that women should be discouraged from working at all. Industrial work disrupted "women's naturally appointed sphere in life" as wife, mother, and homemaker, said one alarmist who went on to argue that wage labor threatened women's reproductive functions. "The wholesale employment of women in the various handicrafts must gradually unsex them," declared another male moralizer who worried about "the hearthstone cruelly dishonored" and charged that employment had stripped women of "that modest demeanor that lends a charm to their kind." Similar concerns encouraged the separate registration of male and female trade unionists, differing scales of dues and strike benefits, and denial of the necessity for equalizing wages.[12]

The nation's chief advocate of organization, the American Federation of Labor, shared this ambivalence toward women in trade unionism. Organized in the mid-1880s, the AFL at first seemed to invite female unionization, but the president was soon lamenting, "We know to our regret that too often are wives, sisters, and children brought into the factories and workshops only to reduce the wages and displace the labor of men." Deciding for a time that organization of women and economic education for children might alleviate this problem, the AFL appointed a committee on women's work and named Mary Kenney (O'Sullivan) as its first female general organizer. Already experienced with the women bookbinders' union and the Chicago Trades and Labor Assembly, Kenney worked for the AFL for five months with New York City garment workers, Troy shirtwaist makers, and Massachusetts printers, binders, shoe workers, and carpet weavers. But the AFL did not renew her contract or employ other women organizers, and throughout the 1890s its spokesmen and journal were increasingly hostile to the employment of women. In 1900 the annual convention considered (although it did not pass) a resolution to demand the firing of all women from federal government employment to "encourage a precedent for the removal of women from the everyday walks of life" and return them to the home.[13] The AFL's attitude may be explained in terms of two of its major priorities. First, the organization existed as a confederation of skilled craft unions; since women rarely possessed the necessary training to work in the crafts, they were employed in unskilled trades and by definition were ineligible for membership in the AFL's affiliates. Second, any organization which struggled as hard as the AFL to achieve middle-class socioeconomic status for its members would naturally adopt a bourgeois view of women. Like the Knights of Labor and the Socialist party, the AFL would only encourage women workers to support the labor objectives of male unionists so that workingmen could achieve sufficient income and economic security to keep their dependent women at home.

Early in the twentieth century, when it appeared that reformers and politicians might seek legislation and the formation of public agencies to deal with the problems of men and women workers, AFL leaders, such as Samuel Gompers, argued that trade unionism rather than public and political action should be the means of securing benefits for workers. And this necessity forced unionists to assume a more open position on organization of women. In 1903 social workers and trade unionists established the Women's Trade Union League during the annual AFL convention; a major purpose of the WTUL included unionization of women workers. By 1906 AFL partisans claimed that it was then the only force in American society which had concerned itself to any great extent with active and practical work for advancement of wage-earning women. Convention after convention went on record as supporting women's suffrage to raise the scale of wages for all. Gompers editorialized in 1915 that the labor movement and the women's movement were "two tremendous movements for freedom at the present time," and extended the AFL organizational hand to all regardless of sex, nationality, politics, race, or creed.[14] But convention delegates noted with alarm the low proportion of women representatives to the large number of working women. Women asked why no women served on the Executive Council. Gompers refused to hire a full-time woman organizer until 1918. Observers labeled AFL campaigns to organize women "puny and half-hearted." And as late as the 1920s, five AFL affiliates denied membership to females.[15]

Despite these obstacles, women had achieved some successful union organization by the early twentieth century. In Chicago, for example, where women were an active rather than a passive force, more than thirty-one thousand women had joined unions by 1903, including eight thousand garment workers and five thousand paper-box makers. As early as 1888 Elizabeth Morgan, wife of socialist Thomas Morgan, organized Ladies' Federal Labor Union No. 2703, a mixed group of clerks, bookbinders, and other women workers, which eventually affiliated with the AFL. Women served as delegates to the city-wide association of trade unions, the Chicago Trades and Labor Assembly. And in at least one union women had learned sufficient organizational sophistication to refuse to strike when a coworker was fired for poor work—because she actually had done poor work. The WTUL organized women in the stockyards when men made no effort to unionize what they called "petticoat butchers." Then their representatives went into the federal courts to demand "that women doing the same class of work as men be paid the same wage." Chicago was the center of women's organization in the glove trade with the national headquarters of the International Glove Workers Union, representing an industry in which women were more heavily organized than men. And the waitresses' local in Chicago was described as "one of the most effective and interesting unions."[16]

But union women in the early twentieth century presented a mixed picture of organization and activity. In the boot and shoe industry, women could follow the example of the Daughters of St. Crispin. After 1895 the Boot and Shoe Workers' Union admitted anyone working in the trade, regardless of sex. Women participated fully in the many strikes organized by the union in its early days and often proved more determined than the men to remain out until they had won their point. The union president declared that it was "harder to induce women to compromise than men." But women had little voice in the management of the union, either locally or nationally. And organizers complained that women workers refused to recognize or use the strength of their numbers in the trade.[17] Among cigar and cigarette makers, women constituted a heavy percentage of the trade—43.9 percent in 1905 —but made up only a tenth of the members in the various unions. Women had declined from the trained Bohemian immigrants of 1869 to unskilled machine operators in factories by 1901. And in their unions, they generally made up small and passive minorities; only the Boston tobacco strippers had a union with women officers and managers. Similarly, women textile workers suffered an erosion in their share of the trade and the lack of a strong union movement. Although more than 330 thousand women worked in textile mills in the United States in 1905, they accounted for only 40.6 percent of workers in that trade (compared with 48.4 percent in 1880). The Northern portions of the industry employed foreigners and significant parts of the trade had moved to the South. The United Textile Workers of America, organized in the 1890s, was intended to include all textile workers, but it suffered from contentions among various branches of the trade, frequent withdrawal of locals who disagreed with national policies, and a lack of coherent organization, which forced it to use strikes rather than more sophisticated means to advance the members' interests. Still, women joined the union in large proportions—about the same as their share in the industry. While unionization itself had not been particularly successful among textile workers, organization had progressed better among women mill-hands than in other trades.

Organization often depended on how work within trades was divided. Women bookbinders, for example, had slightly over half the positions in the industry but seldom did the same work as men. And the usual policy of the International Brotherhood of Bookbinders, founded in 1892, was to organize women separately; 24 of the 130 locals at the turn of the century contained women. One in New York City, with a membership of a thousand, was said to be "the most successful woman's union in the city," winning wage increases of $1.25 per week and reductions of hours from nine to eight per day, without strikes. Although women bookbinders welcomed support from the men's locals, they seemed to prefer task-defined and sex-segregated organization.[18]

The garment workers probably represent the most publicized example of organization and activism among women workers early in the twentieth century. The most important manufacturing trade which employed more women than men, garment work was primarily confined to about eight large cities; New York, for example, produced more than half the total American output in 1905. The trade had evolved into many subdivisions and only cutting of garments still required both skill and strength; hence, recent immigrants flocked into the lower levels of the business, earning while they learned English and saving to become employers themselves or moving into higher levels of the work. Unions were divided by the kind of clothing made, rather than the work skills or sex of the employees; the United Garment Workers' Union organized those working on men's clothing while the International Ladies' Garment Workers' Union dealt with those producing women's wear.

The United Garment Workers, founded in New York City in 1891 and affiliated with the American Federation of Labor, quickly chartered locals, including three composed entirely of women. A woman served on the general executive board from 1897, but women had little part in the general operations of the union and none in its policy-making. Male unionists accepted women into mixed locals out of necessity. The group desired that manufacturers adopt a union label, but employees in the shop had to be organized before the label could be used, and many factories employed only a few men as cutters, with the rest of the workers women. By 1909, 12.9 percent of the more than twelve thousand women in the men's garment trade in New York City and joined the UGW. In Chicago, where ethnic differences, rival unions, and the open shop impeded organization, what had been predominantly a woman's union movement declined drastically after 1903. But some segments of the trade, such as the overalls workers, claimed heavy membership and significant gains, including a reduction in hours—without strikes.

Organization struggled against less favorable conditions in the ladies garment industry. With greater concentration in large cities, workers faced vicious competition from new immigrants; while the number of women in the trade rose between 1900 and 1905, their proportion fell from 68.5 to 62.9 percent. And the turnover of workers was especially high. Organizers also had to contend with a trade conducted in many small shops and with tasks highly subdivided; ten workers produced each shirtwaist, for example. Moreover, seasonal work meant alternative periods of rush and layoff, and workers tended to strain themselves to get maximum earnings under piecework rates while the busy season lasted. Against these obstacles, the International Ladies' Garment Workers' Union began its struggles in 1900 with a treasury of $30 and a few desks in the Cloakmakers' Union office. In particular, the ILGWU had to contend with the sweatshop and the subcontract systems and sought to "civilize the relationship between the jobber, contractor, and worker."[19]

Since so many women in the garment trades were themselves Eastern European Jewish immigrants, ILGWU organizers faced a unique situation of dealing with their previous labor activism and adjustments to American working conditions. These women suffered double discrimination. On the one hand, as recent immigrants from Eastern Europe, they were exploited by the more established German Jews, who owned many of the shops or engaged in subcontract work. On the other hand, while the unions provided a kind of rite of passage into the American labor system, even claiming that "old" immigrant craft unionists extended federation of "new" immigrants, AFL affiliates, including the ILGWU, continued to treat women workers as secondary, supplementary, and subordinate workers. Even on social and religious questions, the Jewish women suffered from both traditional and American attitudes. Many immigrants had become sufficiently Americanized to treat union women who chose to remain single as "marriage rejects or failures."[20]

But unionization profited from the experience and attitudes of these Jewish women. If self-sacrifice prompted a Jewish mother to give first priority to her children's needs, "the Jewish labor union woman put the community and workers' needs first." Perhaps more significantly, Eastern European Jewish women brought two traditions with them when they came to America—work and unionization. Because such a high value was placed on scholarship among Jewish men, women often worked while men studied. Russian and Polish Jewish women had engaged in wage labor before coming to America and expected to continue working here. Second, these women had either experienced or been exposed to trade unionism in Europe and came from a class-conscious culture, which made them interested in unionization.[21]

Between 1900 and 1909 the ILGWU had sporadic success in organizing women in the trade, but working conditions seemed even worse. Garment workers spent from 8:00 A.M. to 6:00 P.M. each day in small, unclean shops, with an hour less on Saturdays, and in rush seasons sometimes worked as late as 10:00 P.M. without overtime pay. A quarter of the women earned less than $4 a week; the average weekly wage was $7 to $12; and workers received nothing during the slack seasons. Garment sewers still bought their own needles and thread, paid for electricity and chairs, and were fined for talking to one another, being late, getting machine oil on fabrics, or taking crooked stitches. Sporadic strikes, such as the reefer makers' in 1907 and the pants makers' in 1908, brought no improvement.

But an enormous walkout by New York shirtwaist makers during the winter of 1909–10 rocked the industry and changed the unionization picture. Employers at the Triangle Waist Company had tried to forestall union organizing by establishing an employees' benevolent society open to "loyal" workers who did not join a union. With the approach of the Jewish holidays in the fall of 1909, workers voted to distribute $10 to each needy member of the association who had a family to support; the company refused this plan, offering instead to make loans to members. Angry employees conferred with representatives of the United Hebrew Trades, and 150 of them soon lost their jobs because of their union sympathies. Triangle claimed that there was no work for them, although the company advertised for workers the next day and refused to rehire the 60 men and 90 women who had been fired. ILGWU local 25 declared a lockout and called a strike of Triangle and the Leiserson shop on September 27. Throughout October the strikers picketed, although Leiserson hired professional thugs to molest strikers and Triangle brought in pimps and prostitutes to harass them. Both union members and sympathetic society women were arrested. Unionists tried to convince strikebreakers to join them, only to find that the Polish, German, Italian, and Slovene women did not understand their pleas in English and Yiddish. By November, as the strikers' resistance was wearing down, the ILGWU and the United Hebrew Trades considered widening the strike to include the thirty thousand shirtwaist workers in the New York shops. Before an audience of several thousand, the leaders debated this issue for half the night at a meeting at Cooper Union on 22 November 1909. Finally, a young working girl, Clara Lemlich, requested permission to speak. Addressing the workers in Yiddish, she offered a resolution for an immediate general strike, launching a five-minute tumult, ending with the audience pledging faith with the old Jewish oath: "If I turn traitor to the cause I now pledge, may this hand wither from the arm I now raise." At dawn the next morning, more than twenty thousand workers—union members and unorganized—left the shops. In order to cheat the bosses of learning who had given the strike signal, it was arranged that the pressers would turn out their lights; the workers then rose in unison and marched out.

The Uprising of the 20,000 lasted thirteen weeks, educated untold numbers of workers in unionization, and sparked a cohesive Jewish labor movement. More than three-quarters of the workers in the trade participated. Russian Jews formed the largest and most faithful contingent. American girls believed they had no personal grievance but struck in sympathy until they became disenchanted by the constant uncompromising ideological pressures of the Russian men. And Italian women appeared and disappeared from the strikers' ranks. The union could offer little material aid; over thirteen weeks, each striker received less than $2 in benefits. Many unmarried women refused even this small sum so that married men could receive more. Men complained of the hardships more than women did. And girls wore their thin best sabbath clothes on picket duty in snow and freezing temperatures. Over six hundred girls were arrested; more than a dozen served five days in the workhouse; several spent ten days in the Tombs, the city prison. In many factories, scabs broke the strike, and workers had to return to "open" or nonunion shops. Only 312 establishments granted union contracts. But the sense of worker solidarity, particularly among the women, had been strong. One analyst noted the fascinating enigma of these workers, "that many of them should be simultaneously inflamed with revolutionary ideas and driven by hopes for personal success and middle-class status."[22]

The following winter, garment workers in Chicago struck the Hart, Schaffner, and Marx factory, largest clothing manufacturer in town, in a walkout which grew to include forty thousand workers in a few weeks. Working conditions in Chicago resembled those of New York, and unions had had a similar lack of success in organizing until the big strike. Most of the strikers left the shops in response to accumulated grievances and turned to the United Garment Workers' Union only after they were out. When the UGW could not handle so many workers, it brought in the Chicago Federation of Labor and Women's Trade Union League; with joint strike conferences, the leaders established committees to deal with grievances, picketing, organization, relief, and publicity. In dozens of meeting halls around the city, organizers struggled for fourteen weeks to keep up the morale of strikers representing at least nine nationalities. Eventually Hart, Schaffner, and Marx agreed to recognize the workers' right to strike, and an arbitration committee with representatives of both workers and employers was established to consider grievances. But many strikers called it a "hunger bargain": the union had not been recognized; it could not represent workers to the employers; hundreds of workers did not get their jobs back; and the Women's Trade Union League had to guarantee the good conduct of the union during the two years covered by the agreement. Even the disgruntled, however, remarked that the Chicago garment strike had produced a sense of mutual understanding "between this huge unorganized group of immigrant workers and the Americanized groups of organized labor."[23]

The inspiring strikes of 1909 and 1910 sparked strong organizing drives in the garment trades but achieved little concrete success. The ILGWU sent out paid organizers like Rose Schneiderman, who took the job because of her commitment to "doing something worthwhile" while she acquired "a little freedom from my family" and saw something of the country. But she soon learned that organizing was an unromantic job, involving recruitment, establishment of a local, and then the nursing of the members "so they won't get discouraged and quit before the union is strong enough to make demands on the employers." She had little success in Cleveland, was unable to rebuild the Chicago Shirtwaist Makers Union, which had collapsed after an unsuccessful strike, and was glad to leave Philadelphia where she had done what she could but was "always under the manager's thumb." Other women organizers reported similar high ideals but few successes.[24]

Clothing workers struck, often in large numbers, sometimes achieving their demands, but rarely retaining a lasting organization. In Cleveland in 1911, workers stayed out for more than ten weeks, drawing even young girls into the strike but not into the labor movement. In 1913 seven thousand New York white-goods workers picketed for five weeks gaining a fifty-hour work week, double pay for overtime, abolition of tenement labor, three legal holidays with pay, slight wage increases, and an impartial wage and grievance board—but not recognition of their union.[25]

After 1910 employers increasingly accepted the trade agreement or protocol solution to labor difficulties. First proposed by Louis D. Brandeis in 1910 to settle the bitter cloakmakers' strike, the protocol was aimed at industrial peace. Provisions usually included the establishment of a preferential union shop (neither union nor nonunion), outlawing of strikes (worker walkouts) and lockouts (employer closings), and the creation of joint labor-management boards to mediate disputes. Partisans praised the protocol as protection for the workers from poor wages and working conditions. Opponents labeled it "class collaborationism."[26]

But male leadership in the unions, reliance on the protocol, and—most significantly—low levels of organization of women meant that even these gains remained beyond the reach and control of most working-class women. Few joined labor organizations outside the garment trades. None influenced policy. And the protocol arrangement itself was the work of middle-class reformers.

The vast majority of working-class women did not yet see a place for themselves in the self-help movement when it focused on organization and unionization. Still regarding themselves as temporary workers and temporary residents in the working class, these women continued to identify with middle-class aspirations in which the trade union movement had little place. Why invest scarce time and effort in organizations to improve the conditions of workers when they, themselves, would soon pass out of that status and into the more secure realm of the middle class?

7. The Progressive Dilemma of Protection

UNTIL THE EARLY twentieth century, working-class women had largely been left to their own devices to survive, cope with poverty and difficult conditions, and struggle upwards toward middle-class security and respectability. In line with the American dream of democracy and opportunity, society assumed that people at all levels could and should take care of themselves, and that everyone possessed an inherent right to independent action. Each person, said the social Darwinists, must bear final responsibility for his or her own status in society, since position was supposedly determined by ability, ambition, and hard work. Consequently, socialists and others who attempted to organize the working classes to make some claims on society were regarded as threatening extremists. Labor unions came under fire for subverting freedom of contract for the individual. And most efforts to help working-class women came under the heading of charity or philanthropy, justifiable only in time of crisis.

Early efforts to establish helpful procedures to aid working-class women through social or public institutions continued to face these prevailing attitudes and obstacles. Moreover, the determination of Americans to succeed on their own often stood in the way of people taking advantage of this kind of help. For a number of years, reformers themselves were determined that their work would be directed at the creation of opportunities in which people could do for themselves, rather than the establishment of custodial protection for the disadvantaged. By the eve of World War I, however, many workers in the cause of reform had become disappointed in the working-class women they sought to help. Increasingly, therefore, the energies of the middle-class reformers focused on changes in the law or in social institu-

132

tions to extend to working-class women the protection they evidently needed but could not secure by their own efforts.

The road to protectionism was not a direct one, however; nor did the protectionists come to it with preconceived notions about that goal. Rather, most reformers hoped simply to help people to help themselves.

At the turn of the century, a new generation of moral activists called "progressives" arose out of the middle class, the colleges, and the professions, vowing to make order out of America's chaotic growth, to redress some of the imbalances in modern society, and to remove artificial barriers which stood in the way of ideal democracy and social mobility. At no time did these reformers constitute a single united group with an agreed-upon agenda of necessary changes. Rather, they formed coalitions, occasionally supporting one another's separate causes in the interest of broad principles of democracy and opportunity. Some concentrated on breaking down political barriers, making war on city machines which robbed the poor ethnic voter of his independence in exchange for an informal network of social services. Others believed that democracy demanded that the vote be extended to women, in fair acknowledgment of their citizenship and contributions to the country, and in hopes that superior female moral standards would help in the fight against corruption. Reformers who saw drunkenness as the "curse of the working classes" sought first temperance and then prohibition of liquor to end the physical and moral effects of drink on the laborer and to close the saloons, which had become recruiting stations for the political machines. Concern for the small farmer and businessman prompted yet other Progressives to demand regulation of railroad rates and public utilities, as well as the establishment of agencies to supervise stock operations, insurance companies, banking, and other business practices. Educators fought for compulsory school for children and night school training in English and citizenship for adult immigrants. Settlement-house workers hoped to impart standards of work, cleanliness, and morality to residents of ghetto neighborhoods. Advocates of democracy introduced the initiative, referendum, and recall to place tools for change in the hands of "the people." Muckrakers exposed vile working and living conditions in city slums, food-processing plants, corporate empires, and other "modern" enterprises. Industrial reformers focused on wages, hours, health, and sanitation standards. Most Progressives agreed that the traditional democracy envisioned by the Founding Fathers for an agricultural society in the late eighteenth century had been altered by the realities of modern expansion, industrialization, and urbanization. And they wished both to restore those original ideals of freedom and democratic participation and to improve the "quality of life" for their contemporaries, especially by improving the efficiency of human effort.

At the same time, these reformers did not wish to assume personal or state control over individual lives. In offering the protection of society or government to the disadvantaged, such as working-class women, Progressives stressed availability and opportunity rather than management and custody. They hoped to create open situations in which people would be free to help themselves. And if their relations with working-class women eventually deteriorated into a "feminism of good works," their initial plans called for independence within a framework of protection. Yet the balance of these two forces—protection and independence—remained a crucial dilemma for the Progressives and their successors.

In approaching any problem, Progressives placed considerable value on orderly, moral, practical, and scientifically sound evaluation and solution. The Gilded Age had generated vague imbalances and discontents. Before launching corrective action, the reformers wanted to know exactly what the difficulties were and how far they extended. For the first time in American history, therefore, reformers began as fact-finders, and for the first time, they developed a significant body of data about the actual living and laboring conditions of working-class women.

Some of the earliest investigators were authors or journalists. Helen Stuart Campbell, for example, had already earned one reputation as a writer of children's stories in the 1860s and another as an activist in the home economics movement in the 1870s before she published *The Problem of the Poor* in 1882, a description of a New York City waterfront mission, which included arguments on the bad effects of low pay for women. She remained with this theme, exposing the impossibility of living decently on such wages, in a magazine series published in 1886 as *Mrs. Herndon's Income.* And in the same year, she began a weekly series of articles for the *New York Tribune* on conditions of women working in department stores and the needle trades; eventually collected as *Prisoners of Poverty: Women Wage-Workers, Their Trades and Their Lives,* the stories were published as a book in 1887. Four years later, the American Economic Association gave an award to her survey of conditions among American and European working women, which was published in 1893 under the title *Women Wage-Earners.* Helen Campbell dramatized working-class women; rather than dealing with them abstractly or statistically, she presented them as Rose Haggerty, seamstress-turned-prostitute to care for her invalid mother and small brothers and sisters, or as Lotte Bauer, who died of hemorrhage over her sewing machine after the foreman had cheated her of wages and seduced her younger sister. The shock value of these pieces began to make middle-class readers aware of living conditions of their "social inferiors."[1] Another journalist, Mary Heaton Vorse, used the same techniques to draw public attention to strikes of textile workers at Lawrence in 1912, steel workers in 1919 and 1937, mill hands in Passaic, New Jersey, in 1926, and the United Textile Workers in North Carolina in 1929.[2]

Some middle-class women, such as Dorothy Richardson and Bessie and Marie Van Vorst, actually entered working-class occupations long enough to gather materials for books on conditions there. Dorothy Richardson produced a particularly sensational account of grim lodging houses, prostitution, drug addiction, alcoholism, death by fire and diphtheria, and insanity as she reported on her work in a paper-box factory, as an artificial flower maker, a white-goods operator, a jewelry-case maker, and a shaker in a laundry, before an old friend rescued her from a white slaver and sent her to a night school stenography course which would open the path to respectable white-collar employment. Mrs. Van Vorst and her sister-in-law also wrote graphic descriptions of their work in a variety of places such as a Pittsburgh pickle factory and pointed up the unequal treatment of men and women workers in each case.[3] Most of these books concluded with a plea for charitable intervention and philanthropy to educate working-class women toward moral uplift and more efficient work habits. Occasionally, an author like Mary Heaton Vorse preached unionization and worker solidarity. But most of these writers believed that working-class women were still unable to help themselves.

Domestic reformers also found themselves investigating conditions while they worked out solutions. In Boston, for example, the Women's Educational and Industrial Union was organized in 1877 "for the advancement of women." After 1890, when Mary Morton Kimball Kehew became director, the Union increasingly moved toward educational work, establishing training programs in housekeeping, dressmaking, and sales while offering job counselling based on its investigations of opportunities for skilled labor among women, jobs for girls in manufacturing, and in such industries as paper-box making. Social fact-finding became more organized when Susan Myra Kingsbury became director of the research department in 1907. A veteran of social research in England and Massachusetts, Kingsbury developed systematic field studies and used Boston area graduate students to compile information, which she analyzed and published as pamphlets and books on such topics as labor laws and industrial home work.[4]

Charitable organizations also began to move in the direction of scientific collection of information to support their good works. When Mary Richmond went to work for the Baltimore Charity Organization Society in the late 1880s as assistant treasurer, she also volunteered as a "friendly visitor" to gather data on the recipients of charitable gifts. At first, charity organization leaders welcomed these case studies as a guarantee that the generosity of wealthy contributors would not be misused, but gradually, thorough research became the basis for perfecting treatment of problems uncovered. Mary Richmond carried this philosophy and method with her to Philadelphia in 1900 and then to New York in 1909, when she was named Director of the Charity Organization Department of the two-year-old Russell Sage Foundation. Under her leadership, the foundation financed studies of communities, ethnic groups, occupations, working conditions, and labor regulations—frequently including or focusing on working-class women.[5]

Between 1907 and 1917 the Russell Sage Foundation sponsored the investigation and distributed the results of a collection of industrial surveys aimed at "improvement of social and living conditions in the United States." The foundation frequently cooperated with other agencies in these studies; the Pittsburgh Survey, for example, used foundation funds for four major and several minor investigations. Similarly, the foundation paid investigators who compiled the materials on standards of living among New York City workingmen's families for the New York State Conference of

Charities and Corrections. In funding and publishing these collections, the Russell Sage Foundation fulfilled the double function of awakening middle-class readers to industrial and working-class conditions and gathering evidence for reformers to use in pressing for state regulation of wages, hours, health, safety, and related standards. Authors of the Pittsburgh Survey learned that not only were the facts of women's work generally unknown outside the industries in which they labored, but employers themselves frequently knew practically nothing about the women who worked for them. In almost every study, the surveyors aimed at a double presentation of evidence: on the one hand numerical compilations of wages, hours, regularity of employment, family budgets, categories of workers, and similar data satisfied the cry of reformers for statistical and scientific weapons for their arguments in favor of protective legislation; on the other hand, personal stories of the survey subjects dramatized the human side of their problems. When Katharine Anthony wrote *Mothers Who Must Earn,* a study of female employment in the West Side district of Manhattan in 1914, she presented tables showing numbers of widows and wives of disabled men working, proportions of households which took in boarders, and ranges of earnings by these women breadwinners. She also reported that almost all of the 370 women investigated had told her, "If I had it to do over, I'd never marry." In addition, the pamphlets and books usually concluded with an appeal for reform. *The Standard of Living Among Workingmen's Families in New York City* (1909) appealed for a scale of wages based on the cost of living; *Women in the Bookbinding Trade* (1913) protested against night work for women; *A Seasonal Industry: A Study of the Millinery Trade in New York* (1917) argued for both minimum wage laws and alternative means of employment to give work during slack seasons.[6]

Various charitable and reform groups conducted similar investigations to bolster their appeals for improvements. The Women's Trade Union League studied the ethnic composition of the white-goods industry and the effects of irregular employment on usable wages. The same group compiled information on wages, hours, working conditions, and length of employment of women in various cities and trades; they exposed inhuman conditions of women and children earning their livings in tenements; and they raised issues of employers' responsibilities for the moral downfall of underpaid workers. Chicago's Juvenile Protection Association surveyed working conditions of waitresses, hotel maids, and other women workers, while the Immigrants' Protective League collected information on Italians, Greeks, Mexicans, and Bulgarians living in Chicago. By 1910 books on working women could draw on materials gathered in New England, New York, New Jersey, Pennsylvania, the Midwest, Oregon, and California.[7]

Eventually, even the United States government joined in the collection of information. The first commissioner of labor, Carroll D. Wright, had employed twenty special investigators as early as 1888 to collect information on industrial hours, wages, employment conditions of women and children, housing, and living costs, for inclusion in his annual reports. At least one of his employees, Mary Clare de Graffenried, publicized this social data in prize-winning essays, which, like the work of Helen Campbell, exposed some of the economic difficulties of women.[8] But the federal government did little beyond the decennial census to gather materials specifically on women. By the early twentieth century, however, pressure had mounted for a thorough investigation of industrial, social, moral, educational, and physical conditions of employed women and children. In 1906 Congress authorized a study,[9] and between 1910 and 1913, the commissioner of labor issued a massive nineteen-volume *Report on Conditions of Women and Child Wage-Earners in the United States.*[10] In addition to historical studies of women in industry and women in trade unions, investigators collected information on age, hours, terms of employment, health, morals, literacy, sanitation, means of protection, organization, and laws for women and children workers in dozens of trades, including cotton textiles, men's ready-made clothing, glass, silk, and laundry work. Although the studies formally involved only employed persons, they also uncovered rich materials about the personal and home lives of members of the working classes, particularly relating low earnings and poor working conditions to family budgets, health, morality, education, and the need for society to be concerned about these women and children.

Pioneer sociologists and social workers also developed casework studies to accumulate factual knowledge and often publicized the results of their social investigations. Teachers of social work began to separate their practical reform-oriented tasks from the theoretical work of the sociologist, and developed schools devoted to the training of professional investigators, analysts, administrators, settlement-house workers, and staffs of the growing number of local and governmental agencies devoted to social improvement. Sophonisba Breckinridge and Edith Abbott worked at the University of Chicago, where they concentrated on housing and juvenile questions. Both wrote extensively, not only out of their own researches but also as publicists making the results of government and foundation surveys available in the popular journals of the day in order to educate middle-class readers to some of the problems of industrial and working-class life. Susan Myra Kingsbury, with her reputation as a social researcher already established by studies of women and children in factories and homes, joined the faculty of Bryn Mawr College in 1915 as professor of social economy and director of the first academic department offering postgraduate training in social services. Kingsbury emphasized practical application of theoretical training, encouraging students in field experience and research; students worked in factories and social welfare agencies during the summers. Later, Kingsbury would also pioneer in worker education.[11] The information gatherers hoped to use their results to press for reforms on behalf of working-class women.

Meanwhile, from the schools, the charities, and the tradition of good works came the settlement-house workers and social housekeepers who would go into the neighborhoods to show working-class women themselves how to improve their lives in practical ways. Dozens of religious and social reformers established social settlements in ghetto areas of large cities, first intending to civilize the immigrants by their middle-class example, and later turning to investigation, lobbying, unionization, and legislation in the attack on urban poverty and impotence. Settlement workers found women especially useful in their efforts to penetrate the ghetto.

The most famous of the Chicago settlements, Hull House, was established in 1889 by Jane Addams and Ellen Gates Starr. Both women were educated in a women's seminary; both had strong leanings toward religion; both travelled abroad and studied European settlements. While Jane Addams handled fund-raising and executive administration, Ellen Starr won support from the city's fashionable elite. Determined to "live with the poor," they rented the dilapidated Hull mansion on Chicago's West Side, surrounded by Sicilian, Italian, Greek, Russian, and German immigrants. At first, the two young women concentrated on acculturation, attempting to share fine art and the literature of Shakespeare and Browning with their new neighbors. But gradually, they came to view the settlement as "an institution attempting to learn from life itself," and within four years

Hull House had become a day nursery, playground, cooperative boardinghouse for working girls, medical dispensary, and cooking and sewing school, as well as a theater, music school, and art gallery. By 1895 the residents had gathered and published an extensive collection of materials on tenement and factory conditions, which they used to press for factory inspection, child labor laws, and a host of other industrial and welfare legislation. Sunday afternoon teas at Hull House brought poor women together with trade unionists and social philosophers; one girl remembered, "We began to feel that we were part of something that was more important than just our own problems."[12]

If settlement workers began with modest middle-class ambitions, their surroundings usually educated them rather quickly to social realities. Hull House provided early training for social activists like Mary Eliza McDowell. In 1894 she was organizing a women's club at Dr. Graham Taylor's Chicago Commons; the dozen immigrant women who met on Monday evenings apparently spent considerable time praising one another as "ladies" and singing patriotic songs. But a few years later "Fighting Mary" McDowell had become the "Garbage Lady" and the "Angel of the Stockyards." Living among the Irish, German, Polish, Lithuanian, Bohemian, and Slavic immigrants in the "back of the yards" district behind the stockyards and meat-packing plants, she directed the University of Chicago Settlement and established day nurseries, English classes, garbage disposal, and a neighborhood playground while unionizing stockyard workers and agitating for the vote for women in municipal elections.[13]

And the work multiplied. So many settlements in so many poor neighborhoods, sometimes more than one in a section. In addition to the prominent Hull House and the Commons, Chicago had Benton House, Gads Hill Center, Olivet Community Center, Erie Neighborhood House, Emerson House, and a dozen others operated by Episcopalians, Presbyterians,

Catholics, universities, and independents.[14] New York City also had many settlement houses, the most famous at Henry Street, where Lillian Wald combined settlement work with her commitment to public health nursing. By 1913 the Henry Street Visiting Nurse Service was organizing two hundred thousand visits each year, maintaining first-aid stations, and providing convalescent facilities—all at fees "most considerate of the dignity and the independence of the patient." As in Chicago, New York settlements combined philanthropy with social work; the Lewisohns, for example, brought dance and theater to Henry Street and built the Neighborhood Playhouse.[15] Every large and industrial city had its settlements, such as Denison House in Boston, Asacog House in Brooklyn, College Settlement in Philadelphia, and Kingsley House in New Orleans.

Settlement workers and other concerned reformers took up a host of issues at the turn of the century, often bringing a professional element of organization to causes which had been in private charitable hands in the past. Immigrants, for example, had drawn on several networks of informal ethnic or religious group support in making their first adjustments to America. Earlier settlers from many districts of Italy met *paisani* at Castle Garden or Ellis Island and helped them find temporary lodging or directed them to transportation to their destinations further inland. The United Hebrew Charities performed similar services for Jewish newcomers, and women's groups assisted with settlement in cities like Pittsburgh. But immigrants sometimes suffered exploitation by older compatriots, losing money or tickets or possessions, and tales increased of innocent country girls lured into white slavery by those who posed as protectors. By 1908 the founders of Hull House and others like Sophonisba Breckinridge and Grace Abbott created the Immigrants Protective League, an agency to aid transient, stranded, bewildered, or unemployed immigrants in the Chicago area. The IPL remained in its headquarters at Hull House for the next eleven years and in 1919 became a statewide operation, often using the University of Chicago Graduate School of Social Service to assist in its investigations and placements.

Educators also tried to assist the assimilation of immigrants through language, civics, and lifestyle training. Preconceived notions about immigrant women led school personnel, social workers, and home visitors to design Americanization programs which offered women domestic instruction, such as cooking, while men learned through work-forms and public involvement. Immigrant women learned English words relating to the household and foodstuffs; men learned words like "machinery" and "foreman" and "vote." In these efforts, the professionals developed programs which were less effective than those structured by the immigrants themselves, in which they learned political awareness and how to use the network of public social services. On the other hand, educators enjoyed more success when they taught immigrant and working-class girls a trade, often combining vocational training in dressmaking or sewing or cord work with citizenship lessons and sometimes religious education as well. Settlement houses also became interested in vocational training. Henry Street, for example, established a model shop in 1897 and offered scholarships to girls who wished to learn there. Lillian Wald and Leonora O'Reilly, veteran of the Knights of Labor and the Working Women's Society of the 1880s, worked on this project and later helped establish the Alliance Employment Bureau, which by 1902 had evolved into the Manhattan Trade School, offering apprenticeships and teaching citizenship. Similarly, Boston's Rutland Corner House offered temporary shelter and employment to women who met its criteria of "poverty, respectability, and ability to work," training inmates in its laundry and sewing rooms.[16]

Reformers showed particular concern for the morals of the

poor, worrying about both exploitation of young women and dangers to the social order. Early in the nineteenth century, the hired prostitute had been the middle-class man's substitute for the wealthy gentleman's kept mistress. By the mid-1800s, with strict Victorian mores required of middle- and upper-class females, the prostitute served as an outlet for men who chose to believe that ladies did not enjoy sex and accepted it only out of duty and for reproduction. Some women voluntarily chose prostitution, trading youth and strength for income during a short career which often ended in crime, disease, and death. Toward the end of the century, however, critics noticed increases in entrapment or "white slavery"; young women felt that they were suited for no other life after they had been raped or seduced. Unsophisticated immigrant girls seemed especially vulnerable, as did factory workers, subject to the whim of foremen who demanded sexual favors if work was not to be rejected. By 1917, for example, the National Council of Jewish Women's Department of Immigrant Aid was taking newly arrived girls and their fiancés to City Hall for a civil marriage ceremony "for their protection." Observers like Jane Addams complained that theatrical melodramas and cheap literature lured girls to the brothel by dazzling them with pictures of a life not possible on their sweatshop wages. After watching a street girl solicit customers, make the mistake of picking up a policeman, go through New York's night court, tell of her desires for pretty clothes and pleasant times, and reject the help of a probation officer, a reporter moralized, "To blame Florence is as impossible as to help her. . . . she has had absolutely no education in the control of natural tendencies by spiritual strength. She wants feathers and fun." Labor reformers frequently connected low wages with immorality, arguing that women were driven to sell their bodies because they could not buy food, clothing, and shelter on their meager wages. Public moralists, clergymen, and charitable groups personally raided red-light districts in attempts to enlighten prostitutes to the evils of their situation. Others established community and state vice commissions to regulate the trade of pimps and madams as well as to arrest and try to rehabilitate girls like "Florence."[17]

Rescue for unwed mothers and delinquent girls also interested moral reformers, who found most of the objects of their charity among working-class women. Kate Waller Barrett, wife of a Virginia preacher, first hoped to save the souls of outcasts and prostitutes but met with little success. Instead she earned a medical degree in Georgia and opened a home for unwed mothers. With financial support from Charles N. Crittenton, she helped organize a memorial to his little daughter, the National Florence Crittenton Mission, a group of more than fifty homes across America. Dr. Barrett established strict rules for the houses, forbidding matrons to listen to the "nauseating details" of the girls' downfall and requiring that every girl work in the home, where she would remain until her child was six months old. Furthermore, Dr. Barrett urged unwed mothers to keep their babies rather than offering them for adoption, although she did suggest that they move to a new place to avoid embarrassing the families they had disgraced. "I am Virginian enough," she said, "to believe that a name should be protected."[18] Like many other reformers, Barrett mingled her concern for the condition of society's outcasts with her interest in sharing her own middle-class and religious values with them.

Most working-class women, however, were more concerned with growing numbers of babies than with the niceties of their genealogy. By 1910, every thousand native-born married women were bearing 3,396 children; foreign-born married women delivered 4,275 babies per thousand. Midwives and visiting nurses sometimes assisted during these births, and a physician might be called in desperate cases. But childbearing in the slums meant great risks of damage and death to both mother and child, and even religious mothers referred to pregnancy as "a curse of God." Many of these women feared conception and used crude methods of abortion, such as jumping off tables and drinking poisons or household chemicals to free themselves of pregnancies they could not prevent. When one woman in miscarriage pleaded with the physician to help her avoid future pregnancies, he advised her to make her husband sleep on the roof; six months later, he attended her again—when she died of an unsuccessful self-induced abortion.

Although the law forbade sale or distribution of information or devices, the middle class had some access to contraceptives. But the working-class remained outside the birth-control movement until Margaret Sanger established the magazine *Woman Rebel* in 1914 to give information to working women. Under federal indictment for violation of the law, she fled to England, learned more about birth control, and returned to open the first birth-control clinic in America in 1916. Margaret Sanger argued that true freedom for women would come only when they controlled their bodies. Various socialists, liberals, anarchists, and utopians agreed and supported the Sanger crusade, especially when it reached out to working-class women. Emma Goldman, long an advocate of birth control and veteran of a jail sentence for lecturing on it, defined birth control as "largely a workingman's question, above all a working woman's question." Other liberals tried to test the obscenity law in court without real success. At the same time, working-class women failed to respond to the Sanger message in large numbers, probably because of ethnic and religious reservations as well as ignorance. Large families meant more earners. The churches forbade contraception. And many women were too modest to inquire about methods. Sanger herself gravitated toward middle-class women, who received her message more eagerly. She had begun by arguing that the lower classes could use birth control as a weapon against the system which oppressed them. But by the 1920s she had moved to a Malthusian doctrine which blamed the working-class's misery on its own fecundity, and she preached birth control as a means for the dominant classes to regulate society by controlling the reproduction of the unfit.[19]

Meanwhile, other reformers aided working-class women in their efforts to deal with the problem of children. Hannah Bachman Einstein established the Widowed Mothers' Fund Association in New York to keep families intact and spare widows the necessity of working outside the home. Concerned with the family as a "fundamental social institution," Einstein believed that society had a duty to protect mothers who would rear healthy, responsible citizens. She urged the organization of a state-sponsored system to aid dependent mothers and participated in the investigation which led to the creation in 1915 of independent local child welfare boards, which would extend public aid to dependent widows with young children—work later expanded in the 1920s.[20] Labor reformers also dealt with child issues, worrying, for example, about Bohemian woman cigar makers who were forced to compensate for lack of male support but earned only slightly more than the housekeepers who cared for their children. Critics praised their ambition to provide for their families but registered concern about the effect of an absent working mother on small children.[21]

Eventually, many of the Progressive reformers who wanted to help working-class women came to believe that reform laws could solve some of these problems. Champions of employed women turned especially to the law and the Progressive Era generated an enormous amount of protective legislation at local and state levels to regulate wages, hours, and working conditions. When the investigations and muckraking exposés revealed the magnitude of the social evils, when working-class women seemed unable to alter their own situations, and when reformers took the position that society and the state held some responsibility for the welfare of their members, a protective framework of law seemed to be the best way to eliminate obstacles and create opportunities for social and economic betterment. Reformers acknowledged that such laws interfered with a totally free labor market, that some even limited freedom of contract, but they argued that society should feel justified in regulating women working because of the social effects of women's work. Although some male unionists fought protective legislation, preferring that workers gain benefits for themselves rather than accepting society's guardianship, many AFL groups supported labor legislation for women to protect the income and employment of adult males, and Samuel Gompers hoped that the state would safeguard the working woman, who was, after all, "a possible mother."[22]

Regulation of women's hours took two main forms: limitation of the workday and workweek, and prohibition of night work. As early as 1845 Massachusetts factory women had argued for a ten-hour workday, but Jacksonian ideas about producers' freedom and nineteenth-century reluctance to interfere in private business arrangements delayed first the legislation and then its enforcement. After 1900, however, reformers' activities stirred the public conscience and forced laws in several states. By 1913 thirty-nine states either regulated the maximum number of hours worked by women or forbade the employment of women at night. Sometimes advocates of protection compromised; unable to overcome legislative indifference and employers' opposition to an eight-hour law in Illinois, its supporters settled for ten hours and promoted the legislation as a health measure to avoid court rulings on freedom of contract which had cast out an earlier eight-hour law.[23] But California and Washington accepted eight hours after waitresses, laundry workers, and factory laborers testified at the hearings.[24] And Oregon not only outlawed night work, but, in the landmark Supreme Court ruling in *Muller* v. *Oregon* in 1908, received the stamp of constitutionality on such protective legislation for women.[25] Between 1913 and 1917 several states, including Wisconsin, Oregon, and Kansas, were persuaded by information on fatigue and efficiency to initiate flexible laws under which industrial commissions could regulate women's hours according to the degrees of strain in various occupations, and studies on the physiological values of a limited (usually an eight-hour) workday were initiated in other areas of the country.[26]

Successes in the hours movement heartened reformers who were working on minimum wage legislation. Women remained clustered in unskilled, low-paying, seasonal trades, where they received unequal wages for equal work, suffered from lack of opportunity to move upward, were not taken seriously as earners, and had their demands for adequate income dismissed on the grounds that they were only working for "pin money." Defenders of freedom of contract and the free labor market continued to argue for individual opportunity, and a few women organizers tried to promote unionization rather than legislation. But critics charged that monopoly rights and special privilege now stood in the way of working women earning a living wage or improving their standard of living by themselves. And investigators frequently linked low pay with immorality, arguing that women who could not survive on their meager earnings had little practical alternative to dishonor and sexual degradation. Advocates of the minimum wage for women argued that it was a "socially just and economically advantageous" means of providing the women with health and moral standards and of sparing society and employers the immorality induced by poverty. In 1911, responding to these accumulated arguments, Massachusetts passed the first state minimum wage law, to be followed by ten other states in the next six years.[27]

Progressives also sought legislation and state-controlled standards of working conditions of industrial women. Massachusetts and other states established licensing of home work, refusing applications from workplaces with sanitation or health problems. New York showed concern for occupational diseases and industrial poisons, such as the use of white lead powder in embroidery factories. Industrial accidents (which often produced the working widow) pointed up the need for compensation laws. And some states required regular inspection of factories.[28]

But it sometimes took a horrifying disaster to teach the public and its legislators what the investigators' statistics and the reformers' theoretical arguments could not. New York State had had factory inspection since the late nineteenth century; investigators looked at fire escapes, sanitation facilities, and general working conditions. But owners of the loft buildings which housed so many factories and sweatshops often failed to meet even the minimal standards set by early state laws. The Asch Building in Greenwich Village, for example, a structure which should have been fireproof, consisted largely of wood and had only two staircases rather than the three required. Moreover, owners of the Triangle Shirtwaist Factory, which occupied the top three floors, kept their doors locked to prevent employee stealing and to keep out union organizers; the managers held no fire drills, and the only access to the one fire escape was through a shuttered window with rusted fasteners. On Saturday afternoon, 25 March 1911, fire broke out in the factory, where five hundred men and girls, mostly Italians and Eastern European Jews, were finishing work. Firemen arrived within three minutes and took another four minutes to assemble their equipment. By then, "bundles of cloth" were hurtling out of the windows;

observers thought that loyal employees were trying to save expensive dress materials. But spectators were horror-stricken when the bundles turned out to be girls who had leaped or fallen a hundred feet to the street—146 died. On Wednesday, April 5, the East Side mourned its dead—eighty thousand marched silently up Fifth Avenue in the rain for four hours in a funeral procession which had been announced in four languages. A crowd of a quarter million looked on. Relief contributions of more than $120,000 poured in, but some workers refused to be grateful. Young Rose Schneiderman said that she would be "a traitor to these poor bodies" if she talked fellowship, and she indicted oppressors and public officials who held the lives of people so cheap and property so sacred.[29]

But the response to the Triangle tragedy highlights the dilemma of the Progressive age—protection or self-protection? The girls who died in 1911 had been among the twenty thousand strikers of 1909–10 demanding safety and sanitation measures in the shops. Rose Schneiderman, in denouncing sentimental sympathy for the dead and their surviving sisters, called for a strong working-class movement as "the only way they can save themselves." The governor of New York responded by appointing the State Factory Investigating Commission, which reported in 1912, 1913, and 1914, offering evidence which supported passage of laws to safeguard life and health of factory workers, shorten the workweek in factories and stores, and enforce existing safety and welfare legislation.[30] In reacting to the growing awareness of the consequences of rapid and unplanned industrial growth, however, reformers had not yet decided who should take responsibility for improving the evil effects of that change. After an investigation of safety and shop conditions affecting eighteen thousand New York workers, a representative of the Women's Trade Union League called both for laws and their enforcement and for organization of the workers.[31]

Middle- and upper-class women particularly found it difficult to find consistent ways to help working-class women
while respecting their personal dignity. The Women's International Union Label League, organized in 1899, attempted to
fight the sweatshop and promote worker welfare by encouraging trade unionism. League efforts concentrated on pro-
moting the use of goods which carried a label showing that
they had been manufactured by organized workers. Leaders
believed that women represented considerable purchasing
power, which they could use to force employers to permit
unionization in order to earn the label for their products.[32]
Similar tactics appealed to early members of the state and
national Consumers' League, who investigated department
stores and published "white lists" of those who treated their
employees fairly, urging that consumers patronize those
merchants and boycott others who did not comply.[33] The
Women's Trade Union League, on the other hand, represented a closer personal interaction between reformers and
workers, but had problems reconciling its objectives of
unionism, feminism, and protectionism.

Established by settlement workers and union leaders during the 1903 annual convention of the American Federation
of Labor in Boston, the Women's Trade Union League sought
economic rights for women through a combination of trade
unionism and political action. From the beginning, the WTUL
had a membership of working girls and "allies," middle- and
upper-class women dedicated to encouraging unionization
and improvement of workers' conditions. Their original concept seemed to favor the independent working woman, since
the constitution called for a majority of trade unionists on
the executive board, and early leaders stressed organization
over legislation. Between 1903 and 1906, the National WTUL
and leagues in Boston, Chicago, New York, and other cities
concentrated on making themselves known to unions and
workers. After 1907, when Margaret Dreier Robins of

Chicago took the presidency, the WTUL became more active, providing speakers and meeting places for new and poor unions, supporting organizers like Rose Schneiderman and Mary Anderson, establishing union locals especially in the garment trades, and supporting strikes such as the Uprising of the 20,000 in 1909–10. While the "allies" endorsed the principle of unionization for working women, many feared the radical tactics of organizations like the IWW; WTUL leaders, therefore, remained close to the AFL, from which they received superficial support. Moreover, League concerns for worker improvement brought them closer to AFL craft unionism than to schemes for industrial organization of all workers, both skilled and unskilled. Since so many working-class women fell into the category of unskilled labor, however, the WTUL had only limited success in convincing them of the need for unionization. Discouraged, many allies turned either to personal rescue efforts (some attempting to "educate" working girls at tea parties or visits to art galleries) or to nonunion means of helping workers. After 1911 conventions spoke of the need for protective legislation, the labor union, and the potential of suffrage to win equity for women. Although the WTUL continued to assert that the problems of working women would only be solved when they became part of the American labor movement, leaders increasingly advanced social welfare rather than labor organization. Finally, workers and allies divided over priorities, and while the WTUL continued in existence for many years, its energies were divided over a broad spectrum of tactics for social betterment.[34]

Many feminist reformers linked the struggle for industrial freedom with the fight for women's political freedom. Progressive organizations devoted to moral or labor or social reform often shared membership with groups working for adoption of the Anthony Amendment to grant women the vote. Suffragists frequently argued that the franchise would give women the means of controlling their destinies while they used the vote to correct society's wrongs. Labor reformers urged working women to support the amendment for their own good; groups such as the AFL and WTUL continually passed prosuffrage resolutions.[35] But recalcitrants like Mother Jones denounced suffrage as a panacea for middle- and upper-class women, without benefit to the working men and women who were (in her terms) "in slavery." She reminded women, "You don't need a vote to raise hell."[36] Moreover, twentieth-century suffragists made no particular effort to include working-class women in their organizations or to promise to use the vote for their benefit.

If the reformers at first hoped that the working-class women themselves would provide solutions to their own problems, solutions which public-spirited citizens could support and facilitate, most reformers eventually came to the conclusion that the women they wanted to help could not or would not generate their own salvation. From the beginning, some reformers probably harbored the fear that open opportunity would fail, and they may have made it a self-fulfilling prophecy. Themselves the products of middle-class homes and schools, the uplifters frequently assumed that their values were both neutral and correct, and they shared (or imposed) these attitudes on the working-class women who became the objects of their good deeds. Many reformers would have preferred that the working-class woman evolve into a good housewife rather than a trade union activist. When she failed to do either, the reformers increasingly turned to protective solutions to give working-class women some of the things they seemed unable to achieve for themselves—home and industrial safety, control of wages and hours, preservation of the family in the face of disaster, and personal morality.

Perhaps working-class women agreed with the shift in the direction of public protection. But few were asked. Reform generally came from the middle-class reformers, who assumed and retained direction of both independent and cooperative efforts. Where the reformers worked alone, they observed, analyzed, and made decisions on behalf of the working-class women they intended to save. Where they engaged in activities with the working-class women, the reformers generally took leading roles because of their greater knowledge and skills in dealing with the public sphere. A few working-class women attempted to facilitate genuine cooperation; some even argued for independent activities. But, on the whole, the reformers prevailed. Neither the investigators nor the social workers nor the moral reformers nor the legislative advocates nor the social feminists nor the suffragists ever established a permanent working relationship *with* working-class women, although these progressives and humanitarians were willing to manipulate the public and political American system to accomplish a great deal *for* working-class women.

8. Confusion between the Wars

THE PROBLEMS OF working-class women intensified in the years following the great reform drives—partly from a lack of internal direction, partly from the impact of war, prosperity, and depression. The years from World War I to the outbreak of World War II were primarily "holding-on times" for working-class women, with a few gains, a few gifts, and many adjustments. The debate over protection and self-help continued. Urbanization increased the concentrations of working-class women within cities. Consumption increased pressures toward middle-class incomes and lifestyles. Rural-urban tension grew as values appeared to change. War brought only temporary changes in attitudes toward employment and the kinds of work women performed. And the apparent benefits which were to result from suffrage had much more meaning for middle-class than for working-class women. But unions began to notice women workers, including the unskilled. And both labor unions and feminists involved working-class women in worker education programs. On the whole, working-class women were probably less affected by the sharp contrasts between prosperity in the 1920s and depression in the 1930s. Depression increased threats of unemployment, but the New Deal revived federal reform and responded to a new political coalition which included blue collar workers. Yet, while these and many other factors affected white working-class women, they remained essentially unaware of themselves as an interest group and did not develop a set of demands like other sectors of American society.

In 1914, as the United States stood on the brink of economic decline and Europe erupted into a world war, President Woodrow Wilson declared progressivism a success. When

Congress had enacted legislation in line with his New Freedom, Wilson felt that the reformers had created the essential structures for political and economic democracy. Almost at the same time, however, meetings of unemployed women reiterated their protests about child labor, excessive hours of work, and low wages, while they called on state and city officials to provide jobs for the unemployed.[1]

During the next five years, as America adjusted to wartime production, first to accommodate expanded trade with European belligerents and then to supply her own war machine, unemployment gave way to a labor shortage. Increased use of machinery and division of labor opened new jobs to women because the tasks now required less skill and physical strength. Support for "the war effort" justified women's search for paid employment outside the home. And both government and private industry recruited female workers. Many women engaged in volunteer activities, knitting and rolling bandages through their clubs or organizations such as the Red Cross. Urban women, including trade union women, joined the Women's Land Army to work on farms. The numbers and proportions of wage-earning women increased from sixty-five per thousand employees in 1914 to one hundred per thousand by 1919. Of the new women workers, however, only a handful went directly into war industries; 95 percent of women war workers transferred from other occupations, often in search of skilled positions and higher wages. Women entered previously "male" job areas, operating drill presses, driving trains, working as stevedores. In Boston and other cities, girls became bootblacks despite the mayor's cries that shining men's shoes was humiliating to women.[2]

The entry of women into new fields raised questions of the effect of that work on their physical, emotional, and economic welfare. Chambers of commerce, committees on industrial welfare, investigative agencies, and even the Congress studied laws, standards, management, training, pay, health, and working conditions of these women war workers.[3] Researchers found some temporary relief from low wages but noted that women were not receiving the same wage rates as men for equal work; their hours continued long and their working conditions poor.[4]

At the same time, government lacked effective machinery to cope with wartime labor problems. Federal and state agencies were poorly organized, inadequately staffed and financed, and lacking in authority to enforce policies. State laws regulating wages, hours, and conditions were spotty, selective, and ineffectively administered in many cases. During 1917 the federal government established agencies to deal with essential war industries such as clothing, food, fuel, and shipbuilding, but each bureau developed its own labor policies, which were often contradictory, wasted money, and led to employer-employee dissatisfaction. In 1918, however, the War Labor Administration, National War Labor Board, and War Labor Policies Board improved upon the heterogeneous and decentralized agencies in an effort to avoid economic waste and industrial disputes.[5] But none of these organizations specifically concerned itself with the woman war worker or with the continuing questions related to female employment. Labor leaders like Samuel Gompers of the AFL maintained that women and men faced the same industrial problems and difficulties, and they denounced as false chivalry efforts to aid women workers.[6]

Sentiment for government regulation of wartime labor grew, however. Even Gompers asked that government, physicians, and scientists determine kinds of work suitable for women. Moreover, those who saw women becoming permanent laborers demanded legislation to protect the results of these adjustments in the factory production system. The nineteen-volume report on women and child wage-earners (1910–13) reinforced desires for a government agency to supervise these categories of workers. The Women's Trade Union League, suffrage groups, settlement workers, and other women's advocates had lobbied for such an agency for over ten years, citing such examples as the Bureau of Women in Industry in New York and the short-lived Women's Division of the Bureau of Labor Statistics in the Department of Commerce and Labor.[7] Wartime necessity clinched the argument. On 1 July 1918 Congress established the Women-in-Industry Service within the Department of Labor to insure effective employment of women, protect their health, and promote their welfare.

Mary Van Kleeck, director of the Women-in-Industry Service, and her assistant, Mary Anderson, immediately began to gather information to develop a set of standards for the employment of women. Based on these investigations, they recommended an eight-hour day, a forty-eight-hour week, half-holidays on Saturday, one day's rest in seven, forty-five minutes for a meal, rest periods, no night work, equal pay for men and women, a minimum wage to cover the cost of living for dependents as well as for the individual worker, safety and sanitation in workplaces, prohibition of work by women in hazardous industries such as lead and poisons, prohibition of home work, worker participation in enforcing the standards, establishment of personnel departments, and rise of women to supervisory positions. They also established an advisory council drawn from all divisions of the Department of Labor and related federal departments, submitted their views on the standards to these and other interested groups, established contact with state labor departments, continued the field investigations, and managed an educational campaign to stimulate interest in the standards. But the Women-in-Industry Service found that it could only recommend the standards; it lacked authority or machinery for enforcement and often encountered resistance from the War Labor Policies Board on subjects such as the substitution of women for men workers at lower wages. As the war ended, the Women-in-Industry Service was fighting for establishment of its standards and concentrated on equal pay for equal work as well as the right of women workers to retain their jobs when the men came home.[8]

Meanwhile, agitation continued for a division within the Department of Labor to do for women what the Children's Bureau was attempting for youngsters. Efforts to reorganize the women's subdivision of the Bureau of Labor Statistics had led to the introduction of legislation in 1916, but the war took precedence, and from 1918 to 1920 the Women-in-Industry Service handled information, advice, investigation, analysis, and the development of and fight for standards. Originally established as a temporary wartime agency, the Women-in-Industry Service continued on a holdover basis after the war, while efforts increased to make its work permanent. Finally, in June 1920, Congress passed the Kenyon-Campbell bill establishing the Women's Bureau of the Department of Labor, "to promote the welfare of wage-earning women, improve their working conditions, and advance their opportunities for profitable employment." Congressmen were still not enthusiastic about women working or government protecting them, but as one representative argued, "We are face to face with a fact of life." The bureau absorbed the organization, staff, research information, and standards of the Women-in-Industry Service. Its first director was Mary Anderson. An immigrant from Sweden, she had begun work as a domestic for $1.50 a week, spent eighteen years as a shoe stitcher, and worked eight years as a labor organizer (often in association with the wtul) before becoming an investigator and labor administrator. Her salary was $5,000 per year, but the original legislation set a ceiling of $2,000 on pay for her staff because, said one senator, "No woman on earth is worth more than $2,000 a year." Mary Anderson continued to press for the adoption of the standards, using a program of information and education which relied on popular exhibits as well as the publication of evidence gathered through surveys and investigations. Like the Progressives, the Women's Bureau saw the power of massive collections of factual information rather than generalizations or hearsay. In particular, the bureau attacked the "pin money" theory: constant investigation proved that families could not live on the husband's or father's wages, that daughters contributed to family income, that married women worked doubly as homemakers and wage-earners. The Women's Bureau also worked for equal pay for women and men, arguing that wages should be based on job content rather than on the gender of the worker. But their efforts met resistance from organized labor and male workers as well as employers, and the slogan "equal pay for equal work" remained unenforceable throughout the 1920s and 1930s.[9]

While the Women's Bureau worked to inform and educate workers and employers about the problems of working women, the issue of protective legislation remained open and took on a new complexion in 1923 with the proposal of an "equal rights amendment" to the United States Constitution. Many proponents of women's suffrage had assumed that the vote would give women the means to defend their own interests; they anticipated the emergence of a women's movement, a set of women's issues, a women's voting bloc, and a kind of social feminism which would press for moral, political, economic, social, and cultural improvements. When these phenomena failed to develop, trade unionists as well as social feminists like the WTUL, the National Consumers' League, and the League of Women Voters (former suffragists) advocated legislation to protect women and children. On the other hand, the Women's Party (former suffragettes) as well as many successful business and professional women supported further amendment to the Constitution to guarantee that "men and women shall have equal rights throughout the United States and every place subject to its jurisdiction."

Working-class women, trade union women, and their defenders especially feared and opposed the equal rights amendment, believing that it would obliterate the preferential protective legislation which they had already won for women workers. Under current industrial conditions, they argued, women were not the same as men; women lacked the skills, organization, and power of male workers and hence needed "differential laws" to remedy their practical inadequacies. Some opponents preferred that such matters be left to the local discretion of the separate states; others worried that destruction of special laws would leave women less protected than men; and most agreed that an equal rights amendment would endanger progress already made. Supporters of the constitutional amendment attacked special legislation as inadequate, as too slow, and as a limitation upon women's freedom to negotiate their own wages, hours, overtime, night work, and the like. Returning to the freedom-of-contract theme of the nineteenth century, this side argued that restrictions perpetuated women's inferior position while the amendment would free women and offer equality in economic situations, professional training, advancement in professions and industries, and give men the same protections as women. Clearly, each group was talking about different categories of women. The protectionists spoke for the young, unskilled, unorganized, weak, working-class woman who lacked individual or collective power to alter or improve her situation and therefore needed the law or some supplementary structure to prevent her exploitation. The equal-rights advocates of the 1920s directed their attention to more autonomous women—professionals, business women, skilled workers, organized groups—on the assumption that these women could take care of themselves if guaranteed the opportunity to do so.

Established progressive reformers and social feminists usually sided with protection. The Women's Trade Union League, National Consumers' League, League of Women Voters, Young Women's Christian Association, and the Women's Bureau, as well as organizations like the National Council of Household Employment and the American Association for Labor Legislation, and settlement and social workers supported laws to protect the home, shelter mothers and children, and remove some of the liabilities of working women. They worked for the Sheppard-Towner Maternity and Infancy Protection Act for pre- and postnatal treatment and infant health care, the Cabell Act to give women separate citizenship so that an American woman would not lose her citizenship by marrying a foreign national, and a wide range of labor reforms including child labor laws, the eight-hour day, prohibition of night work, adequate employment services, social insurance against sickness and accident, public works in depressed times, unemployment relief, and social security. Organized labor generally supported protection for women but not for men.[10]

In 1923, however, protectionists suffered a harsh blow when the United States Supreme Court struck down minimum wage legislation. The Court had upheld hours limitation to protect women's health in the *Muller* v. *Oregon* case in 1908. But a conservative majority declared in the *Adkins* decision that the Washington, D.C., minimum wage law violated a woman's freedom to negotiate freely with employers. The judges used the suffrage amendment to support their argument that women no longer needed special legislation.[11]

Meanwhile, advocates of unionization as well as those who wanted to assist working women in helping themselves saw another avenue for self-improvement—worker education. As early as the 1890s socialists had established schools for workers, and various church and synagogue groups had taught industrial as well as religious subjects in their Sunday school programs. By 1910 more than a hundred New York City public schools offered classes four nights a week for those who wanted to learn language, sciences, commercial subjects, domestic arts, and vocational skills; nearly fifty thousand women attended, for reasons which ranged from having "nothing else to do" to learning "in order to change to better work"; and one girl said that she had been sent by her father "to keep her off the streets." Other cities had similar programs with heavy working-class and immigrant enrollments.[12] By 1913, however, reformers were complaining that workers lacked knowledge of the safety, health, and welfare laws which had been passed for them. Educators proposed courses in the public schools dealing with protective laws, training schools for women union organizers, correspondence courses in trade unionism, and the like. The Women's Trade Union League established a Training School for Active Workers in the Labor Movement in cooperation with Northwestern University; between 1914 and 1926 the WTUL gave scholarships to forty-four girls in seventeen trades to learn economics, civics, trade-agreement, office work, and organization.[13]

In 1921 worker education took a new direction with the opening of the Bryn Mawr Summer School for Women Workers in Industry, an experimental program to bring women workers to live at the school during the summer academic vacation. Largely the brainchild of Dr. M. Carey Thomas, president of Bryn Mawr College, the summer school grew out of her belief that trade unionism could be an effective instrument against war, that study could enrich life, and that industrial women had vested interests in American economic issues. A hundred women from all sections of the country (as well as some from Europe) studied at Bryn Mawr each summer. Almost half were foreign-born. Many worked in the needle trades. Selected for their maturity, industrial experience, and leadership within their local communities, most received scholarships from their unions or groups like the YWCA and WTUL or interested individuals. Faculty from nine prestigious colleges held informal but intensive classes in economics, political and social history, the labor movement, literature, and music appreciation. Daughters of wealthy families served as tutors—young women whose height amazed the working girls, who found it remarkable that such women had never had to bend over a sewing machine. From Bryn Mawr, the summer school movement spread throughout the country to include Brookwood College at Katonah in New York, a nonresident school at New York City's Barnard College, the Southern Summer Schools primarily for textile workers, and the Wisconsin Summer Seminar, which was the first at a state university and the first to make the working girls part of its regular student body in summer session.[14]

Unions also supported worker education, both through the summer schools and in their own programs of publications, lectures, and social and recreational activities. The Educational Department of the ILGWU was particularly active in teaching young women the significance of the union to their hopes for decent lives and the importance of developing leaders from within their own ranks. On the one hand, ILGWU educators sought to disillusion workers of their romantic dreams and provide practical programs such as English language and American history courses for foreign-born members. And on the other hand, they offered art and literature to awaken workers to the possibilities of better lives.[15]

The worker education movement added another dimension in the 1930s, when the summer schools, which had formed the Affiliated School for Women Workers in 1927, evolved into a resource-development organization for local labor education and an in-service training facility for teachers. In 1939 this project became the American Labor Education Service.[16]

Worker education, protective laws, and government agencies all sought to soften the impact of modern industrialization on working-class women. But the underlying problems remained severe. In 1920, for example, the federal census showed that for the first time more Americans lived in cities and towns than in the countryside. But the war had interfered with building activities, leading to a postwar housing shortage, especially in areas where tenements were decaying. Urban landlords took advantage of the growing demand for dwellings to rent out any available property. A Chicago survey in the mid-1920s revealed that a twelfth of the families investigated lived in basements; 11 percent of apartment rooms had no windows; 33 percent of dwellings had no toilets; 85 percent were "cold water flats" heated only by stoves. Investigators described broken windows, missing plaster, dangerous stairs, and poor sanitation.[17]

Urbanization also altered old class and community institutions, offering instead a false sense of democracy based on increased pressures to consume. Working-class women, crowded into poorer areas of cities, became more dependent on modern mechanization to shape their living conditions. Clothing was more likely to be bought in stores than produced at home. Mass production introduced a kind of "democracy of style," whereby a poor woman could achieve dress lines similar to those of the wealthy, but with cheaper fabrics and tailoring. Desire to conform to widely advertised models increased pressure on working-class women to seek store-bought goods. Mass advertising sold labor-saving devices, linoleum floors, running water, electric gadgets, and laundry service, all with the message that success and security depended upon ownership of these "necessities."[18] But a silk dress cost $7.50, a jersey dress $4.50, a winter coat cost at least $39.00 and low-income women spent about $15.00 per year on stockings. When a Cincinnati survey in 1929 estimated that a weekly income of $17.50 would be necessary to maintain health and self-respect, 59 percent of the girls interviewed earned less.[19]

Traditional working-class income problems as well as increased encouragement to spend on material goods brought more married working-class women out into the work force to contribute to family support and income standards. Wives still formed a minority of employed women and retired from paid labor as soon as the family achieved middle-class status, but by 1920, one married woman in fourteen worked outside the home in nonagricultural occupations (compared to one in thirty in 1890), and 90 percent of these women used their wages to support their families, no matter what the amount of their earnings or the size of family income. In a government study of selected communities in Florida, Pennsylvania, Montana, and New Jersey, nearly 53 percent of these married working women had children, 40 percent of the mothers had babies under five years old. And 27 percent lived in families with no male wage-earners, while 21 percent were the sole breadwinners for their families. While most employed, married, working-class women remained secondary or supplementary workers whose wages augmented those of a husband or other family members, their income was nevertheless vital to sustaining their family's standard of living.[20]

In Southeastern cotton textile communities, earnings were so low that even with subsidized housing more than one family member had to work; women worked in about three-fifths of these families. A widow reported earning 90¢ a day as a spinner; her seventeen-year-old daughter made the same wage after six years in the mills; and her twelve-year-old son after three years of employment received 75¢ for replacing ten thousand bobbins each day. Existence revolved around the mill. At 4:30 A.M. the wake whistle sounded, and workers staggered unwashed to breakfast tables which held last evening's supper warmed over. By 6:00 A.M. entire families were at work. Although the dinner whistle did not sound until noon, married women with children could quit fifteen minutes early to go home and prepare a meal of beans cooked for the previous supper, slices of sow-belly bacon, left-over breakfast biscuits or corn pone, and "a nondescript beverage they called coffee." While the rules called for an hour for dinner, the return whistle blew at 12:30 and laborers returned to their tasks, where they remained until 6:00 P.M., when they went home to suppers the same as their dinners. Men's workdays ended there, but the mill women then began their housekeeping duties, mending, cleaning, cutting down clothes for the children.[21]

A wife's work, however, still depended on opportunities available in the community in which her husband found employment. Miners' families, for example, usually lived in villages controlled by the mine companies. Wages were poor. Fewer than a third owned their homes; another 30 percent lived in company-owned houses. More than a fifth of miners' wives and daughters worked to support themselves or to aid in family maintenance. But while daughters often drifted to cities because the mining towns offered few commercial or manufacturing jobs for women, their mothers earned by taking in lodgers or doing laundry or cleaning.[22]

Working-class and other women who were forced to seek paid employment also encountered resistance from employers and male employees. Although women had been expected to show their patriotism by becoming emergency war workers during World War I, and were even brought into skilled and technical crafts, at the end of the war these women workers were expected to relinquish jobs to returning veterans. In Cleveland and Detroit, for example, the street railway unions brought about the dismissal of women conductors and ticket agents in 1918. Protests by the women employees, supported by social feminist groups such as the NWTUL, forced a ruling by the War Labor Board that these particular women could remain. But the same agency approved a contract between employers and the union which effectively prohibited the hiring of any other women. By 1920 the Women's Bureau was trying to recommend a compromise which would leave women some of the gains of the war years but warn them of areas now considered unsuitable for their employment. The best promise for women workers, they said, now seemed to be in machine shops making light parts, assembling and finishing in wood product factories, optical and instrument plants, and sheet-metal shops.[23]

Although the greatest increases in employment opportunities were centered in white-collar rather than working-class occupations, 88.8 percent of wage-earning women were concentrated in nineteen occupations, especially farm-related work, dressmaking, millinery, semiskilled cigar and tobacco work, clothing, food, iron and steel, shoe work, cotton mills, knitting mills, silk mills, and woolen and worsted manufacture. The greatest employment decreases fell among farm workers, servants, dressmakers, laundresses, cooks, and milliners as more of this work went into factories such as clothing or food production or laundry plants, or was affected by labor-saving devices and the domestic revolution.[24]

Wages were low, hours long, and turnover high. Among manufacturing women, wage rates remained abnormally low in states without minimum wage laws. Women earned little more than half of what similarly employed men received. And women still lacked the skill or organization to extract more favorable arrangements. Moreover, women did not remain long in the same occupation. A study of garment, textile, and other workers in 1926 showed that half had held jobs in three or more industries, 60 percent had been in their current positions less than two years.[25] Long hours, fatigue, monotony, and night work also characterized working-class women's occupations. In an eighteen-state investigation, the Women's Bureau learned that two-thirds of the quarter of a million factory women studied worked more than forty-eight hours a week. Workers complained that a reduction in hours was usually accompanied by a speed-up in the pace of work. And even as sentiment for the eight-hour day began to spread, most night employees were working ten hours, significant numbers of them as many as twelve hours a night.[26]

A neckwear-maker, describing herself as "a romantic realist," told of her adjustments to factory life. On the first day, she regarded her task as "a grand game," wondering who would wear the ties she made. But rhythm changed to monotony, all colors became drab, and the threat of a salary cut jeopardized the new coat she wanted. A French immigrant woman, working in a Fifth Avenue dressmaking shop, told of her fear of working on thousand-dollar dresses but had no choice but to do as the forelady told her; she "could have screamed for happiness," she said, when she was told that she would be permitted to come to work again the following week.[27]

Some working-class women did not think their position so precarious. One Southern Illinois daughter of a lumber dealer graduated from high school in 1922, took a more secure year-round job in a store for $12 a week rather than a seven-month appointment as a teacher at $60 a month, married a miner the following autumn and moved into a bungalow built by their fathers. When this new bride heard the news of her first mine fire, she wondered whether she would ever need any of the furniture she and her husband had admired in store windows. By 1927 they had three daughters and were paying $28 a month on a house; the woman now believed that "we lived as well as any other family in Southern Illinois." Two years later, her husband was without work; they had lost the house and were forced to live on a farm where one year's bad crops followed another. But, she speculated, the experience must have been harder for older men than for "those of us who could still hope and had enough health to start over again."[28]

Working-class people shared the general collapse of prosperity when the stock market and the economy deteriorated into the Great Depression of the 1930s. Depression unemployment hit the working classes especially hard. The necktie worker who found her job montonous worried about a layoff, knew that her mother had to pay large coals bills before she could order more, and broke her promise of getting a pair of boxing gloves for her nephew on the next payday. A woman worker in an overall factory had felt proud of earning $30 a week until orders became so slow that she worked only two or three days instead of six. The unemployed miner and his wife lost their uninsured barn to fire in 1929, and with it the tractor, truck, and animals; the mines remained closed, and they stayed on the farm to face dry weather, poor crops, and lower farm prices in 1931, wet weather, poor crops, and lower prices in 1932, and the same in 1933 and 1934, when their life pattern was changed only by the arrival of another baby.[29]

As men lost their jobs, women were forced to enter the paid work force in growing numbers. By 1930 more than a quarter of women sixteen years of age or over were gainfully employed in the United States, and in some communities, like Richmond, Virginia, the figures approached 40 percent. A sixth of the households of Bridgeport, Connecticut, and Fort Wayne, Indiana, were supported by women. And at least a third of working women investigated were also homemakers, many with children under ten years of age.[30]

Despite these realities, the public still opposed work by married women, partly for traditional reasons but increasingly to reserve the available jobs for men. The 1936 Gallup poll showed that 82 percent of Americans opposed employment of married women; 78 percent remained opposed in 1939. The "pin-money worker," said Secretary of Labor Frances Perkins, "ought to be ashamed of herself." And an eighteen-year-old frankly stated that "a girl thought primarily of where she was going to attach herself and find an eligible husband who could make a living." In some cases, laws restricted jobs to men, and few feminists protested. But, in practice, women could get low-paying, unskilled jobs more readily than men, and many wives and daughters on assembly lines supported their "more expensive" skilled husbands, fathers, and brothers. "Working women paid a heavy price during the Depression," one woman recalled, but "many of them actually stood between the coming generation and death." Almost every study of married working women showed that they were working because of need; 19 percent of their husbands had been unemployed from two months to twenty years by 1934, another 6 percent of these men earned less than $1,000 a year, and an additional 25 percent of husbands earned between $1,000 and $2,000 a year.[31]

The women who did find jobs took what they could get, suffered poor conditions, and earned very little. Nearly three-quarters of the industrialized laundry workers in New York City received less than $15 a week by 1936. "I'm as experienced as they make them," said one twenty-eight-year veteran of the trade who made $12.40 a week, in contrast to her $18 wages of earlier years. Average weekly wages for all women industrial workers in Kentucky were $13 in 1937 or $675 for a year. Women also continued to suffer wage discrimination; when they had work, male blockers in the millinery trade earned about $1,927 a year, but women trimmers made only $858. Seasonal industries, depression layoffs, and employer failures caused frequent job changes—nine jobs in eight years, twelve employments in nineteen years, five jobs in seven years, they told investigators. One sixty-five-year-old New York woman told an investigator that she had begun working for a dollar a month scrubbing floors, received 25¢ raises each of the thirty-three years she worked in a factory and never thought of leaving because "at Christmas they'd give you a $5 gold piece and a box of candy." She took her present job because it was around the corner and she could walk to work—she had not been able to save enough for carfare to search for another job. A twenty-one-year-old who said she wanted to get enough education to qualify for a better position found that she was too tired to stay awake during night school classes; "I have ambition," she said, "but it won't do me any good."[32]

Unemployment posed the greatest danger, especially as private and public relief resources ran out. Of more than five thousand unemployed women in Chicago, Cleveland, Minneapolis, St. Paul, and Philadelphia in 1933, from two-thirds to three-fourths had been out of their usual employment for a year, half for at least two years. About a sixth were without work because their firms had gone out of business; half had been laid off. A similar investigation in Chicago four years later showed 12,500 unattached women seeking relief; four-fifths were at least forty years old; many had health problems; most had been in domestic or personal service; only one in eight had held a job which lasted five years. Most had been self-supporting all their adult lives and were driven to seek relief because "low earnings allowed no margin for times of unemployment or illness on the part of the majority of these women." Their relief money went for rent (usually of a room), rather than for clothing, but many lived under threat of eviction and half had been in their present rooms less than a year.[33] Helpful groups like the Women's Trade Union League tried to attract attention to the problems of unemployed women workers and advocated the sharing of available jobs as well as government regulation of wages. In the Boston area, for example, the garment unions devised a sharing plan whereby nearly two thousand members each got ten days' work a month between November 1932 and April 1933. In New York, the WTUL established a revolving loan fund to help unemployed women. Eleanor Roosevelt financed a rest room for unemployed women, where fifty to seventy-five persons a day received meals. Some areas like San Francisco continued to rely on charity agencies, while all other California counties established welfare departments. But the local relief picture had become bleak by the early 1930s.[34]

Hope increased with the arrival of President Franklin D. Roosevelt and the New Deal. Seven state legislatures enacted minimum wage laws. Governors sought regulation of women's working conditions. And the National Recovery Administration possessed authority to establish industrywide codes including standards of wages and hours. Wages increased in the New York dress industry by 30 to 60 percent. The median wage in industries in Michigan ranged from $3.85 to $14.95 per week in 1932 but jumped to $10.00 to $19.65 by 1934. Pay differentials between men and women narrowed in some trades. WTUL and ILGWU veteran organizer Rose Schneiderman served on the Labor Advisory Board, and prominent union women like Agnes Nestor of the glove workers helped devise the codes for their industries.[35]

Despite this surge of emotional recovery, some practical problems weakened the impact of change. NRA codes were enforced unevenly; a quarter of the agreements permitted lower wage schedules for women than for men; and occupations with significant numbers of female employees, such as domestic service, remained outside the codes entirely. Moreover, Roosevelt's secretary of labor, Frances Perkins, the first woman to hold a Cabinet position, was especially conscious that organized labor did not view her kindly, and she hesitated to force profemale positions which would have further antagonized powerful groups like the AFL. Finally, before 1937, the United States Supreme Court struck down both federal and state regulation of wages, even invalidating the NRA.

But the New Deal was essentially shaped by political realities, and Franklin Roosevelt acted as a broker to organized groups which demanded his attention and action. Since women did not constitute a politically self-conscious constituency in the 1930s—and working-class women especially lacked any collective awareness of themselves or any sense of group interest or power—women as women failed to benefit from the New Deal. Rather, whatever relief or gains they enjoyed came from membership in some other group, one which could make itself felt politically, such as organized labor.

Labor had become a recognizable interest group and by 1936 was clearly part of the Democratic New Deal political coalition. One of the most important New Deal policies to affect labor was legislation protecting the right of workers to organize. First under section 7(a) of the National Industrial Recovery Act and then by the Wagner Act, workers were guaranteed the right to select collective bargaining agents. Unions took this incentive and launched active organizing drives.

Unionization had limped along during the 1920s, particularly where women were concerned. Although women's trade union membership had grown fourfold between 1910 and 1920, with most gains in the clothing trades and among railway clerks and electrical workers, women continued to be difficult to organize because of high job turnover, assumptions that they were temporary and secondary employees, and the absence of women from skilled jobs in crafts which drew the attention of union organizers. The AFL leadership paid lip service to organizing women and to efforts by the WTUL, but the male rank and file remained hostile.[36] Even better-organized unions which had devoted efforts toward women workers, like the ILGWU, suffered in the 1920s. That union struggled against internal divisions, mobsters, suspected radicalism, and the failure of male unionists to take women seriously; membership dropped from a hundred thousand members (half of them women) in 1920 to forty thousand by 1933.[37] In areas with a heavy concentration of female labor, such as Southeastern cotton textile mills, management resistance, paternalism, and traditional values defeated organizers. Poor Southern women were told that union membership was "unladylike," "foreign," and "socialist," and mill owners fostered the idea that workers were partners in the mills. Some Southern mill workers did organize and protest, especially as the Depression made bad conditions intolerable; sporadic strikes in North Carolina and Tennessee in 1929 and 1930 resulted in few gains for the workers, although they captured public attention for the presumably unorganizable and passive mill hands.[38]

With the passage of the National Industrial Recovery Act in 1933, unions immediately began organizing. Some groups, especially in the garment trades, hoped to consolidate their strength in time to influence the NRA codes. The New York dressmakers union, for example, grew from ten to seventy thousand members within two weeks, and the ILGWU expanded to two hundred thousand in two years. Organizations which had met secretly now came into the open under protection of section 7(a). Locals encouraged each member to bring in a new member; some held raffles or dances at mass meetings to attract workers to hear the speeches. The WTUL continued to encourage organization and support strikes by textile workers, hotel workers, beauty parlor operators, and others.[39]

But employers, government, and the unions continued to treat women inequitably. Although membership in most of the leading garment unions was about equally divided between men and women, union contracts and NRA codes called for higher wages and separate seniority lists for men. Few women held policy-making positions within unions; only one woman served on the twenty-four-member executive board of the ILGWU, although women constituted three-quarters of the rank and file. In some industries, locals remained sexually segregated. As early as the AFL annual convention in 1933, Elizabeth Christman of the glove workers had questioned the structures which resulted in these arrangements. "While I fully recognize the value of craft unions," she said, "I am in sympathy with the idea now being advanced here and there of a great need for the functional union in such many-sided industries as rubber, textile, automobile, and meat packing, for example."[40]

Organization by industry rather than by craft could take into account the large numbers of unskilled women workers. After 1935 the Congress of Industrial Organizations tried to attract workers in the automobile, electrical, and textile industries. Where the CIO took over an existing organization, such as the United Textile Workers, it included women and unskilled laborers who had been ignored in the past; the Textile Workers Union of America grew from twenty thousand members in 1936 to one hundred twenty thousand by 1943.[41] On the whole, however, even the CIO failed to concentrate on women workers during the 1930s, and, like the AFL, it accepted sex-segregated seniority lists and pay scales. Nor did the CIO enter the clerical and service industries, where so many women had found employment.

The CIO did encourage women's support of men's organizations, however, through women's auxiliaries. Women had formed supportive committees as early as 1934 in New York City in order to work in the open while the men's transit workers' union remained underground. The United Mine Workers, which did not encourage organization of women, also permitted auxiliaries even before it joined the CIO. But the United Auto Workers led the auxiliary movement with its "emergency brigades" during the 1937 sit-down strikes. Each brigade was organized under a general, who commanded five captains, who each had ten subordinates in a hierarchy which could mobilize thousands of women on short notice. Members wore arm bands and berets in the color of their district—green for Detroit, red for Flint, white for Lansing, blue for Ohio. Women in auxiliaries supplemented picket lines, convinced other women to stand by their striking husbands, maintained first-aid stations, worked in communal kitchens to feed strikers and their families, and occasionally engaged in free-for-alls when company police or thugs twisted their arms and took away their pamphlets. One woman, suspicious about her husband sitting-in with women coworkers in his plant, went to complain at the union hall and was thoroughly won over by Walter Reuther, who recruited her for the strike kitchen. Another, worried that her husband was spending too much time at Union Auto Worker meetings, perhaps in beer gardens with a "gang of Reds" being entertained by "plenty of short-haired girls," investigated the union hall, where she found women peeling vegetables and washing dishes; she remained to peel onions and pack pies, often working twelve hours a day seven days a week. "Just being a woman isn't enough any more," she decided, "I want to be a human being."[42]

Even in the face of many grievances on wages, hours, and working conditions—even with the greater economic deterioration wrought by the Great Depression—even with nonexistent or poorly enforced protective legislation—working-class Americans were unwilling to support more extreme solutions than unionization and strikes, and many would not even go that far toward militancy. Depression conditions did perform a slow educational function, awakening laborers, white-collar workers, and farmers to some of their common difficulties, and working people, the poor, and intellectuals all called for a more equal distribution of wealth and power. But that small measure of working-class consciousness and discontent became channelled into traditional political and social outlets. With the encouragement of NIRA

7(a) and the Wagner Act, more Americans accepted the legitimacy of unionization. With the growth of the CIO, some labor leaders recognized the potential for organizing women and unskilled workers. With the formation of the New Deal political coalition, labor and ethnic voters gravitated toward the Democratic Party. None of these groups joined leftist radical organizations in large numbers; communists picked up some of the residue of the shattered socialist movement, but identification with Soviet Russia made the Communist party seem alien to most Americans. If some union members had flirted with radical politics in the 1920s, by the late 1930s they were beginning to distrust all ideologies; the ILGWU, for example, came to loathe any tinge of totalitarianism.[43]

White working-class women hardly recognized themselves at all among the larger and more vocal interest groups seeking to survive and prosper under the American political, social, and economic system. Very little distinguished the working-class woman of 1939 from her counterpart in 1914, except that she had remained alive and come through the changes of war, urbanization, mild prosperity, depression, and the activities of reformers, educators, and unionists on her behalf. Whatever might be the eventual impact of these confusing sets of trends on her, she was not yet in a position to evaluate or even acknowledge them. With the few exceptions of employed women who tried to take advantage of worker education or industrial unionism, the working-class woman of the 1920s and 1930s gave first priority to survival and whatever modest improvements she might be able to eke out for herself and her family in the face of overwhelming social and economic change.

Part Three: "You Would Cry, Too": 1940-77

9. False Promises in World War II

WORKING-CLASS WOMEN appeared to have very little control over their own destinies in mid-twentieth-century America. They adapted, adjusted, and struggled to survive under conditions of immigration, industrialization, urbanization, and even unionization and reform. In good and bad times, they kept families together, supplemented husbands' and fathers' incomes, and tried to advance their households toward middle-class goals. Family- and home-oriented, they seemed to ask little for themselves as individuals, as women, as workers, or as members of the working class. When family needs or society's demands called them, they responded as best they could.

The outbreak of war in Europe again in 1939 had little immediate impact on America's working-class women. They continued to cope with depression unemployment through creative homemaking and sporadic jobs in unskilled trades. A small change began in the spring of 1941, however, when America's commitment to supplying warring European countries called many men back to their jobs; the pressure of the depression had begun to lift. American entry into World War II in December 1941 accelerated this process as the armed forces and war plants rapidly absorbed the five million formerly unemployed.

As the war continued, so did the need for war workers. Government and employers eventually discovered a large and virtually untapped labor supply among women. Before World War II, women with healthy husbands were expected to remain within the home no matter how low the man's income; a widow or wife of a sick or injured man might work, or a woman might seek a job while her man was laid off. But, on the whole, the typical employed woman was young and single, while wives of all classes were expected to devote themselves to housewifery. Some women had been summoned to war work during World War I, but many were women already employed in other fields who transferred into war industries during the emergency with the expectation that they would leave as soon as peace was restored. Although women had proven their ability to perform "men's jobs" even in heavy industry between 1914 and 1920, they made no permanent gains in obtaining access to occupations other than those traditionally defined as women's work. But in World War II, women not only entered the work force in larger numbers and at older ages than previously, but they experienced enormous changes in the kinds of work available to them. Moreover, in 1941 about 7 percent of working women in the United States were married with living husbands and children under ten years of age; in February 1944 that proportion had grown by almost half. Clearly, the war years seemed to represent a watershed not only in women's employment but also in the relationship between home and workplace in women's lives.[1]

World War II gave American women, including working-class women, the opportunity to be patriotic heroines. "What job is mine on the Victory Line?" appeared on roadside billboards and was sung on radio programs across the nation. Newspapers, magazines, and films preached support for the "war effort" through home economics, work on the assembly line, and ideological purity. Propagandists called on women to become antifascist fighters, to take their "place in the war today and in the work of the world tomorrow." Women were told that they were ideally suited physically and mentally for war work. A special bulletin produced by the Women's Bureau of the Department of Labor claimed: "Women excel in work requiring care and constant alertness, good eyesight, and use of light instruments, such as gauges, micrometers, vervier callipers—work calling for little physical exertion. . . . Women excel at work requiring manipulative dexterity and speed, but which permits the individual to set her own tempo and work in a sitting position." Journalists, songwriters, and propagandists glorified the "Janes Who Make the Planes" and the "Woman Behind the Man Behind the Gun," while the media pictured a glamorous Rosie the Riveter with peroxide curls caught in a fashionable snood for safety.[2]

At the beginning of the war, however, the federal government had no clear idea of wartime manpower needs and no effective mechanism for recruiting and training workers or dealing with their problems. The Children's Bureau raised questions of the effect of mothers' employment on the health and welfare of young children and urged employers to adopt liberal maternity policies. Wartime agencies such as the National Defense Advisory Commission, the Office of Production Management, and the War Production Board had too many problems with acquiring and allocating materials to concern themselves with manpower. And it took until April 1942 for harried officials to establish the separate War Manpower Commission.

But this bureaucratic attempt to solve problems of the labor supply meant little recognition and few benefits for the women it would recruit. When officials "spoke of 'the people' they meant the men," complained Mary Anderson of the Women's Bureau. And women also got lost in the tangle of unclear authority, weak enforcement, fragmentation of functions among the military and a host of civilian boards and bureaus interested in everything from agriculture to railroads, and frustrating government and employer suspicions of agency placement procedures. Finally, the War Manpower Commission decided to try labor-management cooperation and established negotiating councils of workers and employers, but the councils included no representatives of women. Under pressure from the Women's Bureau and groups like the Women's Trade Union League to add women to its Management-Labor Policy Committee, in August 1942 the War Manpower Commission established a Women's Advisory Committee to assist in devising policies appropriate to woman war workers. Mary Anderson called its members "a mighty fine lot of women," but from the beginning she wondered whether "those boys over there will let them do anything." Although the Women's Advisory Committee obtained some significant policy statements about recruiting and training of women workers, matching work assignments with women's physical and health conditions, and equal pay for equal work (long a major priority of Women's Bureau), little effective implementation followed. Even within the WMC, the Management-Labor Policy Committee refused to permit a woman representative a vote. Demands for reorganization and recognition of the womanpower issue came to nothing, and recommendations by the Women's Advisory Committee were generally ignored, although the MLPC assured the WAC that its advice was much appreciated. Women were obviously expected to support the war effort by doing what they were told. And if the professional women on the WAC received such treatment, working-class women could expect no consideration at all from those who organized their working lives.[3]

While trying to cooperate with efforts to give women a role in labor policymaking in wartime agencies, the Women's Bureau of the Department of Labor continued to serve as a source of information on working women and tried to use its expertise to convince employers to provide necessary facilities such as rest rooms, establish an eight-hour day and a forty-hour week, be mindful of health and safety hazards on certain jobs, assign women to suitable work, and permit women to rise into supervisory capacities when they had demonstrated their abilities. In particular, the Women's Bureau continued to press for pay rates established on the basis of the task rather than the sex of the worker. While some limited gains were registered, especially in the opening of previously restricted occupations, on the whole, Mary Anderson and her staff, like the women on the Women's Advisory Committee, could not convince either government officials or employers that women constituted a legitimate interest group.

If the managers of the war machine refused to deal with women as an interest group, they did recognize quickly that women would be a commodity to be used in advancing the war. President Franklin D. Roosevelt considered the voluntary registration of women for war work until he learned that the United States Employment Service already had more than a million women waiting to work in the spring of 1942. As the demand for workers increased—for 2.5 million in 1943 and the same number in 1944—propagandists accelerated their message of urgency, directing their recruiting particularly at middle-class housewives and older women. In 1943 Congress considered national service legislation to solve critical labor shortages; the bill called for registration of all persons between eighteen and fifty, arguing for "the equal liability of all" in the war effort. But popular sentiment against universal registration and government belief that voluntary methods would be sufficient killed the legislation. Instead, Secretary of Labor Frances Perkins urged transfer from nonessential to essential jobs and viewed the key problem as one of placement of women and other new workers where they were most needed.[4]

And 5.5 million women responded. Patriotism attracted some. More went to work for personal reasons, to shorten the war in order to bring a loved man back home. For working-class women, wartime employment also meant wages, welcome income after the unemployment days of the depression. No less patriotic than middle-class women, no less worried about their lovers and husbands and sons, women who had struggled against poverty all their lives now had a chance to earn and were actually being encouraged. It looked as if they could enter the factory and still have hope of being "ladies."[5]

War work also provided an opportunity for the unskilled to receive training. Between July 1940 and April 1944, nearly 2.5 million women participated in formal training programs in public vocational schools, federal war production training courses, college classes especially in engineering and management, training within industries, and National Youth Administration courses. Federal, state, and local government jointly financed most of these efforts; faculty salaries alone cost $63.5 million in 1943. One survey indicated that about 60 percent of wartime job openings required six months or less training, about half of these only two months; 16 percent of all employees needed six months to a year of preparation, and 15 percent had to have more than two years' experience. Women were especially attracted to paid-trainee opportunities and made up more than two-thirds of workers learning under salary. A skilled welder, for example, might require from 60 to 270 hours to learn the job. The greatest single training program involving women was in aircraft operations; nearly half a million women took those vocational training courses. Almost two hundred thousand learned machine-shop operations, and over one hundred thousand were trained in shipbuilding. By 1943 women were learning all but the most hazardous and heaviest tasks, and technology opened many occupations which previously required great physical exertion. Significantly, the War Department suggested that women be trained more thoroughly than men, that they first learn things which would give them "the feel of the work," such as plant layouts and production processes. Teachers were also advised to interpret industrial production in terms of household facilities. Trainers cautioned women about safety hazards and tried to relieve their health fears. Women who had never removed their wedding rings took them off in the shipyards. A lecturer tried to disprove the rumor that arc welding caused sterility by claiming that women welders actually had more children, only to have one of his students respond, "No, thanks, I don't like that either!"[6]

With recruitment and training, women entered new occupations. The invasion of the shipyards was especially dramatic. In 1939, only thirty-six women in the United States earned wages in the trade, and a personnel director on tour of a Brooklyn dry dock learned that she was "the first female to set foot on the soil since the yard was opened in 1869." Most yards did not even employ women in their offices. By 1943, however, women made up 4 percent of shipyard employees and constituted nearly a tenth of workers in the trade by the end of the war. Since ship production had been custom work before the war, the impact of mass-production techniques and standardized materials particularly helped to open the industry to women. Women were judged competent in 80 percent of the three thousand pertinent industrial tasks and did assembly work on such varied items as valves, manifolds, couplings, and hoist parts. Large numbers of women worked as fitters, welders, and electrical workers. Women made their first major impact in welding, beginning in the shops and skids, where work was less strenuous, and progressing to work on the ships, where they first tacked seams and later did highly responsible production work, making the final welds which would hold the ship together. Despite male hostility, inappropriate training in the early days, and an initial lack of self-confidence, women learned their jobs and learned to be comfortable and competent. A federal government worker who took a welding job to learn why so many women had quit those jobs shortly after entering the shipyards regarded it as a great personal victory when she

could stop tacking long enough to take a drink of water—
even though the men shipfitters would have to stop work
until she returned.[7]

Women also had to overcome resistance and hostility in
aircraft assembly plants. At the beginning of the war, employers strongly preferred to hire men, although a study by
the Women's Bureau showed that up to a third of aircraft
jobs could be done by women. By the end of 1941, however,
supervisors had discovered that men and women could work
together without jeopardizing discipline or production, and
women could do light work as well as men—"occasionally
better," admitted a few foremen. Since aircraft production
boomed during the war, the demand for workers increased
markedly. By the middle of the war, female employment in
engine plants peaked at 31 percent, and in some tasks women
made up as much as 71 percent of the work force. An industrial relations director estimated that women did about half
the work to construct a modern airplane. Manufacturers
found that women were not only adept at fitting small wires
into junction boxes, but that they could do it in three-quarters of the time it had taken men. And if women excelled in
handling and fitting small parts, one kind of plane had ten
thousand different components in its 20- by 12-foot midsec-
tion alone, while the B-24 bomber included three hundred
thousand rivets. And while Rosie was rivetting, she was also
becoming ambitious; some women claimed that they hoped
to keep their plant jobs after the war, while others hoped for
technical careers.[8]

Overall, the proportion of working women increased to 36
percent of the work force during World War II; by 1945, 19.2
million women worked. More than two-thirds were between
twenty and forty-four years old. Nearly one-third were married with the husband present. They experienced the greatest employment shifts from one occupation to another;
nearly half the women in manufacturing were new to the

labor force, and more than a quarter came from other industries. In essential supply industries, 37 percent were entirely new workers, and only 54 percent had been in the same industry before the war.[9]

More revealing than the statistics on numbers, age, marital status, or occupational history for these women, however, were the social questions raised by their involvement in the war and the temporary efforts of government, business, and society to deal with that set of issues. Training programs instructed women how to dress on the job, pointing out the dangers to safety of high-heeled shoes or uncontrolled masses of hair. The Office of War Information also cautioned that tight sweaters might distract male coworkers and warned women employees not to date the boss or flirt with the foreman. A corporate executive felt that there were only two pertinent social issues: toilet facilities and "an experienced and mature woman as counselor or someone to function in the capacity of Dean of Women."[10]

Employed women in World War II faced the same double job problems which working women had had earlier; in addition to paid work in industry, they remained the principal homemakers for their families. Wartime brought the first real recognition of this dual role, and during the war years, some efforts were made to help women deal with these obligations. In New York and New Jersey plants, managers and unions brought in grocery store representatives to take orders each morning and deliver the food at the end of the shift. Another factory permitted a local department store to maintain a branch within the plant. In the Buffalo, New York, area, where women war workers found shopping bargains gone by the time they quit work, representatives of management and the machinists' union persuaded merchants to hold some of the bargains until the end of the day. Philadelphia butchers did the same. Stores adjusted shopping hours, remaining open one or two evenings a week. The

Pentagon included a shoe-repair shop, and Washington stores sent personal shoppers into the building to take orders from War Department employees.

Family food needs remained a major problem. Women who had to be at work at 8:00 A.M. often left home without breakfast themselves and with little time to prepare meals for their families. A West Coast study discovered that 84 percent of women workers but only 40 percent of men had inadequate breakfasts. Under pressure from groups like the United Auto Workers and the War Production Board, food companies devised carry-out services which could save women up to three hours a day in shopping and preparing food. At the end of her shift, a woman could pick up macaroni and cheese, chili con carne, codfish balls, chicken pie, or a variety of other foods which required only reheating to put a meal on the family table.[11]

Housing also represented difficulties for women war workers. In addition to a general shortage of dwelling units during and after the war, the migrations of large numbers of employees to boom areas like Detroit or the West Coast created intense competition for places to live. Married women who took their children and tried to find work nearest to the base where their husbands were stationed often found local housing projects filled, with long lists of applicants. Unattached women in search of a room learned that landladies frequently preferred to rent to men, who would not clutter the single bathroom with personal laundry. One woman welder in a West Coast shipyard was living in a hotel; when the eldest son of a coworker was drafted, the mother offered the welder a place in her home. The welder protested that with six children still in the house, they could not spare a room for her. But the mother replied that she had not thought in terms of a room; "Just come and live with us, that's all," she said. Occasionally the YWCA or United Service Organization could find temporary living quarters for women in some war-production areas. Government agencies maintained housing referral systems and inspected accommodations for minimum standards such as single beds, no more than two to a room, weekly change of linen, and a bath and toilet for every seven persons. But the housing problem was never really solved.[12]

Care of families, especially young children, was a greater problem for women than for men war workers. The head of the War Manpower Commission spoke for government and society in affirming women's primary responsibility for their own children in war as well as in peacetime. About half the working mothers could rely on relatives to care for their children. School-age children frequently became "latch-key kids" with the door key on a chain around their necks so that they could let themselves into the house when they arrived home from school, often several hours before their mothers finished the shift in the war plants. As public concern over increased juvenile delinquency mounted, society often blamed absent mothers. Similarly, mothers' high absenteeism from their jobs because of child care emergencies highlighted their work-home dilemma. Private nurseries could accommodate only a few children, and costs were high. Some public nurseries had been established under the WPA in the 1930s, and by 1943 small amounts of federal and local money became available for additional child-care facilities. The Los Angeles Board of Education, for example, took in two thousand children of aircraft workers in twenty-one centers in 1943. But the 101 thousand women in airplane plants had 19 thousand children, who would have needed 197 centers rather than 21. Peak enrollment in day care centers in July 1944 showed 129,357 children in 3,102 units, and the federal government estimated that more than half a million different children received some kind of care at some time during the war. But the available centers did not begin to handle the children who might have been in them, and by 1946 most of the programs had been dissolved.[13]

On the whole, community and government responses to the problems of women war workers showed little planning and less realization that these were long-term conditions. In fact, problems which had faced the working-class woman for generations received attention only with the entry of middle-class women into the work force, and then only because the presence of women seemed necessary to fulfill wartime manpower demands. Women obtained jobs because they represented the only available large source of labor rather than because of any significant adjustment of attitudes on the hiring of women. Traditional ideas of sex roles were little affected by changes in employment. Although 38 percent of America's women were employed by the end of the war and a majority of these were married, society continued to see the home as woman's "place" and believed that women were not serious workers and earners. Despite clear prewar evidence that women earners made significant and necessary contributions to family income even where a husband was present, Americans still talked of women working for "pin money" and did not connect women's patriotic service to the war effort with any legitimate economic needs on their part.[14]

The issue of equal pay for equal work best illustrates the 1940s mentality as it affected fair treatment for women workers. Observers reported that women worked well. Women did more than a hundred tasks of varying skills in shipyards, for example. And while they were kept out of some of the heavier jobs because of lack of physical strength, their overall efficiency and resistance to fatigue rated with the men. In factories and foundries, on assembly lines, and in mechanical processes, women not only worked as skillfully as men after adequate training but often proved more durable, especially in repetitive operations. Women rated lower in bench work, but 88 percent of managers found women's production to be equal to or greater than men's on all or most jobs.[15] Yet women workers were judged separately from men in matters of pay and seniority. Although the war brought a general increase in wages, women did not benefit so much as men. War plants paid up to 40 percent more than prewar traditional "women's industries." But wages were fixed to the sex doing the work rather than to the job itself. Employers justified unequal pay with the argument that special arrangements had to be made to accommodate women workers, such as separate toilets, rest rooms, conveyors, and lighter fixtures. Jobs performed by women received separate labor grades with pay rates considerably below those for men in the same job. In electrical plants, for example, women's hourly rates were 12 to 20¢ lower than men's. Women often remained in trainee or apprenticeship classifications after they had acquired full skills and were actually performing the job with complete responsibility.

Some groups protested discrimination. The Women's Bureau had argued for equal pay for more than twenty years. Unions, especially those affiliated with the CIO, pressed for equal pay to maintain wage rates for all workers; they argued that employers might be holding women's wages down in preparation for dropping all wage rates after the war, a threat to returning veterans. Auto workers walked out of a Canadian plant in 1942 over employment of women at rates lower than those formerly paid to men. And while unions in the United States had taken a patriotic no-strike pledge, groups like the United Rubber Workers urged the War Labor Board to act on behalf of equal pay. In 1942 the Board ruled that employers *might* adjust wages, provided the results did not cause an increase in prices, and by 1945 the WLB issued guidelines calling for equal pay for equal work regardless of sex or race. In Congress, Senators Wayne Morse and Claude Pepper and Representative Mary T. Norton introduced legislation guaranteeing equality of opportunity and pay for women in many industries, and giving the Women's Bureau authority to investigate complaints and issue rulings and interpretations. But union and federal activities during the war, as well as these bills introduced in 1945, met with considerable resistance from employers, the American Management Association, and the American Chamber of Commerce. The bills failed.[16]

An alternative approach to equal treatment, the Equal Rights Amendment, received even less support. Originally proposed in 1923, the constitutional amendment surfaced again in 1945 partly as a statement for the development of opportunities for women and partly as a gesture of gratitude for women's contribution to the war. In addition to the forces which opposed equal pay, many women's groups and organized labor were determined that the amendment should not pass. Social workers, trade unionists, the YWCA, the Women's Bureau, the League of Women Voters, and others argued that the amendment would eliminate laws which protected women workers from exploitation. Leaders in both AFL and CIO unions especially pointed out presumed dangers to working women, foreseeing the abolition of widows' pensions, maternity benefits, aid to dependent children, minimum wage and maximum hour legislation, as well as worries that women would be forced to support children and husbands. Like the equal pay question, the equal rights issue advanced little during World War II.[17]

Despite meager gains on social and economic questions, the war did bring some occupational and financial improvement, particularly to many previously employed women. Domestic service and jobs like laundress declined during the war as women left these fields to take better paying war jobs. In 1940 women had made up only 8 percent of workers in durable goods but constituted 25 percent of employees in those industries at the wartime peak and still held 13 percent of the jobs after the war despite heavy layoffs. Working-class women found that they could fulfill the demands of patriotism while upgrading their occupational opportunities and skills. Moreover, just as factory jobs paid more than domestic service, defense industries carried higher wages than nondefense manufacturing. A nondefense factory worker who operated a sewing machine earned between 60 and 85¢ per hour; a defense worker operating a sewing machine averaged 89 to 95¢, and employees sewing in air frame companies received between $1.02 and $1.15. In some plants, such as the Ford works' Willow Run, workers received an average of $1.23 per hour in 1945. But many of these relatively attractive situations did not last beyond demobilization.

As the war ended, America united to thank the women who had contributed to victory. Wanda the Welder and Rosie the Riveter were cultural heroines. Their coworkers, employers, and public officials praised with amazement their unexpected skills and efficiency in performing necessary and temporary wartime tasks. But society assumed that women would prefer to return to their homes after the war.

Conservatives like Secretary of Labor Perkins assumed that women would prefer domesticity to industry and advocated that those who "took jobs only because of the war" should be encouraged to retire. Union leaders like the head of the United Auto Workers hoped that women would get out of the way of returning veterans. In contrast, the Women's Advisory Committee of the War Manpower Commission doubted that many women would leave their jobs voluntarily. Studies conducted toward the end of the war showed that more than 80 percent of employed women wanted to continue working after the war, and many of the nearly 16 million prewar employees probably continued to face the economic hardships which had brought them into the labor market in the first place. Those who planned to withdraw were generally the middle-class housewives. When the United Electrical, Radio, and Machine Workers of America asked more than a thousand women why they were working, investigators learned that one in five was the only wage-earner in her family, that half were the primary support of relatives, that four-fifths planned to continue working, and that 93 percent worked "for financial reasons."[18]

Despite these aspirations, postwar employment of women experienced a sharp drop. By 1946 three million women had left work. Cutbacks began even before the war was over, and women were laid off in greater numbers than men. As early as 1944, 60 percent of workers laid off in aircraft parts plants were women, although women formed only 42.2 percent of employees in that industry; women suffered 86 percent of the layoffs in aircraft engine plants, in which they made up 39.2 percent of the workers. By 1946 women made up only 4 percent of the employees in Ford plants, although they had held as many as 22 percent of the positions there during the war; 58 percent of the women dismissed from the Willow Run operation said that they had wanted to continue working. Moreover, when war plants converted to peacetime production, men were rehired or placed in other jobs in the plant while women were not. Unions occasionally supported women's protests and demands for reinstatement and back pay, but many did not press the issue. And the separate seniority lists—by department, by sex, by race—made it difficult to use union contracts as the basis for more equitable treatment. Moreover, the patriotism argument was now reversed to favor reemployment of all servicemen regardless of seniority; veterans were usually accommodated at the expense of women and minority employees. Despite women's actual work performance during the war, jobs still belonged to men. Women's stated preferences for nonhome labor and women's economic needs for employment were generally ignored.[19]

But the working-class woman who had worked before the war, had taken advantage of wartime industry to improve her earning capacity, and was laid off from her defense plant at the end of the war still needed her income and continued to want employment. Half the women out of work in 1947 were actively seeking jobs. Some found them, at lower pay, in traditional women's employment areas such as service or store work. Some had entered white-collar clerical occupations and could remain there. Others joined the long-term unemployed on welfare rolls, although the number of employed women returned to about 19 million, or a third of all adult females, by the early 1950s. Half were clerical workers or operatives; a fifth were service workers. Half were over 36 years of age; more than half were married, and a quarter had children under 18.[20] The women who wanted or needed to work had found jobs again in less skilled and less highly paid occupations. After five years in men's jobs, they were back in "women's work."

For working-class women, World War II held out the lure and the hope of having their need to earn legitimatized, of obtaining access to training and skilled jobs, and of finding pay which would begin to lift some of the economic restrictions on their lives. When this set of opportunities proved temporary, the middle-class housewives who had chosen to enter the labor market could afford to return home. The working-class women who had been in the work force all along could not, and they were pushed back into their previous poorly paid occupations or faced unemployment with heavy consequences for their own and their family's lifestyle. For the working-class woman, the war meant a promise withdrawn just as it seemed about to be fulfilled.

10. Mixed Signals in Postwar Work

IN THE YEARS after the Second World War, the unresolved tensions of work and home continued for all American women, but especially for working-class women. For generations they had heard that the objective of all families should be an income for the male breadwinner which was high enough to keep his wife and children out of the workplace. Yet for most working-class families, such an arrangement was impossible, and working-class women expected to work openly before marriage and surreptitiously or guiltily after marriage. During and after World War II, however, the greatest change in the female labor force came with the entry of older married women, usually middle-class housewives, whose previous withdrawal from paid labor had established the social norms. This remarkable adjustment left working-class women confused, while it did nothing to alter their need to earn and little to expand their employment opportunities.

Toward the end of the war, a majority of women war workers expressed their desire to continue working, either in their current positions or at something with higher wages and prestige. The greatest number of prospective postwar employees were women who had worked before the war; four out of five intended to remain in the labor market. Moreover, many women who had moved to war production locations hoped to continue in the same place. Industrial women usually wanted to remain in the same industry and occupation, whereas women in service jobs hoped to move into other industries after the war. Virtually all single, widowed, or divorced women intended to remain employed, saying that they would have to support themselves or others, as did 57 percent of the married women; 11 percent of the married women with families were that family's only wage-earner.[1]

The end of the wartime production boom seemed to order women back home. Layoffs and cutbacks hit women harder than men; returning veterans "bumped" women from their jobs. Even when peacetime production increased, women were not rehired. Most government agencies, employers, and popular journals assumed that the woman war worker had been a middle-class drop-in to the labor force who would welcome the opportunity to return to her family. Magazines carried stories of these women's feelings of "guilt and despondency" at leaving small children; confessional writers admitted embarrassment at the "baseless vanity" of feeling that the ability to work was "an additional flower in my wreath of accomplishments." And disciples of the home preached an antifeminist femininity which said, "Being a woman is something in itself." None of the popular literature discussed the working-class woman or the woman who had no choices about working.[2]

Postwar encouragement of consumer spending combined with an inflationary spiral further tightened the grip of poverty on working-class women. At the same time that they were being instructed to leave the paid labor force for marriage and the care of a family, women were being encouraged to buy houses, household goods, and material possessions for their families. The American dream now went beyond an adequate standard of living and into competitive consumption. Simultaneously, with the lifting of wartime wage and price controls, costs mounted; meat prices increased 122 percent in two years. If the working-class woman were to acquire any of the things society said she ought to want, if she were even to keep her family above the poverty level, she had to earn.

Women entered the labor force in increasing numbers and proportions. In 1890 the 3.7 million women workers counted by census takers had represented 18.2 percent of all adult American women and 17 percent of all workers. By 1900 the number observed had grown slightly to 4.9 million, or 21.2

percent of adult women and 18.3 percent of all workers. Increases remained gradual for the next forty years; 23.9 percent of women said they were gainfully employed in 1920, 24.4 percent in 1930, 25.4 percent in 1940. Before American entry into World War II, the 13.7 million employed adult women made up 25.4 percent of all workers. In the main, they were either single, middle-class, white-collar workers who would leave their jobs when they married, or poor, single or married women, working in factories or in domestic service. By 1945 the female labor force numbered over 19.2 million; 38.1 percent of adult women were working and formed 36.1 percent of the work force. With voluntary withdrawals and forced layoffs after the war, the figures had dropped to 16.1 million (30.9 percent of women and 27.6 percent of the labor force) by 1947. In the next three years, the numbers grew slowly. On the eve of the Korean conflict 17.8 million women (33 percent) earned wages as 29.1 percent of all workers. But by 1953, 19.1 million women were gainfully employed and another 870 thousand had jobs by 1955. An even sharper rise characterized the next twenty years as women moved to a third of the work force in 1968 and 38.1 percent in 1970, when 43.2 percent of the nation's adult females were employed. By April 1974, 35,165,000 American women (45 percent of their population) made up an unprecedented 39.3 percent of the labor force. In sum, while the absolute numbers climbed throughout the century (except for the 1945–53 drop), the proportion of women working returned to the World War II level in the mid-1960s, and women surpassed their wartime share of the labor force in 1970.

The participation rate of married women and mothers has risen dramatically, while single, widowed, divorced, and separated women have retained their position within the labor market. The percentage of working married women grew from 36.4 to 62.3 between 1940 and 1974, indicating that the entry or reentry of the married woman into the labor market has been the most remarkable aspect of women's work since the war. Moreover, women with children under six years of age have more than tripled their participation, from 12 percent in 1950 to 37 percent in 1975, and mothers of children under three have doubled their working rate since 1960. The age of employed women has risen; in 1900 half the women workers were under twenty-six; in 1940, under thirty-two; in 1950, under thirty-seven; and in 1960, under forty-one. The rates for women thirty-five and older have increased sharply, although the 1960s rise in participation by young mothers has brought the median age down to thirty-six by 1974. In the same period, 1940 to 1974, the number of employed women grew from 6.2 million to 8.2 million (the change is somewhat greater than the figures indicate since the 1940 count included fourteen- and fifteen-year-olds), while widows, divorcees, and separated women rose from 2.9 million to 6.7 million employees.[3]

Why these women work is a more complex question. Rising earnings and expanded job opportunities in white-collar sectors have lured many women into the labor market, especially married women. Fewer children, postponement of childbearing, or the finishing of childrearing at an earlier age also leave many women free to seek paid employment outside the home. More education increases potential earnings and raises the issue of income forfeited when the woman remains at home. But these reasons apply best to the middle-class woman who is working to supplement a husband's income or increase the family's already-secure standard of living or find fulfillment for herself. In March 1974, most of the 8.2 million single women workers in the United States supported themselves or others, as did most of 6.7 million women workers who had been widowed, divorced, or separated. An additional 3.2 million working women were married to men who earned less than $5,000 a year, and another 2.3 million had husbands who made between $5,000 and $7,000. Therefore, only two-fifths of women workers had husbands with incomes of at least $7,000 per year at a time when the Bureau of Labor Statistics estimated that an urban family of four would require $7,386 a year to maintain even a low standard of living.

Financial need is even clearer in the absence of a male breadwinner. Although about 45 percent of all women currently participate in the labor market, and 43 percent of wives with husbands present are at work, the participation rate for women who head families is 54 percent. In more than a third of the 3.7 million families headed by women, the female family head is the only person employed; another family member also works in about the same number of such families. These women also suffer a higher unemployment rate (6.4 percent) than male breadwinners (2.7 percent). In Virginia in the mid-1970s, for example, families headed by women were four times as likely to be classified as below poverty-level than were families headed by men, and over a fifth of women-headed families received less than half the amount specified as the poverty income threshold.[4]

Although so many women, especially working-class women, work because of need, they remain clustered in traditional female employment patterns. More than half of working women hold clerical, operative, or service positions. The proportion of employed women in clerical or service work grew from 43 percent in 1960 to 48 percent in 1970. In addition, women are concentrated in relatively few occupations; more than 40 percent of women workers in 1973 had jobs in only ten occupations: secretary, retail salesworker, bookkeeper, private household worker, elementary school teacher, waitress, typist, cashier, sewer and stitcher, and registered nurse. About three-quarters of women workers can be found in fifty-seven occupations: thirty white-collar, fourteen service, and thirteen blue-collar or farm work. Women make up at least 90 percent of the workers in seventeen of these occupations and at least 75 percent in the remaining thirty-one.

Educational attainment is a strong influence not only on whether women will seek paid employment but also, of course, on what kinds of jobs they can get. A college graduate is more likely to work than a high-school dropout. But as more students attend college, job requirements are upgraded and managerial, technical, and skilled positions require more training than the working-class woman usually receives. Women with four years of high school and no college are most often found as clerical workers; women with less than four years of high school fall primarily into service occupations and, to a smaller extent, into operative jobs. Thus, the working-class woman may have a chance at a clerical position but is more likely to be one of the 7 million women service workers currently employed in the United States. And, although their numbers are increasing, females remain a small minority in blue-collar or craft categories, where they are most likely to be factory operatives.[5]

Even white-collar status may be an illusion to many women in it. Telephone operators, for example, have begun to complain that while their jobs possess an aura of "niceness" and while many of them work for extra money in order to consume, their labor is highly industrialized, bureaucratic, and paternalistic. Heavily supervised, in some offices they are permitted to go to the bathroom only two at a time and must petition the supervisor for a place on the waiting list. According to two Boston operators, "Supervisors count heads every half hour to make sure no one has escaped!" Wages and status are also problems. Switchboard operators employed full-time earned from $103.00 to $127.50 per week in 1972, or about $5,300 to $6,300 a year. Secretarial workers identify a hierarchy from executive secretaries who have respectable social positions in the office community down to those expected to type rather than think. In 1972 a Class A secretary averaged $169.00 per week, a Class B typist $99.00, and a Class C file clerk $86.50.[6]

Service jobs for women have also increased, although less dramatically. By 1973, 7 million women worked in service, a jump of 52 percent over 1960. Although service has historically implied domestic work in private households, only about 1.3 million women remain in that occupational group and their numbers have declined in the 1960s as they have throughout the twentieth century. Moreover, white working-class women have given way to nonwhites in domestic service and now make up only about a third of such workers, largely because of low pay, lack of benefits, and comparatively better opportunities in other fields.[7] More than a third of women service workers are involved with food—a million waitresses, half a million cooks, and a quarter million counter workers. Potential income attracts some waitresses. One woman, a recent divorcee and veteran of half a dozen war plants by 1945, took a job in Howard Johnson's to earn more money than she could get in an office. Later, after graduating from practical nursing training, she returned to waitressing because she liked movement and meeting new people better than "carrying bedpans or feeding somebody with a spoon." Other women are attracted by hours which permit them to be at home when their children return from school. But recently, part of the restaurant business had become deskilled, with the same person cooking, serving, and taking cash; such places do not hold much incentive in the way of tips.[8] A much faster growing field for women is health service, where opportunities have more than doubled since 1960 and over 1.4 million women now work as nursing aides, orderlies, attendants, practical nurses, health aides, and dental assistants.[9]

Less change has taken place in the factory. Women operatives still concentrate in garment, textile, tobacco, and non-durable goods industries. They continue to do unskilled or semiskilled tasks such as sewing and stitching, assembling, packing and wrapping, and sometimes checking, examining, or inspecting. Rarely are women found among skilled or supervisory employees. Women textile workers averaged $2.22 per hour in 1971; shirtmakers received $2.00; and hand pressers continued on piece rates as an incentive wage system, earning as little as $2.23 in Miami and as much as $3.90 in New York. Assembly line workers tell of the tedium of their routine. One woman in a cosmetics factory fills thirty-three bottles of "blue goop" each minute; workers on the spray mist cologne line envy the "ladies in lipstick," whose department is air conditioned to prevent the lipsticks from melting. Most of the 250 women in filling and finishing in this cosmetics plant are white, middle-aged, secondary earners, but an increasing number are young mothers, the main support of their families. One woman, who began working to put her children through school, stayed to pay for a car, then new rugs, and was still on the assembly line after fifteen years. But whatever their reasons for working, the operatives in that plant are women, the supervisors men. And women remain underrepresented as managers and skilled craft workers.[10]

At the same time that the numbers of working women and their proportion of the labor market grows, recent forecasts indicate that "women's work" will continue to expand. Both white-collar work and service occupations outside private households will grow faster than employment as a whole, although blue-collar jobs will have a slower growth rate. Women are also likely to continue their gradual inroads into "men's" fields, taking jobs as diversified as diesel truck driver, police officer, and construction worker. But opportunities will generally be tied to education or training, placing a premium on college programs and apprenticeships.[11]

Women workers will also have to continue to battle a set of misconceptions which portray them as unserious, temporary, irresponsible workers. Many Americans still believe that women neither want nor need to work, although 46 percent of adult women are currently employed and two-thirds of the adult poor are female, while 40 percent of working women support themselves or their families and another quarter have husbands earning less than $7,000 a year. Women are also accused of higher absenteeism than men, although the rates are approximately equal, and sick male workers are off the job for longer periods than women. Moreover, the job turnover rate between men and women is narrowing, although women remain concentrated in job classifications with less stability. Fewer women leave work for marriage and children, breaking down the myth that women are temporary and irregular workers on whom the cost of training is wasted. Single women average forty-five years in the labor force, two more than the average male worker, while most women who withdraw return when their children enter school. Despite these facts, however, the myths persist.[12]

Kept in low-skilled, low-paying jobs, women suffer especially in their earnings. In 1973 full-time year-round women workers had a median income of $6,488, or about 57 percent of the median for men. The gap has been widening; in 1956 women made 63 percent of men's salaries. Women's relative income position declined in most occupational groups between 1962 and 1973, with sharp drops among clerical workers. Experience, age, education, race, union membership, and women's lower tendency to work full-time all affect the absolute figures and the ratios, but so does sex. A Princeton study estimated that discrimination was responsible for about three-quarters of male-female wage differentials among whites.[13] A major form of wage and occupation discrimination against working women comes from job segregation by sex. In a subtle way, job titles and classifications often hurt women's income. A man and a woman may perform the same task with separate and unequal job descriptions and wages (making minor distinctions in skill, effort, or responsibility), an arrangement which consistently works against the female employee. Technically, equal pay is given for equal work within the same job classification, but equal pay is not attached to work of equal value.[14]

Women also face an unfavorable job structure in which they find more employment opportunities at lower occupational levels, which carry lower rates of pay, in tasks and industries labeled "women's work." With heavy concentration in clerical and service activities, women actually operate in a segregated labor market, one which does not pay well. Moreover, opportunities are increasing in these sex-typed women's jobs much faster than openings in industries or occupations where women are making slow inroads into jobs previously characterized as "men's."[15] Part of the sex-segregation problem rests with traditional cultural assumptions. But women, too, have cooperated in accepting low-prestige, low-responsibility, low-paying employment, and working-class women, especially, do so because they do not expect to find anything better. In addition, women often appear to have shorter-term job goals than men, seeking an immediate income rather than developing a long-range career. Women's work experience differs from men's as well; in 1973, for example, only 42 percent of employed women worked full-time for the full year, while 68 percent of men met those criteria for full employment. For the 11 percent of women workers who hold year-round part-time jobs and the 47 percent who work for only part of the year, clerical and service jobs offer particular opportunities of seasonal or flexible employment.[16]

Women workers are also experiencing an increasing rate of unemployment. Working-class women especially must worry more about finding employment than about job status, wages, benefits, or working conditions. After World War II, when women made up 28 percent of the work force, they accounted for 27 percent of the unemployed. But with increasing female participation, their share of unemployment has also risen, disproportionately. In 1973 women were 39 percent of the labor force but 48 percent of the unemployed, and the unemployment rate for women (6 percent) was higher than that for men (4.1 percent). A major explanation for the higher unemployment rate of women lies in their movement into and out of the labor force, which carries higher risks of unemployment than movement within the labor force; thus, a person seeking a job has a better chance of being hired if he or she is already employed. The higher unemployment rate among women also stems from changing nonwork situations, especially marital and family status, as well as changes in residence, usually because of marriage or change in the husband's job; these factors are especially strong among young women. In periods of economic contraction, women, with less seniority, frequently suffer layoffs first. Some women working part-time would prefer full-time employment but cannot find it. And nearly half a million women are "not in the labor force"; while some believed they would not be hired for reasons of age, lack of education or training, or personal handicaps, three-quarters of them sought work but gave up after not finding a job, or thought no job was available to them.[17]

Despite these obstacles, women, both working-class and others, are seeking employment; mothers are seeking employment. Between 1940 and 1974, labor force participation by mothers increased five times; in the 1940s and 1950s the sharpest rise came from mothers of school-age children, but since the early 1960s mothers of preschool-age children have been moving into the labor force faster. By 1974, 13.7 million American mothers with children under eighteen worked; these constituted 46 percent of all such mothers and 38 percent of female employees. Of these working mothers, 63 percent, or 8.5 million women, had children between six and seventeen. Mothers in fatherless households are much more likely to work than women whose husbands are present, even if the children are very young.

Almost no social questions are raised about the effect of a father's employment on children. Americans assume that men will work and that their children will be better off with an employed than an unemployed father. But the working mother still represents a major subject of debate. Most of the 27 million children of mothers working in the early 1970s were better off in terms of family income; families headed by women (which included 12 million children) had a median income of $3,760 without the mother employed but $6,195 when she had a job. At least one child in twenty with a working mother lived in a low-income family. Yet questions remain about the personal and social effects on children of the mother's employment outside the home. During World War II, when women appeared to make a dramatic departure from the household to the defense plant, speculations about neglect of children and possible correlations of juvenile delinquency with maternal employment abounded. Despite a generation of psychological and sociological studies which show no appreciable difference in personality or social development between young and adolescent children of employed and nonemployed mothers, working mothers are still expected to feel guilty about time spent away from their offspring. Although quality of maternal involvement seems much more significant than quantity of time devoted to interacting with children, the old challenges recur.

On the practical side, working mothers must also arrange to cope with the effects of their dual role in both the labor force and the home. Employers may not treat a women differently because she is a woman, but they feel justified in speculating whether motherhood of preschool children will affect a woman's capacity to work. A mother, especially of school-age children, may have to seek a part-time job or one in areas like service which permit flexible hours or part-of-year work; but adjustable scheduling is not widespread in American occupations. In addition, when the woman does obtain a job, she usually retains full or primary responsibility for household and child-care tasks. A study in the late 1960s showed that women who worked more than thirty hours a week spent about five hours every day on housework while their husbands averaged 1.6 hours daily, the same amount as husbands of nonworking wives. Finally, the largest problem for the employed mother revolves around finding adequate care for her children during working hours.[18]

Child-care arrangements figure prominently in whether or how a mother works outside the home. During World War II, a small amount of federal money funded nursery schools or day-care centers for the children of women who worked in defense industries. But most such facilities in the 1940s and again during the Korean conflict were private and expensive. In peacetime, both government and popular institutions tended to frown upon day-care arrangements, in accord with a general attitude in the fifties and early sixties that children would be better off in the care of their nonemployed mothers. Increasing employment of mothers of school-age (and more recently preschool) children, however, reopened the care issue in the mid-1960s. A joint study by the Department of Labor and the Department of Health, Education, and Welfare in 1965 revealed that nearly half the children of working mothers were being cared for in their own homes, usually by relatives. Another 16 percent were in someone else's home; the figures were much higher for preschool children, almost a third of this category. An additional 15 percent had mothers who worked only during the child's school hours, and 13 percent "went to work" with their mothers. Only 2.2 percent of all the children surveyed and 5.6 percent of those under six were in group care centers. The rest had some other arrangements, often looking after themselves. More recent trends indicate an increase in licensed day-care facilities; more than 81 thousand such centers had space for over a million children in 1972. Modifications in law, especially the Social Security Act, have provided federal funding for child welfare facilities and a Senate investigation in 1974 showed approximately $1.2 billion being spent on child care. Federal and state tax laws now include provisions for child-care deductions by employed taxpayers. And corporations have begun to explore day-care programs for children of employees to increase morale and productivity and to lessen absenteeism and turnover. For working-class mothers, the emotional and financial cost of day care is a key consideration, however; children are frequently left in the custody of relatives when it is necessary for mothers to work. But, on the whole, these women have traditionally preferred to watch over their own children and see less self-fulfillment in employment outside the home than in functioning as traditional wives and mothers of the earlier middle-class type. Therefore, even government-subsidized or employee-sponsored facilities are still less likely to attract this group of mothers than their middle-class counterparts.[19]

In their struggle to deal with problems ranging from discrimination to benefits such as child care, some working women have turned to trade unionism. While few unions actually encouraged women to join during World War II, some CIO unions accepted female members in their drives for industrial organization. But even CIO unions agreed to separate seniority lists. Auto and rubber workers especially welcomed women and made a point of trying to protect their jobs at the end of the war. The United Auto Workers claim leadership in the fight against discrimination, citing UAW contracts since the 1950s which have provided for equal pay, equal job and training opportunity, and maternity benefits.[20] Nevertheless, unionization has proceeded slowly. During the

1940s and 1950s, textile organizers in the South encountered not only employer opposition but also continued resistance from workers. Some women were afraid of losing their jobs; men, concerned only with their own department, offered little support; and women failed to see the need for a union when they received a small increase in pay without union representation.[21]

Women workers remain relatively underorganized despite recent increases in union membership. In 1954, 2.8 million women belonged to unions; in 1962; 3.3 million; and in 1972, 4.5 million. Women's proportion of all union membership rose from 18.6 percent in 1962 to 21.7 percent in 1972. But the percentage of women workers who were unionized declined from 14.1 percent in 1954 to 10.3 percent in 1970, indicating that women are not joining labor organizations as readily as they are entering the labor market. Part-time and part-year women workers are disinclined to join unions, as are women who continue to see themselves as temporary or secondary workers. And women tend to find employment in clerical and service jobs which have not been organized, rather than in blue-collar or other more heavily unionized occupations. More than 20 percent of the unions surveyed by the Department of Labor reported not having a single female member.[22]

Women do account for half the membership of at least twenty-five unions, however, with the greatest numbers still in the garment trades—over 312 thousand in the International Ladies Garment Workers and nearly 274 thousand in the Amalgamated Clothing Workers of America in 1972. Approximately 80 percent of the ILGWU's membership is female; local 22 in New York City, for example, is about 90 percent women. Since 1933 this union has had a thirty-five-hour week; local 22 had the first union health center in the country as early as 1913; the ILG won paid vacations for its members in 1937 and pensions in 1943. But recently, as the dress industry moves out of New York toward nonunion plants in the South and Southwest, local 22 has shrunk from 28,000 to 9,300 members, attendance at meetings is declining, shop stewards are over forty-five and worry about involving younger women in the local.[23] Other unions with heavy female membership include the retail clerks, electrical workers, communications workers, local government employees, and automobile workers. Office workers began to organize in the 1960s, some affiliated with national unions, others in organizations such as New York's Women Office Workers, Boston's Women Employed, and San Francisco's Union Women's Alliance to Gain Equality. But fewer than 10 percent of the women who make up 76 percent of office workers are unionized, although the pace of organization may increase as office employees become more aware of impersonal bureaucracy or realize that their white-collar jobs carry blue-collar or lower wages. Service employees such as office cleaners and health care workers are also beginning to organize. In New York City, for example, 40 percent of the members of a custodial assistants' local are female and the union itself has grown from a few hundred to more than one hundred thousand. Hospital workers have also affiliated, and unions in this occupation are working particularly on training and upgrading of employees.[24]

Increases in the numbers of women in unions have not been accompanied by comparable increases in women assuming union leadership. While groups like the United Auto Workers have women's bureaus to pay attention to the needs of female members, few unions have opened their top councils to women, and where they have, women tend to be in advisory staff positions rather than in policy-making leadership. Although women have a wider local representation as shop stewards or officers of their locals, on the executive boards they are secretaries and trustees more often than presidents or vice-presidents. A recent examination of seven

New York City locals indicates that women do not lack interest so much as information, training, and experience in leadership. The same study showed that both men and women union members hold limiting personal and cultural assumptions about women's role, that women feel they have less time to devote to union activities and have less self-confidence in seeking advancement, and that women desire both education and encouragement. The analysis projected that women could assume leadership positions with appropriate supportive programs.[25] At the same time, women's caucuses within companies, industries, and unions are working to develop awareness of women's problems as workers and to urge action to correct low wages, lack of opportunity, and violations of law and fair play.[26]

Contemporary working women operate within a comparatively recent framework of legislation, directed not so much at protection as at equity. In December 1961 President John F. Kennedy established the President's Commission on the Status of Women to assess the changing position of American women in several major categories, including employment, and to examine ways of eliminating discrimination. Since the 1960s several key laws have emerged to govern the position of women as workers.

Although several states had already enacted statutes providing for equal pay and the Women's Bureau had been arguing for the principle since its inception, the first federal law against sex discrimination in employment as the Equal Pay Act of 1963, specifying that jobs of equal skill, effort, and responsibility performed under similar conditions shall carry the same wages regardless of the sex of the employee performing the task. While seniority, quantity of work, and quality of production may all affect pay, sex cannot. The Department of Labor's Wage and Hour Division administers the law, which has been upheld and defined in several landmark court cases; the United States Supreme Court has used the rule of "substantially identical" in applying the law.[27]

Women also benefited from a last-minute addition to Title VII of the Civil Rights Act of 1964, in which "sex" was added to race, color, religion, and national origin as an area in which employers, employment agencies, and labor unions may not discriminate in hiring or firing, wages and salaries, promotions, conditions of employment, classifying or referring for employment, membership, training or apprenticeship, or advertising. Exceptions cover only those situations in which sex would be a genuine occupational requirement for the normal operation of the business, as in the hiring of a wet nurse, for example. The Equal Employment Opportunity Commission administers Title VII; because the EEOC engaged primarily in investigation and conciliation in the 1960s, its enforcement powers were strengthened in 1972. But the enforcement record remains poor and some judges have ruled that in specific cases discrimination is not solely by sex but by sex plus some other factor. Conversely, EEOC has been accused of setting quotas which prevent employers from hiring the most qualified applicants. Moreover, advocates of protective legislation for women see Title VII as a threat to state laws regulating such areas as physical facilities and rest and meal periods. And unionists worry about the effect of increasing federal specifications on the free collective bargaining process.[28]

Several other federal actions affect working women. Two executive orders issued by President Lyndon Johnson forbade sex discrimination by employers working under government contract. Federal contractors were also obliged to analyze whether minorities or women were being underutilized and to pursue affirmative action to rectify such imbalances. In view of the number of older women entering or reentering the job market, the Age Discrimination in Employment Act of 1967, prohibiting discrimination by employers, employment agencies, and labor unions against persons forty to sixty-five years old, is significant. The Fair Labor Standards Act, originally passed in 1938, has been amended to increase the minimum wage and to broaden the categories of employees protected by it. The Department of Health, Education, and Welfare now includes the National Institute of Occupational Safety and Health to conduct research into job environment hazards.

In addition, the states have expanded equality and protective legislation. In 1975, forty states and the District of Columbia prohibited sex discrimination in private employment; thirty-seven states forbid sex-based pay differentials for equal or substantially equal work in private employment. Minimum wage laws have been enacted in forty states and the District of Columbia, and most of these now extend to men as well as women.

Finally, the Equal Rights Amendment, first proposed in 1923, has reemerged in the 1970s. On 12 October 1971 the House of Representatives approved the amendment; the Senate followed on 22 March 1972; and the amendment went to the states for ratification. During and since its passage through Congress, the ERA has raised questions similar to those first posed in the 1920s. In particular, defenders of women have expressed concern over the impact of the amendment on protective legislation. The AFL-CIO, for example, originally objected that the amendment would cost working women the hard-won gains of minimum wage, maximum hours, weight lifting, and other protective laws, but after 1973, the unionists withdrew their objections and supported ratification. Three-fourths of the states must ratify the amendment for the ERA to become part of the United States Constitution.[29]

These legal and social advancements reflect a dramatic change in the activities of American women since World War II. More women are working. More married women are working. More working-class women are working after marriage—and they are no longer obliged to be ashamed of that fact. But the actual circumstances of their employment frequently remain limited. Most women, particularly working-class women, work out of necessity. Yet a combination of educational levels, lack of marketable skills, and family obligations restrict their job opportunities. Clustered in service, clerical, and operative positions known as "women's work," they remain the lowest paid workers at the lowest occupational levels. And while they hold such jobs, most working-class women retain primary responsibility for their homes and children, performing all the tasks of the woman who "does not work."

For the woman in the work force, there are avenues for improvement. On the one hand, some women have turned to trade unionism; some unions have expressed greater interest in women members or in the organization of job sectors where women are heavily employed; and in a few cases the possibilities of women in leadership positions in unions are being explored. On the other hand, laws and court decisions have tried to provide equity for women in access to employment and in treatment on the job. Some combination of these factors may bring employed working-class women to the point envisioned by the early progressives who hoped to provide a framework of protection to equalize opportunity for people to help themselves.

The impact of these social, economic, and legal changes has been particularly great on working-class women. The old rules appear to have changed. For at least a century and a half, these women were told to leave the workplace, to find legitimacy within the home. Now, a new set of goals, applauding self-fulfillment and economic advancement urges them to move back into the labor market, where, however, they continue to find few real opportunities. The conflict is often painful.

11. Postwar Challenges to Home and Community

As THE United States entered World War II, Mary, the nine-teen-year-old daughter of a tenant farmer, left home to be married to an army private. She never returned, following her soldier husband first to New Jersey, where she worked in a factory which made flame throwers, then to ¯ xas, where she sold Christmas cards in the PX, then to Spokane, where she was an airplane mechanic, then to Battle Creek, where she found a job on the air base, then finally to Ann Arbor, where, after five years of marriage, she obtained a divorce. "Took me three years to get that divorce," she said, "but I said I was gonna get it and I got it." Mary then worked as a wait-ress in Maryland to support herself and her son as well as her former husband's mother and stepfather. Although she re-married and lived in suburban Chevy Chase, she was still working as a waitress in 1970, "because I've never done noth-ing else." Without a job she "wouldn't be happy." Mary saw society divided into rich, poor, and middle-class, and placed herself in that last category, proud of her independence but concerned with the enormous rise in costs, afraid of debt and illness but proud of the house her second husband had been working to pay for since he was sixteen years old.[1]

Like many other American women, Mary's adult life has been lived during a period of striking social change and ap-parent improvement. Since 1945 women have outnumbered men in the United States; the estimated female population of 109,337,000 in 1975 represented 51.3 percent of the total popu-lation. Women are also living longer; while the median age for women was 22.4 years in 1900, it increased to 30 years by 1975. Nearly a fifth of all women are between 15 and 24 years of age, a quarter between 25 and 44, and a fifth between 45 and 64. Birth rates are declining, particularly the number of third and subsequent children. And while nearly all women in the middle years are married, younger women are not entering marriage so rapidly as they did in the past and increasing numbers of older women are divorced, separated, or widowed.[2] These contemporary women have experienced an increasing list of options and alternatives in life- and workstyles: sexual freedom, opportunities for controlling family size, new occupations, rising employment outside the home, consumerism, and the increase in labor-saving devices and household aids. And like most groups, the working class seems to have participated in a growing prosperity, which shows itself in increased purchasing power, a shorter workweek, and more leisure time.[3]

But as historian William Chafe has argued, changes for women have been tolerated only insofar as they fail to challenge the economic and sexual status quo.[4] The working-class woman in particular remains in a network of subordination—in the home and in the workplace as a woman, socioeconomically and culturally as working-class.[5] Mary has traveled far from the tenant farm of her childhood. She lives in an affluent suburb of Washington, D. C., in a $30,000 house, and considers herself middle class. If offered $25,000, she says she would be suspicious, would regard the money as "hot" or having strings attached, and would refuse it; if offered a million dollars, she says she might buy some new furniture or a car for her husband. But she works nine hours a day for low pay and tips, refuses the opportunity of a supervisory position because it carries more responsibility, expresses defensive and critical attitudes about youths and nonwhites, feels threatened by government involvement in issues such as education and welfare, is horrified at credit buying, and varies from her mother's life only in her divorce, urban setting, and service occupation.[6]

For the working-class woman in post–World War II America, as before, marriage and motherhood remained the ultimate career. Throughout American history, at least since the impact of industrialization, she had been instructed to seek the ladylike middle-class female status of "unemployed" caretaker of a man's person, residence, and offspring. Her own extramarital earning endeavors, however vital they might be to her family's survival or progress, remained illegitimate. In the 1950s particularly, women experienced strong pressures toward "femininity," with magazine fiction preaching against the folly of women "denying their sex" by pursuing careers or sports or unattached lives. These stories usually ended with the tomboy crumpling under a returning soldier's kiss or the career woman capitulating before the picture of a "real" woman cuddling a child.[7] Working-class women in the late 1950s and early 1960s gave sociologists a strong impression that they would not feel comfortable without a clear-cut familial role, that their husbands and children and households were central to their lives.[8]

But the manner in which these working-class marriages came about was casual, almost accidental; both men and women indicated that they just drifted together when they decided that it was about time to get married. Marriage seemed to provide the most acceptable escape from an unhappy home; a thirty-two-year-old man endorsed married life because a wife could not boss him around the way his parents did. Working-class men distrusted women, finding them unpredictable, moody, inquisitive, and devious. A veteran of the occupation forces in Japan praised the Japanese woman for only inquiring "how high" when he told her to "jump," and he saw no reason why an American woman should ask "why?" Another denounced his wife for crying at the death of her ninety-four-year-old favorite uncle— "Women cry over the damndest things," he said, recalling that the last time he had shed tears was "when the Packers lost the championship." His male listeners laughed, while a woman observed, "If you were married to some of these dumb bastards you would cry too." The distrust was mutual. When women referred to men as "dumb," they meant that men engaged in excessive drinking, spending, and chasing of other women; but the same women agreed that they themselves had married such men, usually because "the other men aren't any better." Working-class men described the ideal woman as reliable, faithful, sexually responsive, neat and clean, willing to spend time and effort on the family and household, and primarily one who would not interfere with the world of men. The "good wife" would be a mother-housekeeper to whose children a husband could be a good father. Conversely, women spoke of their desire for attention, the value they placed on affection, but most admitted that they did not actually expect such treatment. Working-class wives hoped that their husbands would be good providers or good lovers to whom they could be lovers and companions, but in practice, they expressed disappointment at not receiving affection, and they worried about risking too many complaints. They would settle for permanence in the less-than-happy relationship, emotionally isolated from their husbands, because they felt that nothing better could be expected from a man. Similarly, they doubted their own ability to "hold" a husband's affections. Many tried to get closer to their men by submissiveness or acceptance of rough or distant behavior. Each sex tended to find companionship with its own gender, leaving marriage in the realm of complementary tasks (work and housework) and sexual union.[9]

While specific statistics on white working-class women are not yet available, the working class, like the rest of American society, has experienced an increase in marital instability. While the rates of first marriages declined in the 1950s, 1960s, and early 1970s, the divorce rate doubled between 1960 and 1974, and the remarriage rate rose by about a fourth. One observer, in a blue-collar suburb of Washington, D.C., found that most couples had had previous marriages, and that where current marriages appeared stable, the parents were often concerned about their children's troubled marriages or separations. Moreover, since the divorce rate has increased so much more than the remarriage rate, the proportion of unattached women has grown; in 1950, 38 percent of all American women twenty to twenty-four years of age were single; in 1975, 40 percent. Simultaneously, divorced women twenty-five to thirty-four years old who had not remarried rose from 2.5 percent in 1950 to 6.8 percent in 1975. And the 7.2 million families headed by women in 1975 represent an increase of 73 percent over 1960.[10]

Despite these problems, working-class women of the post-war period remained strongly oriented toward marriage and motherhood. Although they may have drifted into specific marriages because they wanted the married state and may have drifted into pregnancy—again, without making a conscious decision—most working-class mothers embraced pregnancy and childbirth as the most vital experience of their lives, a natural affirmation of their femininity. If the working-class husband proved his masculinity by having a pregnant wife, even more so, the wife established both her female legitimacy and her respectability by becoming a mother. The absence of children indicated a spiritual and practical emptiness in her life, since investigators learned during the 1950s and the early 1960s that working-class women without children did not fill their days with meaningful activity, were bored, and did not leave the house more than young mothers. If bearing children established the worth of the working-class woman, she often made their care the central activity of her daily life, finding much of her own fulfillment through her children and perhaps using them to compensate for her husband's lack of demonstrated affection. These women wanted to protect their children; many expressed fears for the child's physical safety in the outside world, and some praised television as a device to keep youngsters "out of harm's way." Working-class women told interviewers that they were more interested in a happy, contented life for their children than in mobility or accomplishment, and they expressed goals for their children in moral terms—respectability, decency, honesty, and being good Christians. But many working-class mothers were uncertain about discipline, and while they strongly desired that the children know and practice the distinction between right and wrong, many felt that punishment should not be applied to a first offense; in practice, working-class parents seemed more concerned with the results of a child's behavior than with the motivations for it.[11]

Since they find so much satisfaction in motherhood, working-class women generally do not resist or reject it. As early as the World War I years, Margaret Sanger abandoned working-class women as unreceptive objects of her birth-control information campaign. And working-class couples continued to elect or accept larger families than their midddle-class contemporaries. Many working-class men and women traditionally regarded family planning and contraception as unnatural, believing that married people should have as many children as God sent them, although working-class wives, especially those with several children, expressed concerns about another pregnancy and often claimed that those fears spoiled their chances of enjoying a sexual relationship with their husbands. But contraceptives carried a variety of threats. If husbands had accepted responsibility for preventing conception, wives sometimes did not trust them to actually do so. Lower-class men expressed strong fears of emasculation by a male birth control pill, and wives sometimes wondered whether an oral pill for women might desex or poison them in some way. Moreover, many such women were too reticent to discuss methods of limiting family size with a physician.[12]

More recently, however, working-class women have

placed children in a less central (though still highly important) role. Both in current goals and long-term aspirations, these women—who continue to be wives and mothers—are including other interests in their personal lives. In some cases, husbands are displacing children as the primary source of satisfaction; these wives are speaking of their husbands as friends, companions, and sex mates. Others are adding an employment or community dimension to their home roles.[13]

Traditionally, the titles "wife" and "mother" have also implied "housewife" for the working-class woman. A life centered in husband-servicing and child-rearing requires great concentration on homemaking activities. A typical daily routine encompasses getting children out of bed, washed, dressed, and to the breakfast table, a husband off to work, clothes laundered, the house cleaned, dishes washed, lunch, clothes ironed, beds made, dusting and mopping done, clothes mended, windows washed, kitchen and bathroom scrubbed, groceries purchased, snacks and supper prepared, and perhaps yard work and new clothes or curtains sewn. A working-class wife could honestly say, "I haven't ever caught up with myself since the twins were born four years ago." Another, admitting exhaustion after fourteen hours of housekeeping, realized that the day just completed would be repeated tomorrow; her solution was to postpone the mending and ironing "until it's an emergency." And a student-mother-housewife and part-time worker recorded a 5:30 A.M. to 9:00 P.M. day of drudgery, which included the joy of cleaning a cereal bowl her husband had left in his car the day before; at midday she valiantly resisted the impulse to dump Bosco on her son's head. Those working-class women who confessed to disliking housework in the late 1950s tended to feel guilty at their failure in this "normal feminine responsibility"; but most working-class wives spoke positively of their tasks. These women had clear ideas about the appearance and organization of their homes as well, stressing plain, simple, all-American standards of house, furniture, food, and clothes. They desired a "homey" rather than a "showy" house and preferred current "modern" styles over "old-fashioned" surroundings. At the same time, they attempted to "pretty up" their homes, adding decorative items often purchased on impulse and at considerable damage to the family budget. Increasingly, in the 1960s and 1970s, working-class housewives also sought equipment and appliances which would lighten the burden of housekeeping chores, no longer feeling that they had to make a show of hard labor to emphasize their value.[14]

The burdens of homemaking, husband-tending, and child-rearing left little time or energy for outside contacts for the postwar working-class wife, and when she did move outside her own home, it was usually within a restricted neighborhood and circle of friends. In the late 1950s working-class women reported crowded, busy, dull, humdrum existences, which they assumed were the same for all women. Weekends were little different from weekdays, since their husbands frequently held extra-income jobs at that time. Even the changing seasons were more similar than different; a few women noted that autumn was distinguishable from summer because their husbands would be hunting instead of playing baseball. Their social lives were segregated from those of their husbands; men seemed to operate in a world of work and male companionship, often in neighborhood taverns, while women were relegated to home life and child care. Even outside the home, the woman's social life was family-oriented. These women told interviewers that they liked their own relatives best, that they visited a mother or sister most frequently, that whole families automatically got together on weekends and holidays. Even when they did not want to live too close to parents or other relatives who might interfere in their lives, they remained family-type people through default, feeling insecure in the world outside their relatives. One study found that 92 percent of wives married less than seven years whose mothers lived in the same community saw their mothers daily or at least several times a week. In the same group, over a third of the wives confided most fully in someone other than their husbands, usually their mothers, to whom they talked about everything except sex.[15] From the late 1950s to the early 1970s, however, changes in lifestyle have required working-class women to adjust their families' social relations. A steady movement of young people away from their parents' neighborhoods in search of employment or housing makes day-to-day family contact more difficult. Some working-class women, unprepared for suburban living, have found themselves isolated not only from their husbands but also from their neighbors, who are no longer relatives or companions since childhood. They have not made friends easily or quickly and miss the emotional support which used to be so close at hand.[16]

Income and employment have also had a significant influence on working-class women in postwar America. Since the 1950s the popular imagination has gradually blended working class into middle class. And, in fact, both groups did experience a rise in real, spendable wages during the 1950s and 1960s, and increasing numbers held white-collar jobs. But mobility was more apparent than concrete. In 1970, 30 percent of employed American workers earned less than $7,000 per year. Moreover, many fell below the federal government's established income level for middle-class status. In 1973, for example, an urban family of four was classified "poverty level" at $4,200 per year, "low income" at $7,486, and "intermediate" at $11,446. But 12 percent of families placed between "poverty" and "low," and more than 25 percent were between "low" and "intermediate." A majority of working-class families, therefore, remain subaffluent, usually somewhere between poverty and security. Only families of skilled workers or households with employed wives and mothers find stability of income and spending power.[17]

The condition of women heads of households is usually much worse. Again, white working-class women have not been segregated in the statistics, which undoubtedly reflect strong trends in black families. But during the 1960s overall, families headed by women increased ten times as fast as two-parent families, and in 1971, 40 percent of families living in poverty were headed by women. Desertion, illegitimacy, divorce, separation, and widowhood have increased dramatically in the postwar years, making many women into breadwinners of some sort. Federal programs such as Aid for Dependent Children originally hoped to permit mothers to remain at home during their children's early years, but such payments rarely ensure a decent living standard. When women seek paid employment, they have been handicapped by lack of skills and find either low-paid service jobs or none at all. Moreover, welfare payments have become a particular concern to working-class people, who have strong traditions of independence and suspicions of government control.[18]

Whatever the source of income in a working-class household, women have frequently managed it, and women, particularly, have had to deal with postwar mass consumerism. Consistently throughout the 1950s, 1960s, and 1970s, working-class women have had primary control over the day-to-day spending of their families. As consumers, their first priority has been security—physical, social, and economic. Since they are not especially optimistic about the economic future, they would like to save money, whether or not they actually achieve that goal. Moreover, they look for esteem by trying to earn reputations as thrifty housewives, seeking a "good buy" which has value; therefore, they are afraid to buy cheaply and prefer safe, guaranteed, nationally known products. In addition, they would like to enhance family status while remaining within a respectable, simple, "common man" sphere; modern rather than ornate styles appeal to them, and they value equipment within the home over exterior appearance. Since the working-class woman seeks affection from those around her, she sometimes tries to buy it, winning praise by "doing for others" or indulging children. But increasingly, she has felt the desire to free herself from the monotonous chores of household labor and may purchase an item for its work-saving rather than its aesthetic qualities; at the same time, she may give in to urges to decorate or "pretty up" her environment. But throughout her spending, she is conscious that she is dealing with a limited income; working-class wives continually assess their families' incomes as average or below, even when real wages have risen. This consciousness of economic restriction leaves them with the feeling that they will never come out ahead. But they hope for the security of always knowing their current financial situation; therefore, they strongly prefer cash to credit buying, and since they are not conditioned to abstract thinking, they use a variety of devices in budgeting, such as keeping money in separate drawers or in tin cans.[19]

A growing number of working-class women have become so aware of their family income limitations that they have tried to solve the problem by seeking paid employment. Because of inflation, American families had less spendable income in 1970 than in 1967, unskilled workers were being replaced by machines, and a wife's paycheck often meant the difference between poverty and "just getting by." While fewer working-class women have had to work to bring their families up to bare subsistence, two-thirds of working women are either the only supporter of themselves and their children or are married to men who earn less than $7,000 a year. Women who remained employed at the end of World War II generally belonged to the latter group, although they struggled to get out of the work force under pressures of 1950s domesticity-femininity, and as their husbands' income rose. But almost as soon as working-class women seemed to be catching up to the middle-class position of remaining at home, middle-class women entered the work force in pursuit of added family income or self-fulfillment or putting education and skills to use. At first confused by the shifting trend, working-class women clung to the home. By the late 1960s, however, they were facing economic realities which made their wage-earning absolutely necessary.[20]

Many working-class wives entered the labor market at considerable personal cost, often over their husbands' strong objections. In opinion polls gathered from the 1940s to the 1970s, working-class men were consistently least favorable to the idea of married women working. "A man should be able to make enough money to take care of things," they asserted, both in protest against their own low wages and in embarrassment that their wives should have to supplement those incomes. Working-class women agreed in part, stating that a wife should not work unless her husband could be persuaded to give his consent. But when the issue of additional income was raised, women were less willing than men to sacrifice the higher standard of living which came from the wife's wages. And by the early 1970s working-class women were adding the argument that earning money had become a source of pride which was rewarding in itself, unlike earlier women who felt compelled to mask their earnings.[21]

Even if the husband's opposition can be overcome, working-class women still pay a practical and emotional price for seeking jobs. Women at all levels are confronted with dual allegiance if they work: they retain the home and family commitments alongside a major relationship with the source of their earnings. Housewives spend from five to twelve hours per day on household work if they do not also hold a paying job, and from four to eight hours if they do;

husbands spend one-half to three hours daily on house-related tasks whether or not they are married to earning women.[22] Moreover, employed working-class mothers often feel guilty about time spent away from their children, while they must also cope with the practical question of child care. In the 1950s and the early 1960s, the working-class generally resisted day-care programs, primarily on the assumption that mothers were the most appropriate caretakers of their children, and therefore, ought to be at home caring for them, and partially out of concern for what appeared to be yet another government welfare drain on their tax dollars. As late as 1973, over two-thirds of mothers interviewed said that they preferred having the child cared for at home and 57 percent actually had that arrangement. But increasing numbers are finding day care a realistic and respectable alternative if a mother must go to work. And their children are changing their attitudes on working women; fewer working-class daughters now say that they expect to become housewives with or without children and more are thinking of themselves as future married career women with children.[23]

Once out of the house, having made whatever compromises are necessary to leave, however, the employed working-class woman faces continuing limitations. She will be a temporary worker; she will have a high absenteeism rate; she will change jobs frequently—or so her potential employers assume. While none of these assumptions remains valid, they are among the forces keeping women in low-level positions. Working-class women particularly tend to accept such explanations, claiming to be working "only" until a car is paid for or a child educated—the same statements made by similar women twenty years ago, women who are still in the job market. Moreover, as education increasingly becomes a criterion for employment, and working-class women still have high-school diplomas or less, they are relegated to positions requiring minimal skills.[24]

Some changes seem to be taking place at present. Although schools are still frequently tracking working-class children into vocational or commercial programs, when working-class daughters elect to go beyond high school, many are choosing community college classes which will prepare them for skilled jobs at higher rates of pay. Similarly, some businesses are evaluating new employees with an eye toward potential for supervisory positions and are offering in-house training or educational subsidy programs. And a variety of governmental, union, and private sources are pressing for the opening of the skilled trades to women through apprenticeship, placement, and application of existing laws.[25] The same beginnings of adjustment appear within the trade union movement. While some working-class women continue to regard union membership as unladylike, or give in to employer intimidation, or find few models among the limited number of female union leaders, some women's caucuses and departments within unions have turned their attention to concerns of employed women, including day care, maternity benefits and leave, family health care, legal services, and equality in pay and seniority systems. Finally the issue of part-time work or flexible hours to accommodate mothers of young children is beginning to be addressed.[26]

By all indicators of lifestyle, work force participation, and their own responses to interviewers, however, working-class women in postwar America have been anxious and insecure, feeling that they have relatively little control over their own lives and none over the outside world. While these concerns have modified slightly by the 1970s, the essential fear remains. Bounded by the endless chores of homemaking and child-rearing, having little spare time to visit neighbors and less communication with husbands who can only report the same old routine on the job, hearing political leaders and pollsters and even their soap operas completely enchanted with the middle class, working-class women acquired a negative way of thinking, accepting life as it was offered but fearing that it would become worse. A miner's wife recalled eating Christmas dinner in 1951 with part of a funeral procession parked in front of her house; an explosion had killed 118 men; her husband was not one of them, this time.[27] Frequently threatened with unemployment through economic shifts or automation or similarly uncontrollable forces, the working class lacked any basis for faith in its own effectiveness, or even any awareness that it constituted a group which might influence its own destiny. Some working-class women quite frankly coped by not coping. Others clothed themselves in pity for the less fortunate, finding comfort that they were not alone in a capricious and hostile world. Still others tried to soften the harsher aspects of life by prettifying their surroundings. And many became fiercely protective of their families, especially the children, of their possessions, and of their sense of values. On the whole, they remained alienated from external institutions such as politics, professionals, and social services.[28]

By the 1960s working-class people began to feel that they had not achieved the American Dream despite the promises and popular concepts of the 1950s. Life was less stable, more confusing, less safe, more costly, and people who seemed less "worthy" appeared to be getting more of the world's benefits than hard-working, clean-living, patriotic working-class Americans. Vague threats and insecurities began to focus on issues like race, war, morality, welfare, and women's liberation.

An increasingly vocal black identity movement, as well as the arrival of black neighbors, sharpened fears of those who found their own social position to be only marginal. A middle-aged white waitress complained that it was almost impossible to get rid of a black girl who "just won't work." Whites resented hiring programs which appeared to place race before job qualifications. Blacks sought racial pride with assertive slogans and actions. But out of reactions to "Black Power" and "Black Is Beautiful" also came affirmations of white ethnicity, which went beyond the traditional New York City St. Patrick's Day Parade to plastic buttons reading "Kiss Me, I'm Italian" and a Richmond, Virginia, restaurant called O'Brienstein's, where young waiters and waitresses wear buttons claiming "St. Patrick Eats Bagels."

Working-class women also reacted strongly to the Vietnamese conflict and contemporary social questions; like their men, they set forth traditional, straightforward patriotic values. For many working-class observers, John Kennedy would never have permitted such a drawn-out and unsatisfying war as the one in Indochina, but since the country had made the commitment, students and radicals and Communists (the terms were often used interchangeably) should not bother the government about something which was none of their business, since they were not responsible, tax-paying citizens. To the working-class mind, youth had overthrown oldtime religious holiness in favor of sexual promiscuity and a kind of blackmail of their parents for immediate satisfaction of their every whim. "If the young people today had to work as hard as we did," one woman said, "they wouldn't have no damn time to do all this demonstrating." The poor and the middle class also seemed to be thriving at working-class expense, purchasing on credit rather than paying in hard-earned cash. And welfare recipients "just don't care" and "live like rats" on working-class tax dollars, they argued. The "new politics" of people like George McGovern seemed to have something for everyone except the working class; and George Wallace appeared to give voice to their concerns about busing, civil rights, protection of property, and federal government interference in local or private matters. On the whole, working-class people saw too much upset in the natural order of things for their liking.[29]

One of the greatest recent threats felt by the working class, particularly working-class women, has come from women's liberation. The late 1950s and 1960s witnessed the emergence of a variety of social movements: civil rights, New Left, anti-war, and women's liberation, among others. In 1963 Betty Friedan exposed a dismal picture of educated middle-class women suffering from "the disease that has no name," while others rushed to point out the range of political, social, economic, and cultural oppressions suffered by females. Sensational accounts of supposed bra-burning and protests against the exploitation of women as "sex objects" followed. But in leadership, goals, and tactics, the women's liberation movement seemed to speak to and for a middle- and upper-class educated elite, and the media encouraged that impression. The independent, assertive, self-determined, equal role put forth for liberated women especially threatened the working-class housewife, who already felt insecure about her husband's lack of affection, changes in her neighborhood, uncontrollable economic conditions, and the lack of rewards for her hard work, religious devotion, and patriotism. Working-class women had been educated to be passive, dependent on men, nurturing to others. In particular, the implied assault on housework created severe problems for the housewife whose homemaking skills were one of her few claims to value. Therefore, while the early women's liberation movement made little effort to reach out to this group of women, they in turn rejected the movement as illegitimate and thought of "women's libbers" as unfeminine failures who attacked husbands, children, and homes out of frustration since they were not "women enough" to win those prizes. Working-class women also saw no reason to fight for entry into exclusive men's bars since the sexes had separate social lives anyway; they could not appreciate the demands of women to have credit cards in their own names when they disliked the uncertainty of credit buying; and they opposed the revived Equal Rights Amendment in fear that not only would it cost them the few privileges and protections they presently enjoyed, but also it might subject them to the military draft, unisex public toilets, and requirements that they contribute equally to child support.[30]

In the late 1960s and 1970s, however, the women's liberation movement has had considerable impact on the working class. As working-class women seek employment, they have added other feminist priorities to the commitment to equal pay for equal work, such as health and day care. As labor unions retreated from opposition to the ERA in 1973, many trade union women no longer view the amendment as a threat to protective legislation. As working-class mothers move into the larger world through parent-teacher and child recreational groups and become more like middle-class women of a previous era, they are less homebound and begin to acquire a measure of self-assurance. Some have embraced a middle-of-the-road consumerism. And in areas which touch their lives directly, attitudes are softening. Working-class women are adopting those aspects of liberation which seem appropriate and useful, while continuing to reject extremist positions.[31]

Working-class women have also become more analytic about social mobility. Long educated to believe that complete assimilation into American society meant the discarding of all "alien" influences and adoption of middle-class culture and values, they frequently felt obligated to seek the external signs of middle-class status, such as suburban houses or higher education for their sons. But they did not readily follow middle-class women into clubs, volunteer organizations, jobs, or community activities. When asked about their aspirations in the 1950s, many gave proper middle-class-oriented responses but continued to live working-class lives. More recently, the responses have begun to agree with lifestyles, and working-class people affirm their uniqueness, show less inclination toward entering the middle-class, and are developing or joining institutions which will serve working-class goals. Working-class women in 1972 told interviewers that they wanted to enjoy life now without bearing the burdens of middle-class moral codes or work standards. Using terms like "me" and "now," they indicated less feeling of obligation to sacrifice for their own or their children's future. Resenting ethnic stereotypes such as Italian gangsters or Poles in undershirts, they are rediscovering their ethnic identity.[32]

Some working-class women are also changing their social circles and community involvement. In the 1950s working-class women remained homebound; the clubs which a few of them participated in were usually related to their churches or their children's schools. Many claimed that club women probably neglected their families, since the burden of homemaking left working-class women little time or energy for such activities. They felt isolated from the larger society, and their social contacts were limited to family and neighbors, often out of shyness, sometimes because husbands opposed contact with outsiders. The working class in general expressed cynical views of the political process and few women engaged in formal political community organization.[33] During the 1960s working-class women remained alienated from community services, saying that they were too shy to ask about birth control at the clinic or believing that family services or employment agencies were for those economically beneath them. Still proud that they could "take care of themselves," they were bewildered by problems which they could not handle. Crime, drugs, busing, changes in the neighborhood, the threat of urban renewal all showed the working class that they were no longer to be "left alone" to struggle through a presumably pre-middle-class period. Some reacted by giving in to helplessness. Others, especially those who were emerging into jobs and wider social contacts, united to fight for their neighborhood against city councils' plans for urban renewal, to force sanitation departments to collect garbage, to become informed and share information on issues of employment, legal aid, and social services. Committed to remaining in their neighborhoods, but feeling their old sense of community threatened, they have engaged in assertive community organizations to preserve and improve where and how they live here and now.[34]

Overall, the last generation has been a difficult one for working-class women, bombarding them with massive social and economic changes which have dramatically challenged their attitudes and lifestyles. On the one hand, some working-class women belong to families which have finally reached the outer fringes of the middle class. But social norms always seem to be one step ahead of these women. Just as they have arrived in the group which told them to seek the home, to become a housewife, and to avoid the workplace and the community, older members of that class have begun to leave the home, even to denigrate the role of housewife, and to involve themselves in jobs and public activities. It hardly seems fair to change the rules at the last minute. On the other hand, women who are still in the working-class are increasingly becoming aware of themselves as working-class women and face the frustrations of a society which has long ignored their special characteristics. Caught between poverty, which might entitle them to public benefits, and the middle class, which could mean greater economic and social security, many react with anxiety to the insecurities of their position. Long schooled in concepts of isolated self-reliance, they are confused by increasing government involvement, demands by already-organized interest groups, and apparent threats from the women's liberation movement. But as working-class women make practical adjustments to the new realities, some are finding ways to take advantage of recent trends. On a selective basis, these working-class women are taking up such causes as employment, job training, unionization, day care, ethnic pride, and community preservation. They do not want to be anything other than what they are, but they are quite willing to use contemporary means to improve what they have.

12. Contemporary Beginnings of Awareness

THE PRIMARY characteristic which distinguishes American working-class women of the mid-1970s from their historical counterparts is the beginning of identity and recognition. Although at least one of the first two female immigrants to the New World was a working-class woman, she and her successors neither singled themselves out as working-class women nor were recognized as such by their contemporaries. Even occasional efforts to learn more about women subsumed working-class women under the larger category of sex, and attempts to deal with the working class subordinated gender to class membership. More recently, however, blue-collar women, white ethnic women, and working-class women have begun to emerge in all their facets—sex, race, class, caste, minority, organized and unorganized, single and married, private and public, employed and nonearning, and even historical. While an enormous lack of awareness remains, the beginnings of self- and external analysis are currently offering some insights into who they are now and how they have come to their present condition.

From concern over neighborhood and local issues, groups of working-class women have developed both analysis and organization to deal with their own issues and priorities. As Barbara Mikulski of Baltimore points out, the white ethnic woman in America is not a dingbat, however warm and humanistic may be the character of Edith Bunker, nor is she limited to "tacky clothes," "plastic flowers," *True Confessions,*" and an "I.Q. of 47."[1] Rather, she is Maria Fava and Ann Giordano, who travelled to Albany to express parent and community concern over limitations on day care. She is Rosemarie Reed, who attended a Washington conference on community organizing. She is Marie Anastasi, who is work-

241

ing with senior citizens as well as a "mothers' morning out" group. She is one of dozens of women who have joined with Monsignor Genno Baroni of the National Center for Urban Ethnic Affairs to deal with housing, redlining by banks, and neighborhood preservation.[2] And since 1974, she may be a member of the National Congress of Neighborhood Women, a nationwide organization with chapters in at least thirty cities. The NCNW is committed to working on issues which affect the lives and communities of working-class ethnic women, such as education, employment, health, housing, legal services, and welfare. Their activities include workshops and speakers' bureaus to educate the women, their communities, and the government on legal and consumer rights, political awareness, and the like. Members have formed block associations, worked on poverty boards, exchanged information on women's organizations, and demonstrated against cutbacks in social services and insensitive urban renewal programs.[3]

Similarly, among employed working-class women, interest has grown in trade union membership and in the responsiveness of organized labor to women's issues. Union women, including representatives of the United Automobile Workers and the Communications Workers of America, helped found the National Organization of Women in 1963 (although most publicity in the 1960s went to middle- and upper-class feminist leaders). Within their own unions, while women constitute only 4.6 percent of union officials, their numbers are growing, as is their awareness of the education necessary to qualify for leadership. Trade union women attend programs such as the one organized by Barbara Wertheimer at the New York State School of Industrial and Labor Relations. Growing numbers of unions have women's departments and address themselves to equality and feminist issues in contract negotiations. And at the same time that the AFL-CIO withdrew its opposition to the Equal Rights Amendment, it amended its own constitution "to encourage all workers without regard to race, creed, color, sex, national origin, or ancestry to share equally in the full benefits of union organization."

Working women of the 1970s have met in caucuses and have founded organizations to identify and advance their interests. In 1971, for example, women in the San Francisco–Berkeley area established the Union Women's Alliance to Gain Equality, which emphasizes collective advancement for low-level employees in the expectation that women can revitalize unions to lead the struggle to alter basic social conditions.[4] The following year in Chicago, representatives of thirty unions formed United Union Women to lobby for unemployment compensation for pregnant women, a higher minimum wage, and the Equal Rights Amendment. This group persuaded the AFL-CIO to hold its first conference on women's rights. On 22 March 1974 the Coalition of Labor Union Women convened with 3,200 delegates from fifty-eight unions to hear Myra Wolfgang of the Hotel and Restaurant Employees' and Bartenders' International Union tell them, "We didn't come here to swap recipes." Committed to working within the labor movement, CLUW determined to encourage women to join unions, to increase women's involvement within their unions, to seek union support against employer discrimination, and to lobby for the ERA as well as legislation in such areas as child care.[5] Despite internal conflicts, differing goals, and traditional problems of reconciling feminism and trade unionism, organized women workers, like the neighborhood groups, are coming to define themselves as working-class women and are seeking an agenda which will accommodate their own interests.

Working-class women are also attracting the attention of outsiders. In the 1950s the MacFadden-Bartell Corporation, publishers of a number of women's magazines, hoped to convince advertisers that working-class women constituted an available market. They commissioned Social Research, Inc., to investigate the psychological, sociological, and consumer profile of working-class women. The results were published as *Workingman's Wife* by Lee Rainwater, Richard P. Coleman, and Gerald Hanley in 1959.[6] Follow-up studies were conducted in 1965 and 1972, the most recent published as "Working-Class Women in a Changing World."[7] While the objective of these surveys was the working-class woman as a consumer, the underlying assumptions indicated that America does, indeed, have working-class women who possess unique and changing characteristics. Significantly, the interviewers in 1959 approached their subjects as wives of working-class men; in 1972, stressing the impact of the women's liberation movement, they established the category of working-class woman in her own right.

Elsewhere, media responses seem slower to take note of the working-class woman. On television, for example, only "One Life to Live" among long-running daytime serials included ethnic working-class characters, although more recently "The Young and the Restless" has shown a female breadwinner who worked as a domestic to raise three children after her husband abandoned the family. Significantly, in that scenario one son becomes a doctor, the other a lawyer, and the daughter enters the "pink-collar" world of hairdressing. "Both sides of the tracks" received more attention on evening viewing, however, from "Peyton Place" to "Soap." And working-class stereotypes have produced such culture heroines as Edith Bunker and Alice the waitress. Television and magazine advertising also present the working-class woman as cheerful Maxine of the coffee-cart or Rosie who banishes diner-counter tragedies with half a paper towel. On the whole, media remains primarily middle-class, and current portrayals of working-class women have not moved far from the tokenist, patronizing, and simplistic.[8]

On the other hand, scholars, especially social scientists, have shown a growing interest in women. In the early twentieth century most of the useful research came through charitable or reform organizations such as the Russell Sage Foundation or the Consumers' League; data thus assembled were analyzed to bolster arguments for improvement in wages, hours, and working conditions. Similar motivations guided collection and study of information by the Women's Bureau of the United States Department of Labor and equivalent agencies of state and local government. In general, these investigations concentrated on employed females, burying working-class women in the broader category of working women and excluding those women of the working class who were not earning wages. While valuable information can be extracted from these sources, as it can from labor union analysis, the point remains that those who conceptualized the gathering, discussion, and use of the evidence did not elect to study working-class women as a separate group. Later books, when they did examine industrialization, occupations, and even working-class life, usually concentrated on men,[9] just as studies of women focused on middle- and upper-class females, frequently those in professional or executive positions.[10]

But in the 1970s academics are investigating working-class women as a unique group, both by themselves and in relation to such fields as worker education, working-class studies, and women's studies. In these enterprises, they are aided by relatively new methodologies such as quantification, demography, and oral history. Universities have continued to serve the needs of worker education and to cooperate in the development of curricula which will serve both academic and practical objectives. The Institute of Labor and Industrial Relations at the University of Michigan and Wayne State University, as well as the New York State School of Industrial and Labor Relations at Cornell University, for example, offer workshops, single courses, summer schools, and degree programs for women workers. At the same time, faculty within such institutes frequently develop, analyze, and distribute information such as the examination of women in seven New York City union locals prepared by Barbara Wertheimer and Anne Nelson in *Trade Union Women,* a project designed to learn about women's participation and leadership in their unions.[11] Often information in such contemporary studies is obtained through questionnaires, statistical analysis, and interviewing. Since, by definition, American working-class women have been both numerous and anonymous, several modern techniques have been applied to extracting information about them. Computers, for example, make census data and other wide-ranging surveys more manageable. Oral history projects such as those at Roosevelt University in Chicago, Sangamon State University, Wayne State University, and the University of Michigan, and the "Radical Women and Women Labor Leaders" project at the California Historical Society, among others, are breaking ground in soliciting information from working-class women who might otherwise leave no records. Publishers such as Arno Press have reprinted rare historical materials on working-class women. And meetings of scholars are including papers, panels, and even entire conferences on working-class women, such as "Class and Ethnicity in Women's History" at SUNY-Binghamton in 1974. Recent doctoral dissertation topics range from studies of Frances Perkins and Mary Anderson to women in the Socialist party to the New York Women's Trade Union League to participation of working-class women in grass-roots political organizations. Historians dealing with women's issues have established no consensus philosophy as yet and continue to debate whether sex, class, caste, oppression, race, or various other factors are the key operating principles in that analysis. In the case of working-class women, gender and class, at least, are generic to the discussion.

Beyond the campuses, working-class women have been the subject of a number of recent policy studies and recommendations for social change. Nancy Seifer of the National Project on Ethnic America developed a study of white ethnic women since the 1950s, incorporating psychological and sociological research and concluding with recommendations of ways in which the women's movement, government, and trade unions can deal with working-class women. She urges new thinking to devise definitive solutions to questions of work, education, family, community, and society. Among her specific proposals are flexible work schedules, community-based programs of guidance and training, mid-career grants for women workers, an end of the mythology of women as "poor risks," expanded awareness of academic counselors, multiservice health care, community skills programs, reasonable commercials, and "public policy concepts related to the particular social and economic needs of working class women." Perhaps most significantly, Seifer entitled her exposition "Absent from the Majority" to pinpoint the spiritual and cultural isolation felt by working-class women in recent times.[12] Similarly, Pamela Roby, working for the Russell Sage Foundation, has investigated past and current research on women in blue-collar, industrial, and service jobs. Her study goes beyond the workplace into the lifestyle and broader concerns of working class women. Because she believes that policy-making should rest on research and because the material presently available is such a small portion of the pertinent analysis, she has presented a research agenda aimed at gathering information which can be used to improve wages, working conditions, job training, work opportunities, living conditions, and attitudes.[13] Working-class women themselves are also developing responses and recommendations. In 1975, for example, the Institute of

Pluralism and Group Identity of the American Jewish Committee brought together white ethnic, Southern, working-class, Jewish, Catholic, and black women to share their differing and overlapping perceptions of their concerns, especially in response to the United States National Women's Agenda.[14]

Government, too, has paid some attention to working-class women in recent years, although they generally remain buried in the broader female category. In the early 1960s the President's Commission on the Status of Women dealt with American women in general, touching on education, social insurance, law, leadership, citizenship, and employment. Similarly, the Citizens' Advisory Council on the Status of Women, in its annual reports in the early 1970s, grouped all women, although it did include treatment of issues such as pensions, maternity leave, equal pay, credit, and training as well as progress reports on the Equal Rights Amendment and recent rulings of the Supreme Court. While the Advisory Committee on the Economic Role of Women of the Council of Economic Advisers treated working women at all levels, it has also analyzed low-level jobs in which working-class women predominate. Therefore, though working-class women are still often hidden in the aggregate data and policy recommendations, many of their concerns are beginning to be identified and addressed. An agency which is particularly conscious of the special concerns of working-class women is the Women's Bureau of the Department of Labor. While the bureau sets broad objectives of improving the employability of women, increasing their employment opportunities, and eliminating sex discrimination in employment, its specific applications of these goals frequently speak directly to the needs of working-class women. In addition to its documentation of conditions in the workplace, the bureau has increasingly sponsored workshops, projects, and information centers which touch on apprenticeship, day care, referral service, employment rights and benefits, and vocational counseling.[15]

With the women's liberation movement and International Woman's Year commanding attention for women, the United States Congress issued an unprecedented call to "identify barriers that prevent women from participating fully and equally in all aspects of national life" and to recommend means for overcoming them. In response, over 1,800 delegates and 12,000 observers of all personal and political complexions went to Houston, Texas, in November 1977 for the National Women's Conference. Representatives included feminist luminaries, "total women," housewives, and proponents and opponents of issues like the ERA, abortion, homosexual rights, federally funded child care, and a Cabinet-level women's department. The Equal Rights Amendment received highest priority, and its endorsement convinced Liz Carpenter, leader of the ratification drive, that "we can no longer be accused of being a middle-class white women's cause." While most publicity focused on ERA, abortion, and lesbianism, and no specific set of working-class issues was discussed, the conference produced a twenty-five-point National Plan of Action with aspects for many categories of women. The plan included ratification of the Equal Rights Amendment, free choice on abortion and public funds for those who cannot afford it, national health insurance with special provisions for women, Social Security benefits for housewives, elimination of discrimination against lesbians in jobs and housing and credit as well as their right to custody of their children, federal and state-funded programs for victims of abuse, education in rape prevention, and a rural program to fight isolation and poverty and underemployment. Not all delegates supported every aspect of the National Plan, but the strength of the conference lay in its willingness to incorporate diverse views from many sectors, including those of working-class women. Moreover, women who did not feel part of the white, middle-class, elitist feminism of the 1960s could find places for themselves within a women's movement and are beginning to learn how proposals like those of the Houston meeting can accommodate their particular needs. *Time* magazine concluded that "over a weekend and a day, American women had reached some kind of watershed in their own history, and in that of the nation."[16]

For working-class women in particular, the 1970s are a watershed. Awakening to consciousness and acceptance of who they are, recognized by many who would help them improve within their own sphere, included in the broader issues and concerns of modern American women, working-class women have begun to step beyond stereotypes and have reached the point of asking, "Where do we go from here?"

Notes

1. Women, Girls, and Ladies in Early America

1. H. R. McIlwaine, "The Maids Who Came to Virginia in 1620 and 1621 for Husbands," *The Reviewer* 1 (1 April 1921): 109–13.

2. Julia Cherry Spruill, *Women's Life and Work in the Southern Colonies* (Chapel Hill: University of North Carolina Press, 1938), p. 9.

3. Wesley Frank Craven, *White, Red and Black: The Seventeenth Century Virginian* (Charlottesville: University Press of Virginia, 1971), pp.1–38; Philip Alexander Bruce, *Social Life in Virginia in the Seventeenth Century* (New York: Capricorn Books, 1965), pp.224–26; George Alsop, "Character of Province of Maryland," in *Narratives of Early Maryland,* ed. Clayton Colman Hall (New York: Barnes and Noble, 1910), pp.335–87; Spruill, pp.136–37.

4. Elizabeth Anthony Dexter, *Colonial Women of Affairs: Women in Business and the Professions Before 1776* (Boston: Houghton Mifflin Company, 1931), ch. III.

5. Gerda Lerner, ed., *The Female Experience: An American Documentary* (Indianapolis: Bobbs-Merrill, 1977), p. xxviii; Roger Thompson, *Women in Stuart England and America: A Comparative Study* (Boston: Routledge & Kegan Paul, 1974), pp.60–81; James K. Somerville, "The Salem (Mass.) Woman in the Home, 1660–1770," *Eighteenth Century Life* 1 (September 1974): 11–14; Edith Abbott, *Women in Industry: A Study in American Economic History* (New York: D. Appleton and Co., 1910), p.12; John Demos, *A Little Commonwealth: Family Life in Plymouth Colony* (New York: Oxford University Press, 1970), pp.82–95.

6. Eleanor Flexner, *Century of Struggle: The Woman's Rights Movement in the United States* (Cambridge: Harvard University Press, 1959, pp.7–8; Mary P. Ryan, *Womanhood in America: From Colonial Times to the Present* (New York: New Viewpoints/ Franklin Watts, Inc., 1975), pp.25–26.

7. Ryan, p.24; Walter Hart Blumenthal, *Brides from Bridewell: Female Felons Sent to Colonial America* (Rutland, Vermont: Charles E. Tuttle Co., Inc., 1962); Flexner, pp.5–6; Rosalyn Baxandall, Linda Gordon, and Susan Reveby, eds., *America's Working*

Women (New York: Random House, 1976), pp.24–26; Richard Morris, *Government and Labor in Early America* (New York: Octagon Books/Farrar, Straus & Giroux, Inc., 1946), pp.11, 15, 320, 347; Helen Sumner, *History of Women in Industry in the United States,* vol. IX of *Report on Conditions of Woman and Child Wage-Earners in the United States* (Washington, D.C.: Government Printing Office, 1910–13), p.30.

8. Blumenthal, pp.13–14; Baxandall, pp.26–29.

9. Page Smith, *Daughters of the Promised Land: Women in American History* (Boston: Little, Brown and Company, 1970), pp.57–76.

10. *New York Mercury,* 27 August 1770, in Baxandall, pp.22–23; Samuel McKee, *Labor in Colonial New York, 1664–1776* (New York: Columbia University Press, 1935); Alice Morse Earle, *Home Life in Colonial Days* (New York: Grosset & Dunlap, 1898).

11. Morris, pp.32, 41, 42; Alice Clark, *Working Life of Women in the Seventeenth Century* (New York: E. P. Dutton & Co., 1919), p.197.

12. Charles Francis Adams, ed., *Familiar Letters of John Adams and His Wife Abigail Adams During the Revolution* (New York: Hurd and Houghton, 1876), pp.286–87; Elizabeth Commetti, "Women in the American Revolution," *New England Quarterly* 20 (September 1947): 329–46.

13. Walter Hart Blumenthal, *Women Camp Followers of the American Revolution* (Philadelphia: George S. MacManus Company, 1952), pp.15–16, 37, 60, 72–76, 83; John Todd White, "The Truth About Molly Pitcher," paper, Conference on Women in the Era of the American Revolution, Washington, D.C., 1975.

14. Julia Ward Stickley, "The Truth about Deborah Sampson Gannett," paper, Conference on Women in the Era of the American Revolution, Washington, D.C., 1975; Vera O. Laska, *"Remember the Ladies": Outstanding Women of the American Revolution* (Massachusetts Bicentennial Commission, 1976), pp.61–94.

15. *Virginia Cavalcade* 3 (Autumn 1953): 18–21.

16. Linda Kerber, "The Republican Mother," paper, Southern Historical Association meeting, Washington, D.C., 1975; commentary on same by Anne Firor Scott; Ryan, pp.146–48.

17. Abbott, pp.32, 265; Raymond A. Mohl, *Poverty in New York, 1783–1825* (New York: Oxford University Press, 1971), pp.25–44, 85–95; Stephen Robert Davis, "From Plowshares to Spindles: Dedham, Massachusetts, 1790–1840" (Ph.D. diss., University of Wisconsin, 1973).

18. Elizabeth Faulkner Baker, *Technology and Woman's Work* (New York: Columbia University Press, 1964), pp.5–7; Helen Campbell, *Women Wage-earners: Their Past, Their Present, and Their Future* (Boston: Robert Brothers, 1893), p.68.

19. Lerner, p. xxx.

20. Edward Shorter, "Women's Work: What Difference Did Capitalism Make?" paper, Conference on Class and Ethnicity in Women's History, SUNY-Binghamton, 1974; Ryan, pp.118–19.

21. Gerda Lerner, *The Woman in American History* (Reading, Mass.: Addison-Wesley Publishing Company, 1971), pp.29, 32–33, 53; Barbara Welter, "The Cult of True Womanhood: 1820–1860," *American Quarterly* 18 (Summer 1966): 151–74.

22. Daniel Scott Smith and Michael Hindus, "Premarital Pregnancy in America 1640–1971: An Overview and Interpretation," *Journal of Interdisciplinary History* 5 (Spring 1975): 537–70.

23. Gerda Lerner, "The Lady and the Mill Girl: Changes in the Status of Women in the Age of Jackson," *Midcontinent American Studies Journal* 10 (Spring 1969): 5–14; Lerner, *Female Experience*, p. xxxi.

2. Temporary Working-Class Women

1. Elizabeth Faulkner Baker, *Technology and Woman's Work* (New York: Columbia University Press, 1964), p.3; David Montgomery, "The Working Classes of the Pre-Industrial American City, 1780–1830," *Labor History* 9 (Winter, 1968): 17.

2. Helen Sumner, *History of Women in Industry in the United States,* vol. IX of *Report on Conditions of Woman and Child Wage-Earners in the United States* (Washington, D.C.: GPO, 1910–13), pp.37–44.

3. Sumner, pp.47–50.

4. Sumner, p.50; Baker, p.24.

5. Caroline F. Ware, *The Early New England Cotton Manufacture: A Study in Industrial Beginnings* (Boston: Houghton Mifflin, 1934), pp.199–200, 210–11.

6. Hannah Josephson, *The Golden Threads: New England's Mill Girls and Magnates* (New York: Duell, Sloan, and Pearce, 1949), pp.18–22, 24–28.

7. Ware, p.226.

8. *Lowell Offering,* 1:169, 4:89; *Voice of Industry,* 2 January, 17 April, and 22 May 1846; *Massachusetts House Documents,* 1845, no. 50; Ware, pp.214–22.

9. General Rules of the Lowell Manufacturing Company; Regulations to be observed by all persons employed in the factories of the Hamilton Company (1848); Rules of the Merrimack Company; *Lowell Offering,* 1:364, 4:45, 5:282; Sumner, pp.84–88; Josephson, pp.68–70; Helen Wright, "The Uncommon Mill Girls of Lowell," *History Today* 33 (January 1973); 10–19.

10. Harriet H. Robinson, *Loom and Spindle: or, Life Among the Early Mill Girls* (New York: Thomas Y. Crowell & Company, 1898), chs. 4, 5.

11. Report of Committee on Hours of Labor, *Massachusetts House Documents,* 1845, no. 50; Sumner, pp.88–89; Robinson, ch. 3; Lucy Larcom, *A New England Girlhood* (New York: Houghton, Mifflin, 1889).

12. *Lowell Offering,* Series 1, nos. 1–4 (1840–41), Series 2, vols. 1–5 (1841–45); Robinson, chs. 6, 7; Bertha Monica Stearns, "Early Factory Magazines in New England: The Lowell Offering and Its Contemporaries," *Journal of Economic and Business History* 2 (August 1930): 685–705.

13. *Mind Among the Spindles: A Miscellany Wholly Composed by the Factory Girls, Selected from the Lowell Offering* (Boston: Jordan, Swift and Wiley, 1845), pp.81–92.

14. Stearns, pp.699–702; Sumner, pp.89–94; *Lowell Offering,* 2:280; 3:48, 96; 4:262; 5:190; *New England Offering,* December 1849, p. 176.

15. *Boston Daily Times,* July 13–18, 1839.

16. *Lowell Courier,* July 1839; "A Vindication of the Character and Condition of the Females Employed in the Lowell Mills against the Charges contained in the Boston Times and Boston Quarterly Review" (Lowell: Leonard Huntress, Printer, 1841).

17. (Lowell: Samuel J. Varney, Printer, 1843).

18. Rev. James Porter, *The Operative's Friend, and Defence: or, Hints to Young Ladies, Who Are Dependent on Their Own Exertions* (Boston: Charles H. Peirce, 1850).

19. Rosalyn Baxandall, Linda Gordon, and Susan Reverby, eds., *America's Working Women* (New York: Random House, 1976), pp.42–45.

20. Larcom, *New England Girlhood,* pp.44, 137, 146, 150, 153, 155, 182; Lucy Larcom, "Among Lowell Mill- irls: A Reminiscence," *Atlantic Monthly,* November 1881; David Baldwin, "Lucy Larcom," *Notable American Women* 2:368–69.

21. Harriet Hanson Robinson papers, Arthur and Elizabeth Schlesinger Library on the History of Women in America, Radcliffe

College, scrapbook, vol. 30; Geoffrey Blodgett, "Harriet Hanson Robinson," *Notable American Women* 3:181–82.

22. Robinson, ch. 8; George Rogers Taylor, "Harriet Farley," *Notable American Women* 1:596–97.

23. Robinson, ch. 8.

24. Ibid.

25. Sumner, pp.62–73; Ware, pp.249–51.

26. Ware, pp.222–29; *Massachusetts House Documents,* 1845, no. 50.

27. Robinson, p.7; Ware, pp.236–48; Sumner, pp.73–79; "Corporations and Operatives."

28. *Lowell Offering,* 3:240; 4:45, 282; 5:239, 281; *Voice of Industry,* 19 June and 11 September 1846, 12 February 1847; Sumner, pp.94–100; Ware, pp. 260–68.

29. John B. Andrews and W. D. P. Bliss, *History of Women in Trade Unions,* vol. X of *Report on Woman and Child Wage-Earners in the United States* (Washington: GPO, 1911), pp.23–26; Ruth Delzell, *The Early History of Women Trade Unionists in America* (Chicago: National Women's Trade Union League of America, 1919), pp.2–5; Alice Henry, *The Trade Union Woman* (New York: D. Appleton and Company, 1915), pp.1–3.

30. Andrews and Bliss, pp.22–36; Henry, p.308; M. E. J. Kelley, "Women and the Labor Movement," *North American Review* 166 (March 1898):408–17.

31. Josephson, pp.207–15, 219, 221; Laurie Nisonoff, "Bread and Roses: The Proletarianisation of Women Workers in New England Textile Mills, 1827–1848," paper, Conference on Class and Ethnicity in Women's History, SUNY-Binghamton, 1974; H. M. Gitelman, "The Waltham System and the Coming of the Irish," *Labor History* 8 (Fall 1967):236–39; Ware, pp.251–56, 269–98; Andrews and Bliss, pp. 45–49, 53, 61–69; Lise Vogel, "Their Own Work: Two Documents from the Nineteenth Century Labor Movement," *Signs: A Journal of Women in Culture and Society* 1 (Spring 1976): 787–802.

32. Andrews and Bliss, pp.69–70.

33. *Massachusetts House Documents,* 1845, no. 50.

34. Andrews and Bliss, pp.71–78; Josephson, ch. 7; *Voice of Industry,* 15 May and 18 September 1846.

35. Andrews and Bliss, pp.45–46, 78–82.

36. *Voice of Industry,* 15 May 1846; 8 January, 12 and 19 February, and 2 April 1847.

37. *New York Weekly Tribune,* 15 September 1847.

38. Thomas Dublin, "Women at Work: The Transformation of Work and Community in Lowell, Massachusetts, 1826–1860," Ph.D. diss., Columbia University, 1975; Dublin, "Women, Work, and the Family: Female Operatives in the Lowell Mills, 1830–1860," *Feminist Studies* 3 (Fall 1975): 30–39; Dublin, "Women, Work, and Protest in the Early Lowell Mills: 'The Oppressing Hand of Avarice Would Enslave Us,'" *Labor History* 16 (Winter 1975): 99–116; Vera Shlakman, "Economic History of a Factory Town: A Study of Chicopee, Massachusetts," Smith College Studies in History, vol. 20, no. 1 (1935).

39. Josephson, p.216; Gitelman, pp.239–40; Caroline Ware, p.230; Norman Ware, *The Industrial Worker, 1840–1860: The Reaction of American Industrial Society to the Advance of the Industrial Revolution* (Boston: Houghton Mifflin Company, 1924), p.150; W. Eliot Brownlee and Mary M. Brownlee, *Women in the American Economy: A Documentary History, 1675 to 1929* (New Haven: Yale University Press, 1976), pp.17–18.

40. Gitelman, pp.239–43; Caroline Ware, pp.228–35; Dublin, "Women, Work, and the Family," pp.30–39.

3. Immigrant Women from Several Cultures

1. Helen Sumner, *History of Women in Industry in the United States*, vol. IX of *Report on Conditions of Woman and Child Wage-Earners in the United States* (Washington: GPO, 1910–13), pp.81–83; C. G. Sargents Sons, Graniteville, Massachusetts, papers, Merrimack Valley Textile Museum.

2. Bruce Gordon Laurie, "The Working People of Philadelphia, 1827–1853" (Ph.D. diss., University of Pittsburgh, 1971); Susan Eleanor Hirsch Bloomberg, "Industrialization and Skilled Workers: Newark, 1826 to 1860" (Ph.D. diss., University of Michigan, 1974); Joan Younger Dickinson, "The Role of the Immigrant Women in the U.S. Labor Force, 1890–1910" (Ph.D. diss., University of Pennsylvania, 1975).

3. H. M. Gitelman, "The Waltham System and the Coming of the Irish," *Labor History* 8 (Fall 1967):249–52.

4. Stephen Dubnoff, "Mill Women of Lowell, Massachusetts in the 1860s," paper, Third Berkshire Conference on the History of Women, Bryn Mawr, Pa., 1976; Dubnoff, "The Family and Absence from Work: Irish Workers in a Lowell, Massachusetts Cotton Mill, 1860," paper, Eastern Sociological Association Meeting, 1976; Cath-

erine Mattis, "The Irish Family in Buffalo, New York, 1855–1875: A Socio-Historical Analysis" (Ph.D. diss., Washington University, 1975).

5. Carol Groneman, "The 'Bloody Ould Sixth': A Social Analysis of a New York City Working-Class Community in the Mid-Nineteenth Century" (Ph.D. diss., University of Rochester, 1973); Groneman, "She Earns as a Child; She Pays as a Man: Woman Workers in a Mid-Nineteenth Century New York City Community," paper, Conference on Immigrants in Industrial Life, 1850–1920, Eleutherian Mills Historical Library and the Balch Institute, 1973.

6. Charles Chauncey Bell, "The Workers of Worcester: Social Mobility and Ethnicity in a New England City, 1850–1880" (Ph.D. diss., New York University, 1974).

7. Judith Smith, "Work Patterns of Italian Emigrant Women in Early Twentieth Century Providence, Rhode Island," paper, Third Berkshire Conference on History of Women, Bryn Mawr, Pa., 1976; Virginia Yans-McLaughlin, "Italian Women and Work: Experience and Perception," paper, Conference on Class and Ethnicity in Women's History, SUNY-Binghamton, 1974.

8. Louise C. Odencrantz, *Italian Women in Industry: A Study of Conditions in New York City* (New York: Russell Sage Foundation, 1919).

9. Virginia Yans-McLaughlin, "Patterns of Work and Family Organization: Buffalo's Italians," *Journal of Interdisciplinary History* 2 (1971): 199–314.

10. Rosa Cavalleri, *Rosa: The Life of an Italian Immigrant,* ed. Marie Hall Ets (Minneapolis: University of Minnesota Press, 1970).

11. The Pittsburgh Section, National Council of Jewish Women, *By Myself, I'm a Book! An Oral History of the Jewish Immigrant Experience* (Waltham: American Jewish Historical Society, 1972), ch. 1; Rose Pesotta, *Bread upon the Waters,* ed. John Nicholas Beffel (New York: Dodd, Mead and Co., 1944), pp.4–8; Rose Schneiderman, with Lucy Goldthwaite, *All for One* (New York: Paul S. Eriksson, Inc., 1967), pp.11–15.

12. Pesotta, pp.8–9; Pittsburgh Section, ch. 2.

13. Pittsburgh Section, ch. 2; Schneiderman, pp.18–22; Pesotta, pp.9–11.

14. Schneiderman, pp.23–34.

15. Ruth Heller Steiner, "The Girls in Chicago," *American Jewish Archives* 26 (April 1974): 5–22; Charlotte Baum, Paula Hyman, and

Sonya Michel, *The Jewish Woman in America* (New York: The Dial Press, 1976), pp.92–98.

16. Schneiderman, pp.23–47.

17. Baum et al., pp.56, 67–68.

18. Baum et al., pp.98–109.

19. Alice Kessler-Harris, "Wage-earning Women," paper, Third Berkshire Conference on the History of Women, Bryn Mawr, Pa., 1976; Baum et al., pp. 109–16, 144.

20. *New York Times,* 23 and 26 May 1902; Irving Howe, *World of Our Fathers* (New York: Simon & Schuster, 1976), pp.124–25.

21. Kessler-Harris, "Wage-earning Women"; Baum et al., pp. 121–29; Mary Van Kleeck, *Working Girls in Evening Schools: A Statistical Study* (New York: Russell Sage Foundation, Survey Associates, Inc., 1914).

22. Isaac Metzker, ed., *A Bintel Brief: Sixty Years of Letters from the Lower East Side of the Jewish Daily Forward* (Garden City: Doubleday and Company, Inc., 1971), pp.109–10.

23. Babbette Inglehart, "Daughters of Loneliness: Anzia Yezierska and the Immigrant Woman Writer," *Studies in American Jewish Literature* I (Winter 1975):1–10; Howe, pp.268–70.

24. Metzker, pp.9–15, 35, 38–49, 56–59, 72, 83–84, 103–10.

25. Howe, pp.254, 265, 267.

26. Kessler-Harris, "Wage-earning Women."

27. Thomas Kessner, *The Golden Door: Italian and Jewish Immigrant Mobility in New York City, 1880–1915* (New York: Oxford University Press, 1977), pp.166–67.

28. Mary Antin, *They Who Knock at Our Gates: A Complete Gospel of Immigration* (Boston: Houghton, Mifflin Company, 1914).

4. Industrialization and Organization

1. Helen Campbell, *Prisoners of Poverty: Women Wage-Workers, Their Trades and Their Lives* (Boston: Robert Brothers, 1887), pp.30–32; *The Revolution,* 1 October 1868.

2. Gerda Lerner, *The Woman in American History* (Reading, Mass.: Addison-Wesley Publishing Company, 1971), pp.99–102; Bernice M. Deutrich, "Propriety and Pay," *Prologue* 3 (Fall 1971): 67–72.

3. Helen Sumner, *History of Women in Industry in the United States,* vol. IX of *Report on Conditions of Woman and Child Wage-Earners in the United States* (Washington, D.C.: GPO, 1910–13),

p.16; Cincinnati sewing women to Abraham Lincoln, 1865, in "Lincoln and Labor," *Life and Labor* 1 (February 1911):40; "The Working Women, White Slavery in New England," in *America's Working Women,* ed. Rosalyn Baxandall, Linda Gordon, and Susan Reverby (New York: Random House, 1976), pp.105–108.

4. Decennial censuses, 1850–1900 (note changing definitions of employment and categories); Ethelbert Stewart, "Trend of Employment of Men and Women in Specified Industries," *Monthly Labor Review* 20 (April 1925): 739–50; Sumner, pp.17–18; United States Commissioner of Labor, *Fourth Annual Report: Working Women in Large Cities* (Washington: GPO, 1888), pp.18–19.

5. Ray Ginger, "Labor in a Massachusetts Cotton Mill, 1853–60," *Business Historical Society Bulletin* 28 (March 1954): 67–91.

6. Anne Firor Scott, *The Southern Lady: From Pedestal to Politics, 1830–1930* (Chicago: University of Chicago Press, 1970), pp.188, 121; Jack Blicksilver, *Cotton Manufacturing in the Southeast: An Historical Analysis* (Atlanta, Ga.: Bureau of Business and Economic Research, School of Business Administration, Georgia State College of Business Administration, 1959), pp.28–29; Elizabeth Faulkner Baker, *Technology and Woman's Work* (New York: Columbia University Press, 1964), p.113.

7. Baxandall et al., pp. 85–87; Daniel Jay Walkowitz, "Working Class Culture in the Gilded Age: The Iron Workers of Troy, New York, and the Cotton Workers of Cohoes, New York—1855–1884" (Ph.D. Diss., University of Rochester, 1972); Tamara K. Hareven, "Industrial Work and the Family Cycle," paper, Conference on Class and Ethnicity in Women's History, SUNY-Binghamton, 1974.

8. Sumner, pp.113–74; Edith Abbott, "Women in Industry: The Manufacture of Boots and Shoes," *American Journal of Sociology* 15 (November 1909): 336–60; "The Boot and Shoe Industry in Massachusetts as a Vocation for Women," *Life and Labor* 6 (June 1916): 88–89.

9. Decennial census, 1850–1900; Edith Abbott, "Employment of Women in Industries: Cigarmaking—Its History and Present Tendencies," *Journal of Political Economy* 15 (January 1907): 1–25; Sumner, pp.193–205.

10. Decennial census, 1850–1900; Baker, p.54.

11. Susan J. Kleinberg, "Technology and Women's Work: The Lives of Working Class Women in Pittsburgh, 1870–1900," *Labor History* 17 (Winter 1976); 58–72.

12. Rebecca Harding Davis, "Life in the Iron Mills; or, the Korl Woman," *Atlantic Monthly,* April 1861 (reprinted New York: The Feminist Press, 1972).

13. Clarence D. Long, *Wages and Earnings in the United States, 1860–1890* (Princeton: Princeton University Press, 1960), pp.104–18.

14. Carrol D. Wright, *The Working Girls of Boston: From the Fifteenth Annual Report of the Massachusetts Bureau of Statistics of Labor for 1884* (Boston: Wright & Potter, 1889); Campbell, pp.120–22; Robert W. Smuts, *Women and Work in America* (New York: Columbia University Press, 1959), pp.91–93.

15. Caroline Dall, *Women's Right to Labor* (Boston: Walker, Wise and Co., 1860); Catherine G. Waugh, "Women's Wages" (Rockford, Ill.: Daily Gazette Book and Job Office, 1888).

16. Campbell, pp. 10–17; Louis Levine, *The Women Garment Workers* (New York: B. W. Heubsch, Inc., 1924).

17. John D. Andrews and W. D. P. Bliss, *History of Women in Trade Unions,* vol. X of *Report on Conditions of Woman and Child Wage-Earners in the United States* (Washington, D.C.: GPO, 1910–13), pp.21, 36–40; Alice Henry, *The Trade Union Woman* (New York: D. Appleton and Company, 1915), pp.6–8; Ruth Delzell, "1825–1851—Organization of Tailoresses and Seamstresses," *Life and Labor* 2 (August 1912):242–44.

18. Andrews and Bliss, pp.58–60; Dolores Janiewski, "Making Common Cause: The Needlewomen of New York, 1831–1869," *Signs: Journal of Women in Culture and Society* 1 (Spring 1976): 777–86.

19. Andrews and Bliss, pp.102–103.

20. Ibid., pp.106–107.

21. Ibid., pp.89–94, 101–102, 107; Victor R. Greene, *The Slavic Community on Strike: Immigrant Labor in the Anthracite* (South Bend: University of Notre Dame Press, 1968); *Boston American Workman,* 8 and 15 May, 20 November 1869, 31 December 1870.

22. Andrews and Bliss, pp.41–45, 60–61, 108–10; Ruth Delzell, *The Early History of Women Trade Unionists in America* (Chicago: National Women's Trade Union League of America, 1919), pp.13–14; Mary Blewett, "The 'Newer Woman' and Trade Unionism: The Haverhill, Massachusetts Stitchers and the Formation of the Boot and Shoe Workers Union, 1895," paper, Third Berkshire Conference on the History of Women, Bryn Mawr, Pa., 1976.

23. Andrews and Bliss, pp.90–91; *The Revolution,* 24 September 1868, 13 May 1869; Sumner, p.25; Mary Ogden White, "Susan B. Anthony, Labor Leader," *Life and Labor* 9 (April 1919): 89–90.

24. Andrews and Bliss, pp.87–88; Sumner, pp.212–21; Israel Kugler, "The Woman's Rights Movement and the National Labor Union (1866–1872): What Was the Nature of the Relationships between the National Labor Union and the Women's Rights Movement and What May Serve to Explain Periods of Cooperation and Subsequent Divergence?" (Ph.D. Diss., New York University, 1954).

25. *The Revolution,* September and October 1868; Eleanor Flexner, "Augusta Lewis Troup," *Notable American Women* 3: 478–79; Andrews and Bliss, pp.103–105; Belva Mary Herron, "Labor Organizations among Women," *University of Illinois Bulletin* 2 (1905): 16–24; George A. Stevens, *New York Typographical Union No. 6.: A Study of a Modern Trade Union and Its Predecessors* (Albany: J. B. Lyon Company, 1913), pp.421–40.

26. Andrews and Bliss, pp.111–32; Norman J. Ware, *The Labor Movement in the United States, 1860–1895: A Study in Democracy* (New York: Appleton-Century-Crofts, Inc. 1929), pp.346–49; Henry, pp.25–34; Sue Levine, "'Strive for Your Rights, Oh Sisters Dear': The Carpet Weavers Strike and the Knights of Labor, 1885," paper, Third Berkshire Conference on the History of Women, Bryn Mawr, Pa., 1976; Flexner, pp.194–200; Flexner, "Leonora Marie Kearney Barry," *Notable American Women* 1:101–102.

5. Working-Class Women Become Working Women

1. Dorothy Bass Fraser, "The Feminine Mystique: 1890–1910," *Union Seminary Quarterly Review* 27 (Summer 1972): 225–39.

2. U.S. Department of Commerce, Bureau of Census, *A Statistical Portrait of Women in the United States,* Current Population Reports, Special Studies, Series P-23, No. 58 (Washington, D.C.: GPO, 1976); U.S. Department of Commerce, *Occupational Trends in the United States, 1900–1950* (Washington, D.C.: GPO, 1958); U.S. Department of Labor, Bureau of Labor Statistics, "Special Labor Force Report," nos. 13 and 50; U.S. Department of Health, Education, and Welfare, National Center for Health Statistics, *Vital Statistics of the United States, 1970* (Washington, D.C.: GPO, 1971); W. Elliot Brownlee and Mary M. Brownlee, *Women in the American Economy: A Documentary History, 1675 to 1929* (New Haven: Yale University Press, 1976), p.3.

3. Mary Heaton Vorse, "Making or Marring: The Experience of a Hired Girl," in Vorse papers, Archives of Labor History and Urban

Affairs, Wayne State University, box 19; Florence S. Wright, "The Visiting Nurse in Industrial Welfare Work," *Fifth Safety Council Proceedings* (Detroit: National Safety Council, 1916).

4. New York State Legislature, "Conditions of Female Labor in New York," quoted in Robert W. Smuts, *Women and Work in America* (New York: Columbia University Press, 1959), pp.43–44.

5. Smuts, pp.51–55; Mary E. Richmond and Fred S. Hull, *A Study of Nine Hundred and Eighty-five Widows Known to Certain Charity Organization Societies in 1910* (New York: Charity Organization Department of the Russell Sage Foundation, 1913).

6. Smuts, pp.14–17; Richmond and Hull, pp.27–28; Margaret Byington, *Homestead: The Households of a Mill Town* (New York: Russell Sage Foundation, 1910), pp.107–109, 148–49, 179.

7. Mary Van Kleeck, *Artificial Flower Makers* (New York: Russell Sage Foundation, Survey Associates, Inc., 1913), pp.94–95.

8. Dr. Henry Moscowitz, testimony quoted in *The Tenement House Problem,* ed. Robert W. DeForest and Lawrence Veiller (New York: The Macmillan Company, 1903); Edgar Fawcett, "The Woes of the New York Working-Girl," *Arena* 5 (1891–92): 25–35; Edith Abbott, *The Tenements of Chicago, 1908–1935* (Chicago: University of Chicago Press, 1936); Mrs. John Van Vorst and Marie Van Vorst, *The Woman Who Toils: Being the Experiences of Two Gentlewomen as Factory Girls* (New York: Doubleday, Page and Company, 1903); Roy Lubove, *The Progressives and the Slums: Tenement House Reform in New York City, 1891–1917* (Pittsburgh: University of Pittsburgh Press, 1963); Robert Coit Chapin, *The Standard of Living Among Workingmen's Families in New York City* (New York: Charities Publication Committee, 1909).

9. Smuts, pp.25–26; Esther Packard, *The Organized Homes, A Study of Living Conditions of Self-Supporting Women in New York City* (New York: Metropolitan Board of the Young Women's Christian Association, 1915); Caroline Manning, *The Immigrant Woman and Her Job* (New York: Arno Press, 1970); Helen Campbell, *Prisoners of Poverty: Women Wage-Workers, Their Trades and Their Lives* (Boston: Robert Brothers, 1887).

10. Campbell, pp.18–29.

11. Helen L. Sumner, "Historical Development of Women's Work in the United States," *The Economic Position of Women, Proceedings of the Academy of Political Science* 1 (1910):11–26; Margaret Dreier Robins, "Women in American Industry," *Life and Labor* 1 (November 1911): 324–35; Edith Abbott and Sophonisba P. Brecken-

ridge, "Employment of Women in Industries: Twelfth Census Statistics," *Journal of Political Economy* 14 (January 1906): 14–40.

12. Van Vorst and Van Vorst, pp. 117, 181–82, 222; Dorothy Richardson, *The Long Day: The Story of a New York Working Girl* (New York: The Century Company, 1905), pp.204–205, 231–33; Manning, pp.22, 98, 118, 212; Rheta Childe Dorr, "Bullying the Woman Worker," *Harper's Weekly* 51 (30 March 1907): 458–59.

13. Campbell, p.180; Smuts, pp.85–89; Charlotte Baum, Paula Hyman, and Sonya Michel, *The Jewish Woman in America* (New York: The Dial Press, 1976), pp.130–36; Philip Davis, "Women in the Cloak Trade," *American Federationist* 12 (October 1905): 745–47; Sue Ainslie Clark and Edith Wyatt, *Making Both Ends Meet: The Income and Outlay of New York Working Girls* (New York: Macmillan Company, 1911), p.5.

14. Grace Scribner, "Those Who Serve—How Long Is Their Day?" *Life and Labor* 9 (April 1919): 88; Manning, p.98; "Women on the Night Shift," *Life and Labor* 4 (December 1914): 377–79; "Why I Oppose Night Work," in *I Am a Woman Worker: A Scrapbook of Autobiographies,* ed. Andria Taylor Hourwich and Gladys L. Palmer (New York: The Affiliated Schools for Workers, Inc., 1936), p.50.

15. Davis, pp.745–47; Paul Brissenden, *Earnings of Factory Workers, 1899–1927: An Analysis of Pay-Roll Statistics* (Washington, D.C.: Government Printing Office, 1929), pp.94, 155; Abbott and Breckenridge, pp. 14–40; Kate Stevens, "Women's Wages," *North American Review* 162 (March 1896): 377–79; S. Webb, "The Alleged Differences in the Wages Paid to Men and to Women for Similar Work," *Economic Journal* 1 (December 1891): 635–62; Clara E. Laughlin, *The Work-a-Day Girl: A Study of Some Present-Day Conditions* (New York: Fleming H. Revell Company, 1913), p. 16.

16. Helen Sumner, *History of Women in Industry in the United States,* vol. IX of *Report on Conditions of Woman and Child Wage-Earners in the United States* (Washington, D.C.: GPO, 1910–1913), pp.177–83, 185; Smuts, pp.17, 72–73, 79–80; Margaret Maher to Mrs. Lucius Boltwood, letters, 1867–1869, passim, Boltwood Family papers, Burton Historical Collections, Detroit Public Library.

17. Louise de Koven Bowen, *The Girl Employed in Hotels and Restaurants* (Chicago: Juvenile Protection Association, 1912).

18. "Behind the Scenes in a Restaurant" (New York: Consumers' League of New York City, 1916).

19. Sumner, pp.183–84; Mary E. Dreier, "To Wash or Not to Wash:

Aye, There's the Rub," *Life and Labor* 2 (March 1912): 68–72; Jane Filley and Therese Mitchell, *Consider the Laundry Workers* (New York: League of Women Shoppers, Inc., 1937), pp.7–14.

20. Mary Trueblood, "Housework vs. Shop and Factories,"*Independent* 54 (13 November 1902): 2691–93.

21. Agnes Nestor, "A Day's Work Making Gloves," *Life and Labor* 2 (May 1912): 137–39; Charlotte Teller, "Women in Unions (Cloth Hat and Cap Makers)," *American Federationist* 13 (April 1906): 222–24; Sumner, pp.142–55.

22. Edna Bryner, *Dressmaking and Millinery* (Cleveland: The Survey Committee of the Cleveland Foundation, 1916); Mary Van Kleeck, "Wages in the Millinery Trade," appendix to *Fourth Report of the New York State Factory Investigating Commission* (Albany: J. B. Lyon Company, 1914); Van Kleeck, *A Seasonal Industry: A Study of the Millinery Trade in New York* (New York: Russell Sage Foundation, 1917); Mabel Hurd Willett, *The Employment of Women in the Clothing Trade* (New York: Columbia University Press, 1902).

23. John R. Commons, "Women in Unions," *American Federationist* 13 (June 1906): 382–83; Edith Abbott and Sophonisba P. Breckinridge, "Women in Industry: The Chicago Stockyards," *Journal of Political Economy* 19 (October 1911): 632–54; Sumner, pp.189–91; "Pilgrim's Progress in a Packing House," *Life and Labor* 10 (February 1920): 35–38; "The Day's Work in a Cannery," *Life and Labor* 2 (November 1912): 326–28.

24. Sumner, pp.238–41; David L. Kaplan and M. Claire Casey, *Occupational Trends in the United States, 1900 to 1950* (Washington, D.C.: GPO, 1958); Smuts, pp.22–23.

25. Sumner, pp.241–42; Caroline Crawford, "The Hello Girls of Boston," *Life and Labor* 8 (September 1918): 260–64; "Pilgrim's Progress in a Telephone Exchange," *Life and Labor* 11 (January, February 1921): 11–14, 48–52.

26. Sumner, pp.234–38; Smuts, p.22; Elizabeth Beardsley Butler, *Saleswomen in Mercantile Stores: Baltimore, 1909* (New York: Russell Sage Foundation, Survey Associates, Inc., 1912); Louise deKoven Bowen, *The Department Store Girl, Based Upon Interviews with 200 Girls* (Chicago: Juvenile Protection Association, 1911).

27. Elizabeth Beardsley Butler, *Women and the Trades: Pittsburgh, 1907–1908* (New York: Charities Publication Committee, 1909).

28. Van Vorst and Van Vorst, pp.68, 82, 159; Robert A. Woods and Albert J. Kennedy (eds.), *Young Working Girls: A Summary of Evidence from Two Thousand Social Workers* (Boston: Houghton Mifflin, Publishers, Inc., 1913), pp.11–17, 35, 37; Smuts, pp.84–85; Lizzie M. Holmes, "Not By Bread Alone," *American Federationist* 9 (January 1902): 11–14.

29. Clara E. Laughlin, *The Work-a-Day Girl: A Study of Some Present-Day Conditions* (New York: Fleming H. Revell Company, 1913), pp.127–55.

6. Self-Help without Self-Awareness

1. Theresa Schmidt McMahon, "Women and Economic Evolution, or the Effects of Industrial Changes upon the Status of Women" (Ph.D. Diss., University of Wisconsin, 1908); Katherine Anthony, *Mothers Who Must Earn* (New York: Russell Sage Foundation, Survey Associates, West Side Studies, 1914); Daniel J. Walkowitz, "Working-class Women in the Gilded Age: Factory, Community and Family Life among Cohoes, New York, Cotton Workers," *Journal of Social History* 5 (Summer 1972): 464–90.

2. Mabel Hurd Willett, *The Employment of Women in the Clothing Trade* (New York: Columbia University Press, 1902); Mary Van Kleeck, *Artificial Flower Makers* (New York: Russell Sage Foundation, Survey Associates, Inc., 1913), pp. 36–37, 67.

3. William I. Thomas and Florian Znaniecki, *The Polish Peasant in Europe and America* (New York: A. A. Knopf, 1927), pp.1800–21, 1935, 2225; Helen Campbell, *Prisoners of Poverty: Women Wage Workers, Their Trades and Their Lives* (Boston: Robert Brothers, 1887), pp.133–34.

4. Philip S. Foner, *The Industrial Workers of the World, 1905–1917,* vol. IV of *History of the Labor Movement in the United States* (New York: International Publishers, 1965), pp.306–72; Elizabeth Gurley Flynn, *I Speak My Own Piece: Autobiography of the Rebel Girl* (New York: Mainstream, 1955).

5. Mari Jo Buhle, "Feminism and Socialism in the United States, 1820–1920" (Ph.D. Diss., University of Wisconsin, 1974); Buhle, "Women and the Socialist Party, 1901–1914," in *From Feminism to Liberation,* ed. Edith Hoshimo Altbach (Cambridge, Mass.: Schenckman Publishing Company, 1971), pp.65–86; Max Fruchifer to Rose Schneiderman, 5 March 1911, Schneiderman papers, Tami-

ment Library, New York University, box 1; "Socialism and Feminism," *Socialist Revolution* 4 (January–March 1974): 59–82.

6. Priscilla Long, *Mother Jones, Woman Organizer* (Cambridge: Red Sun Press, 1976); Dale Feterling, *Mother Jones, the Miners' Angel: A Portrait* (Carbondale and Edwardsville: Southern Illinois University Press, 1974), pp.163–66, 202–203; Mary Jones, *Autobiography of Mother Jones* (Chicago: Charles H. Kerr and Co., 1925), pp.146–47.

7. E. M. Phillips, "Progress of Women's Trade Unions," *Fortnightly Review*, n.s. 54 (July 1893): 92–104; Belva Mary Herron, *The Progress of Labor Organizations among Women Together with Some Considerations Concerning Their Place in Industry* (Urbana: University of Illinois Press, 1905); Lillian R. Matthews, *Women in Trade Unions in San Francisco* (Berkeley: University of California Press, 1913), pp.88–91; E. Barnes, "Women in Industry," *Atlantic Monthly* 110 (July 1912): 116–24; Alice Henry, "Women and the Trade Union Movement in the United States," *The Economic Position of Women, Proceedings of the Academy of Political Science* 1 (1910); 109–18; Agnes Nestor, "The Experiences of a Pioneer Woman Trade Unionist," *American Federationist* 36 (August 1929): 926–32; Margaret Dreier Robins, "Self-government in the Workshop: The Demand of the Women's Trade Union League," *Life and Labor* 2 (April 1912): 108–10.

8. John B. Andrews and W. D. P. Bliss, *History of Women in Trade Unions*, vol. X of *Woman and Child Wage-Earners in the United States* (Washington, D.C.: GPO, 1910–13), pp.145–52; Leo Wolman, *The Growth of Trade Unions, 1880–1923* (New York: National Bureau of Economic Research, 1924), pp.98–99; Wolman, "Extent of Trade Unionism," *Annals of the American Academy of Political and Social Sciences* 69 (January 1917): 118–27; C. E. Persons, "Women's Work and Wages in the United States," *Quarterly Journal of Economics* 29 (February 1915): 201.

9. Mary Anderson, with Mary N. Winslow, *Woman at Work* (Minneapolis: University of Minnesota Press, 1951), pp.25–26, 62–70; Helen Marot, *American Labor Unions* (New York: Holt and Company, 1914), pp.65–77; Alice Henry, *The Trade Union Woman* (New York: D. Appleton and Company, 1915), pp.142–45; Theresa Wolfson, "Trade Union Activities of Women," *Women in the Modern World, Annals of the American Academy of Political and Social Science* 143 (May 1929): 120–31; Ellen M. Henrotin, "Organizing for Women," *American Federationist* 12 (November 1905): 824–27; Wil-

liam English Walling, "Fields of Organization for Women Workers," *American Federationist* 12 (September 1905): 625–27.

10. Andrews and Bliss, pp.140–45; Mary Kingsbury Simkovitch, *The City Worker's World in America* (New York: The Macmillan Company, 1917), pp.93–95; Anderson, pp.20–24, 62–63; Lillian D. Wald, "Organization Amongst Working Women," *Annals of the American Academy of Political and Social Science* 27 (1906): 638–45; Edward A. Filene, "The Betterment of the Conditions of Working Women," *Annals,* pp.613–23; Jacob M. Budish and George Soule, *The New Unionism in the Clothing Industry* (New York: Harcourt, Brace and Howe, 1920), pp.40–42.

11. Sophie Yudelson, "Women's Place in Industry and Labor Organizations," *Annals of the American Academy of Political and Social Science* 24 (September 1904): 343–53; Yudelson, "Women in Unions," *American Federationist* 13 (January 1906): 19–21; Edith Abbott, "The History of Industrial Employment of Women in the United States; An Introductory Study," *Journal of Political Economy* 14 (October 1906): 461–501, and 15 (December 1907): 619–64; Frank P. Walsh, "Women and Labor," *Life and Labor* 5 (November 1915): 165; "Female Labor Arouses Hostility and Apprehension in Union Ranks," *Current Opinion* 64 (April 1910): 292–94; Alice Kessler-Harris, "Where Are the Organized Women Workers?" *Feminist Studies* 3 (Fall 1975): 92–110.

12. F. M. Thompson, "The Truth about Women in Industry," *North American Review* 178 (May 1904): 751–60; Edward O'Donnell, "Women as Bread Winners," *American Federationist* 4 (October 1897): 186–87; Esther Taber, "Women in Unions," *American Federationist* 13 (February 1906): 85–86; Lillian Matthews, *Women in Trade Unions in San Francisco* (Berkeley: University of California Press, 1913).

13. Andrews and Bliss, pp.155–57; Eleanor Flexner and Janet Wilson James, "Mary Kenney O'Sullivan," *Notable American Women* 2:655–56; Henry, pp.51–56.

14. Eva McDonald Valesh, "Wage Working Women," *American Federationist* 13 (December 1906): 963–67; Elizabeth J. Hauser, "Women Workers and the Labor Movement," *American Federationist* 17 (April 1910): 305–306; Samuel Gompers, "Women's Work, Rights, and Progress," *American Federationist* 20 (August 1913): 624–27; Gompers, "Coming into Her Own," *American Federationist* 22 (July 1915): 517–19.

15. S. M. Franklin, "The American Federation of Labor Conven-

tion," *Life and Labor* 4 (December 1914): 361–64; "Why Not Women on A.F. of L. Executive Council?" *Life and Labor* 8 (July 1918): 138; James J. Kenneally, "Women and Trade Unions, 1870–1920: The Quandary of the Reformer," *Labor History* 14 (Winter 1973): 42–55.

16. Lake Grant, "Women in Trade Unions," *American Federationist* 10 (August 1903): 655–56; Ralph Scharnau, "Elizabeth Morgan, Crusader for Labor Reform," *Labor History* 14 (Summer 1973): 340–51; Anderson, pp.26–31; Andrews and Bliss, pp.186–88; Olive M. Sullivan, "The Women's Part in the Stockyards Organizational Work," *Life and Labor* 8 (May 1918): 102; Agnes Nestor, *Woman's Labor Leader* (Rockford, Ill.: Bellevue Books, 1954).

17. Andrews and Bliss, pp.172–75; C. L. Baine, "Women in the Shoe Industry," *Life and Labor* 3 (June 1913): 164–67.

18. Andrews and Bliss, pp.175–83.

19. Ibid., pp. 159–70; Dorothy Rabinowitz, "The Case of the ILGWU," in *The World of the Blue-Collar Worker,* ed. Irving Howe (New York: Quadrangle Books, 1972), pp.49–52; Morris Kotchin, "The Ladies Garment Industry," *American Federationist* 36 (December 1929): 1472–77; Julius Hockman, "Organizing the Dressmakers," *American Federationist* 36 (December 1929): 1462–67; Isidore Negler, "Wages, Hours, and Employment," *American Federationist* 36 (December 1929): 1468–71.

20. Moses Rischin, "The Jewish Labor Movement in America: A Social Interpretation," *Labor History* 4 (Fall 1963): 232–35; Charlotte Baum, Paula Hyman, and Sonya Michel, *The Jewish Woman in America* (New York: The Dial Press, 1976), pp.144–48, 160–62; Alice Kessler-Harris, "Organizing the Unorganizable: Three Jewish Women and their Union," *Labor History* 17 (Winter 1976): 5–23.

21. Baum et al., pp.137–49, 160–62; Alice Kessler-Harris, "Wage-earning Women," paper, Third Berkshire Conference on History of Women, 1976.

22. Helen Marot, "A Woman's Strike—An Appreciation of the Shirtwaist Makers of New York," *The Economic Position of Women, Proceedings of the Academy of Political Science* 1 (1910): 119–28; Rose Schneiderman, with Lucy Goldthwaite, *All for One* (New York: Paul S. Eriksson, Inc., 1967), p.97; "A Woman's Strike," *Outlook* 92 (11 December 1909): 799–801; Constance D. Leupp, "Shirtwaist Makers Strike," *Survey* 23 (18 December 1909): 383–86; William Mailly, "The Working Girls Strike," *Independent* 67 (23 December 1909); 1416–30; S. C. Comstock, "Uprising of the Girls," *Colliers* 44 (25 December 1909): 14–16; Ida M. Tarbell, "The Shirt-

waist Strikers," *American Federationist* 17 (March 1910): 209–10; Philip Davis, "The Shirtwaist Makers' Strike," *The Chataquan* 59 (June 1910): 99–106; "Shirt Shops after the Strike," *Survey* 25 (1 October 1910): 7–8; Irving Howe, *World of Our Fathers* (New York: Simon and Schuster, 1976), pp.296–302, 306–10.

23. "Chicago at the Front: A Condensed History of the Garment Workers' Strike," *Life and Labor* 1 (January 1911): 4–13; "Holding the Fort: The Chicago Garment Workers' Strike," *Life and Labor* 1 (February 1911): 48–50; Alice Henry, "The Hart, Schaffner, and Marx Agreement," *Life and Labor* 2 (June 1912): 170–72; Anderson, pp.38–49.

24. Schneiderman, pp.110–14.

25. "On the Picket Line," *Life and Labor* 3 (March 1913): 71–73; Martha Bensley Bruere, "The White Goods Strikes," *Life and Labor* 3 (March 1913): 73–75; Rose Schneiderman, "The White Goods Workers of New York," *Life and Labor* 3 (May 1913): 132–36.

26. Hyman Berman, "Era of the Protocol: A Chapter in the History of the International Ladies' Garment Workers' Union, 1910–1916" (Ph.D. Diss., Columbia University, 1956): Samuel Gompers, "The Struggles in the Garment Trades—From Misery and Despond to Betterment and Hope," *American Federationist* 20 (March 1913): 185–202; "Minimizing the Controversy," *Life and Labor* 3 (April 1913): 105–107; "The Protocol Meeting the Cost of Living," *Survey* 38 (June 9, 1917): 249; Harry Best, "Extent of Organization in the Women's Garment Making Industries of New York," *American Economic Review* 9 (December 1919): 776–92; Morris Sigman, "Ladies Garment Workers Gain," *American Federationist* 30 (September 1923): 742–43.

7. The Progressive Dilemma of Protection

1. Charlotte Croman, foreword to reprint of *Prisoners of Poverty* (New York: Garrett Press, Inc., 1970), pp. v-x; Ross E. Paulson, "Helen Stuart Campbell," *Notable American Women* 1:280–81.

2. Articles on strikes, Mary Heaton Vorse papers, Archives of Labor History and Urban Affairs, Wayne State University.

3. Dorothy Richardson, *The Long Day: The Story of a New York Working Girl* (New York: The Century Company, 1905); Mrs. John Van Vorst and Marie Van Vorst, *The Woman Who Toils: Being the Experiences of Two Gentlewomen as Factory Girls* (New York: Doubleday, Page and Company, 1903).

4. Women's Educational and Industrial Union papers, Arthur and Elizabeth Schlesinger Library on the History of Women in America, Radcliffe College; Robert Sklar, "Mary Morton Kimball Kehew," *Notable American Women* 2:313–14; Mildred Fairchild Woodbury, "Susan Myra Kingsbury," *Notable American Women* 2:335–36.

5. Muriel W. Pumphrey, "Mary Ellen Richmond," *Notable American Women* 3:152–54.

6. "Industrial Studies of the Russell Sage Foundation, 1943," Mary Van Kleeck papers, Wayne State, box 10; Van Kleeck, "Industrial Investigations of the Russell Sage Foundation" (New York: Russell Sage Foundation, Committee on Women's Work, 1915).

7. "The Stress of the Seasons," *Survey* 29 (8 March 1913): 806; Lola Carson Toex, "Working Women in Maryland," *Life and Labor* 3 (April 1913): 100–104; Ethel Mason and S. M. Franklin, "Low Wages and Vice—Are They Related?" *Life and Labor* 3 (April 1913): 108–11; Louise deKoven Bowen, *The Girl Employed in Hotels and Restaurants* (Chicago: Juvenile Protection Association, 1912); Annie Marion MacLean, *Wage-Earning Women* (New York: The Macmillan Company, 1910).

8. Lola Carr Steelman, "Mary Clare de Graffenried," *Notable American Women* 1: 452–54.

9. "Women Wage-earners," *Nation* 82 (22 February 1906): 152–53; "Women and Children in Industry," *Outlook* 83 (5 May 1906): 12.

10. (Washington: GPO, 1910–13).

11. Christopher Lasch, "Sophonisba Preston Breckinridge," *Notable American Women* 1: 233–36; Jill Ker Conway, "Grace Abbott," *Notable American Women* 1: 2–4.

12. Christopher Lasch, ed., *The Social Thought of Jane Addams* (Indianapolis: The Bobbs-Merrill Company, 1965); Allen F. Davis, *Spearheads of Reform: The Social Settlements and the Progressive Movement, 1890–1914* (New York: Oxford University Press, 1967); Mary Anderson, with Mary N. Winslow, *Woman at Work* (Minneapolis: University of Minnesota Press, 1915), p.32.

13. "Commons Women's Club" in Chicago Commons papers, Chicago Historical Society, box 11; Mary McDowell papers, Chicago Historical Society; Caroline M. Hill, *Mary McDowell and Municipal Housekeeping: A Symposium* (Chicago: Millar Publishing Company, n.d.).

14. Settlement house papers at the Chicago Historical Society and the University of Illinois at Chicago Circle.

15. Allan Edward Reznick, "Lillian D. Wald: The Years at Henry Street" (Ph.D. Diss., University of Wisconsin, 1973); Marian Rich, "Irene Lewisohn," *Notable American Women* 2:400–402.

16. Maxine Seller, "The Education of the Immigrant Woman, 1890–1935," paper, Third Berkshire Conference on the History of Women, 1976; Columbia Religious and Industrial School for Jewish Girls papers, American Jewish Historical Society, annual reports, 1909–11; Francis Hovey Howe, "Leonora O'Reilly, Socialist and Reformer, 1870–1927," (Honors Thesis, Radcliffe College, 1952), pp.20–55.

17. Charlotte Baum, Paula Hyman, and Sonya Michel, *The Jewish Woman in America* (New York: The Dial Press, 1976), p.169; Rosalyn Baxandall, Linda Gordon, and Susan Reverby (eds.), *America's Working Women* (New York: Random House, 1976), pp.91–100; Grace Abbott, *The Immigrant and the Community* (New York: The Century Company, 1917), pp.55–80; Jane Addams, *A New Conscience and an Ancient Evil* (New York: The Macmillan Company, 1913), pp.28–29, 56–57; Clara E. Laughlin, *The Work-a-Day Girl: A Study of Some Present-Day Conditions* (New York: Fleming H. Revell Company, 1913), pp.22–40; Samuel Gompers, "Women's Wages and Morality," *American Federationist* 20 (June 1913): 465–67.

18. Kate Waller Barrett, *Some Practical Suggestions on the Conduct of a Rescue Home* (Washington: National Florence Crittenton Mission, 1903); Carol L. Urness, "Kate Harwood Waller Barrett," *Notable American Women* 1:97–99.

19. Margaret Sanger papers and Planned Parenthood Federation of America papers, Smith College and Library of Congress; David M. Kennedy, *Birth Control in America: The Career of Margaret Sanger* (New Haven: Yale University Press, 1970), pp.70–71, 76, 112–14; Sanger, *Margaret Sanger: An Autobiography* (New York: W. W. Norton & Co., 1938); Emma Goldman, "Testimony Before a Court on April 20, 1916," *The Masses* 8 (June 1916): 27.

20. Roy Lubove, "Hannah Bachman Einstein," *Notable American Women* 1: 566–68; Ellen Malino James, "Sophie Irene Simon Loeb," *Notable American Women* 1: 416–17.

21. Alice Gannett, "Bohemian Women in New York," *Life and Labor* 3 (February 1913): 49–52.

22. Claire de Graffenried, "Conditions of Wage Earning Women," *Forum* 15 (March 1893): 68–82; Annie Marvin MacLean, "Factory Legislation for Women in the United States," *American Journal of*

Sociology 3 (September 1897): 183–205; Josephine C. Goldmark, "The Necessary Sequel of Child-Labor Laws," *American Journal of Sociology* 11 (November 1905): 312–25; Frank P. Miles, "Statutory Regulation of Women's Employment—Codification of Statutes," *Journal of Political Economy* 14 (December 1906): 109–18; "May the Legislature Protect Women and Children," *Outlook* 83 (11 August 1906): 824; Sophonisba P. Breckinridge, "Legislative Control of Women's Work," *Journal of Political Economy* 14 (February 1906): 107–109; Ernst Freund, "The Constitutional Aspect of the Protection of Women in Industry," *Proceedings of the Academy of Political Science* 1 (1910): 162–84; Samuel Gompers, "Good Work for Women by Women," *American Federationist* 17 (August 1910): 685–86.

23. Alice Henry, "The Campaign in Illinois for the Ten-Hour Law," *American Federationist* 17 (August 1910): 669–72; Josephine Goldmark, "The Illinois Ten-Hour Decision," *Proceedings of the Academy of Political Science* 1 (1910): 185–87; Sophonisba P. Breckinridge, "The Illinois Ten-hour Law," *Journal of Political Economy* 18 (June 1910): 465–70.

24. Irene Osgood Andrews, "Diary of Judicial Decisions," *Life and Labor* 2 (July 1912): 213–14.

25. Josephine C. Goldmark, "Labor Laws for Women," *Survey* 29 (25 January 1913): 552–55; Goldmark, *Fatigue and Efficiency: A Study in Industry* (New York: Russell Sage Foundation, Survey Associates, 1912); Louis D. Brandeis and Josephine C. Goldmark, *The Case Against Nightwork for Women: The People of the State of New York, Respondent, Against Charles Schweinler Press, A Corporation, Defendent-Appellant; Summary of "Facts of Knowledge" Submitted on Behalf of the People* [1914] (New York: National Consumers' League, [1918]).

26. Agnes Nestor, "The Trend of Legislation Affecting Women's Hours of Labor, *Life and Labor* 7 (May 1917): 81–82; *Hours and Health of Women Workers: Report of the Illinois Industrial Survey* (Springfield, Ill: Schnepp and Barnes, 1919); "Regulation of Women's Working Hours in the United States," *American Labor Legislation Review* 8 (December 1918): 339–54; Jacob Andrew Lieberman, "Their Sisters' Keepers: The Women's Hours and Wages Movement in the United States, 1890–1925" (Ph.D. Diss., Columbia University, 1971).

27. "Women in Economics," *American Federationist* 9 (July 1902): 366–67; "American Women at Men's Work," *Harper's Weekly*

51 (8 June 1907); 831; Irene Osgood Andrews, "Relation of Irregular Employment to the Living Wage of Women," *American Labor Legislation Review* 5 (June 1915): 287–418; Annie Marion MacLean, *Women Workers and Society* (Chicago: A. C. McClurg and Co., 1916), pp.2–3; Margaret Dreier Robins, "The Minimum Wage," *Life and Labor* 3 (June 1913): 168–72; Brandeis, et al., "Case for Minimum Wage, A Symposium, *Survey* 33 (6 February 1915): 487–515; "Women's Right to a Living Wage," *The Independent* 81 (4 January 1915): 4–5; James T. Patterson, "Mary Dewson and the American Minimum Wage Movement," *Labor History* 5 (Spring 1964): 134–52.

28. Susan M. Kingsbury and Mabelle Moses, "Licensed Workers in Industrial Home Work in Massachusetts," Commonwealth of Massachusetts, State Board of Labor and Industry, Industrial Bulletin No. 4 (Boston: Wright and Potter Printing Co., 1915).

29. Martha Bensley Bruere, "The Triangle Fire," *Life and Labor* 1 (May 1911): 137–41; William Mailly, "The Triangle Trade Union Relief," *American Federationist* 18 (July 1911): 544–47; Rose Schneiderman, with Lucy Goldthwaite, *All for One* (New York: Paul S. Erikkson, Inc., 1967), pp. 100–103; Tom Brooks, "The Terrible Triangle Fire," *American Heritage* 7 (August 1957): 54–57, 110–11; Leon Stein, *The Triangle Fire* (Philadelphia: Lippincott, 1962); Corrine J. Naden, *The Triangle Shirtwaist Fire, March 25, 1911: The Blaze that Changed an Industry* (New York: Franklin Watts, 1971).

30. New York State Factory Investigating Commission, *Preliminary Report of the Factory Investigating Commission, 1912* (Albany: The Argus Company, 1912); *Second Report, 1913* (Albany: J. B. Lyon Company, 1913); *Third Report, 1914* (Albany: J. B. Lyon Company, 1914); *Fourth Report, 1914* (Albany: J. B. Lyon Company, 1915).

31. Alice Henry, "The Way Out," *Life and Labor* 2 (April 1912):120–21.

32. John B. Andrews and W. D. P. Bliss, *History of Women in Trade Unions,* vol. X of *Report on Conditions of Woman and Child Wage-Earners in the United States* (Washington: GPO, 1910–13), p.159; Mamie Brettel, "Woman's Union Label League," *American Federationist* 12 (May 1905): 276; Anna Fitzgerald, "Woman's International Union Label League and Trades Union Auxiliary," *American Federationist* 22 (September 1915): 731.

33. Maud Nathan, *The Story of an Epoch-Making Movement* (Garden City: Doubleday, Page & Co., 1926); Nathan, *Once Upon a Time and Today* (New York: G. P. Putnam's Sons, 1933); Josephine

Goldmark, *Impatient Crusader: Florence Kelley's Life Story* (Urbana: University of Illinois Press, 1953); Dorothy Ross Blumberg, *Florence Kelley: The Making of a Social Pioneer* (New York: Augustus M. Kelley, Publishers, 1966); Allis Rosenberg Wolfe, "Women, Consumerism, and the National Consumers' League in the Progressive Era, 1900–1933," *Labor History* 16 (Summer 1975): 378–92.

34. For internal commentary on the Women's Trade Union League, see articles and reports on conventions in *Life and Labor* 1–10 (1911–21) and *Life and Labor Bulletin* after 1921; also Gladys Boone, *The Women's Trade Union League in Great Britain and the United States of America* (New York: Columbia University Press, 1942); Alice Henry, *The Trade Union Woman* (New York: D. Appleton and Company, 1915), pp.61–65, 70–71, 89–114; Anderson, pp.32–39, 50–60; Schneiderman, pp.77–82; Mary E. Dreier, *Margaret Dreier Robins: Her Life, Letters and Work* (New York: Island Press Cooperative, Inc., 1950); James J. Kenneally, "Women and Trade Unions, 1870–1920: The Quandary of the Reformer," *Labor History* 14 (Winter 1973): 42–55; Allen F. Davis, "The Women's Trade Union League: Origins and Organization," *Labor History* 5 (Winter 1964): 3–17; Alice Kessler-Harris, "Organizing the Unorganizable: Three Jewish Women and their Union," *Labor History* 17 (Winter 1976): 5–23; Agnes Nestor, *Women's Labor Leader: An Autobiography* (Rockford, Ill.: Bellevue Books, 1954); Nancy Schrom Dye, "The Women's Trade Union League of New York, 1903–1920" (Ph.D. Diss., University of Wisconsin, 1974); Dye, "Creating a Feminist Alliance: Sisterhood and Class Conflict in the New York Woman's Trade Union League," *Feminist Studies* 2 (1975): 24–38; Dye, "Feminism or Unionism? The New York Women's Trade Union League and the Labor Movement," *Feminist Studies* 3 (Fall 1975): 111–25; Robin Miller Jacoby, "The Women's Trade Union League and American Feminism," *Feminist Studies* 3 (Fall 1975): 126–40.

35. Lillian Carr, "Women of the World Unite: The Lesson of the Washington Parade," *Life and Labor* 3 (April 1913): 112–16; Agnes O'Brien, "Suffrage and the Woman in Industry," *Life and Labor* 5 (August 1915): 132–33; Mabel Kanka, "Women's Struggle for Emancipation," *One Big Union Monthly* 12 (December 1920): 22–23; Samuel Gompers, "Labor and Woman Suffrage," *American Federationist* 27 (October 1920): 937–39; Agnes Nestor, "Ushering in the New Day," *Life and Labor* 11 (June 1921): 168–71.

36. Mary Jones, *Autobiography of Mother Jones* (Chicago: Charles H. Kerr & Co., 1925), p.202.

8. Confusion between the Wars

1. "Protest of the Working Women of New York," *Survey* 31 (14 February 1914): 605–606.

2. "Women in the Industries," *Scientific American* 116 (3 February 1917): 127; Nancy E. Malan, "How'ya Gonna Keep 'Em Down?: Women and World War I," *Prologue* 5 (Winter 1973): 209–39; "What Shall Be Done with Women Who Have Replaced Men in Industry?" *Current Opinion* 66 (February 1919): 124–25; H. S. Gillespie, "Where Girls Are Really Doing Men's Jobs and the Woman Who Is Responsible for It," *Ladies Home Journal* 34 (November 1917): 83; Esther Harney, "Boston's Shine Girls," *Life and Labor* 7 (December 1917): 186–88; Harry L. Morrison, "Trade Organizations and War Problems—Laundry Workers' International Union," *American Federationist* 24 (September 1917): 732–33.

3. Cleveland Chamber of Commerce, Committee on Industrial Welfare, "The Substitution of Woman for Man Power in Industry" (Cleveland: Chamber of Commerce, 1918); Annette Mann, "Women Workers in Factories: A Study of Working Conditions in 275 Industrial Establishments in Cincinnati and Adjoining Towns," (Cincinnati: The Consumers' League of Cincinnati, 1918); Mary Anderson, "Organizing the Bureau of Engraving and Printing Girls," *Life and Labor* 8 (January 1918): 11–12.

4. "Are Many Women Replacing Soldiers in Industrial Work?" *Current Opinion* 64 (January 1918): 60–61; Florence C. Thorne, "Women's War Service," *American Federationist* 24 (June 1917): 455–56; Josephine C. Goldmark, "Some Considerations Affecting the Replacement of Men by Women Workers," *Monthly Review* 6 (January 1918): 56–64.

5. Leonard Philip Krivy, "American Organized Labor and the First World War, 1917–1918: A History of Labor Problems and the Development of a Government War Labor Program" (Ph.D. Diss., New York University, 1965).

6. Samuel Gompers, "Women Workers Organize and Win," *American Federationist* 23 (March 1916): 199–201.

7. Samuel Gompers, "Don't Sacrifice Womanhood," *American Federationist* 24 (September 1917): 747–49; Gertrude Bedell, "A Present Need," *Survey* 38 (18 August 1917): 448; Mary Van Kleeck, "Trade Union Women," *New Republic* 17 (16 November 1918): 74–75; Marie L. Obenauer, "What Is the United States Bureau of Labor Statistics Doing for Women in Industry?" *Life and Labor* 6 (May 1916): 67–70.

8. Ethel M. Smith, "At Last—A National Women's Labor Bureau," *Life and Labor* 8 (August 1918): 159–60; Mary Van Kleeck, "The Government and Women in Industry," *American Federationist* 25 (September 1918): 788–90; Mary Anderson, with Mary N. Winslow, *Woman at Work* (Minneapolis: University of Minnesota Press, 1915), pp.88–113; "Women in Industry," *New Republic* 16 (26 October 1918): 365–66; "Gravity of the Woman Labor Problem After the War," *Current Opinion* 66 (January 1919): 61–62.

9. "Senate Bill 5408," *Life and Labor* 6 (May 1916): 70; Alice Henry, *Women and the Labor Movement* (New York: George H. Doran Company, 1923), pp.113–15, 134–50; Sister John Marie Daly, "Mary Anderson, Pioneer Labor Leader" (Ph.D. Diss., Georgetown University, 1968); Mary Van Kleeck, "Federal Policies for Women in Industry," *Annals of the American Academy of Political and Social Sciences* 81 (January 1919): 87–94; Mary Anderson, "What Use is the Women's Bureau to the Woman Worker?" *American Federationist* 36 (August 1929): 939–42.

10. Julia E. Johnsen, *Special Legislation for Women* (New York: H. W. Wilson Company, 1926), pp. 9–24, 45–48; J. Stanley Lemons, "Social Feminism in the 1920s: Progressive Women and Industrial Legislation," *Labor History* 14 (Winter 1973): 83–91; Lemons, *The Woman Citizen: Social Feminism in the 1920s* (Urbana: University of Illinois Press, 1973), pp.62–68, 137–47; Lucy Randolph Mason, "The Shorter Day and Women Workers," (Richmond: Virginia League of Women Voters, 1922); Agnes Nestor, "The Women's Industrial Conference," *American Federationist* 33 (March 1926): 196–304; V. Bari, "Shall Women Be Protected?" *Nation* 124 (9 February 1927): 143–44; E. E. Witte, "The Effects of Special Labor Legislation for Women," *Quarterly Journal of Economics* 42 (November 1927): 153–64; Cornelia Bryce Pinchot, "Women Who Work," *Survey* 62 (15 April 1929); Florence Kelley and Marguerite March, "Labor Legislation for Women and Its Effects on Earnings and Conditions of Labor," *Annals of American Academy of Political and Social Science* 143 (May 1929): 286–300.

11. William H. Chafe, *The American Woman: Her Changing Social, Economic, and Political Role, 1920–1970* (New York: Oxford University Press, 1972), pp.79–81; Mollie Ray Carroll, "Women Workers and the Minimum Wage," *American Federationist* 32 (December 1925): 1155–58; Ethel M. Smith, "The Supreme Court and Minimum Wage Legislation," *American Federationist* 33 (February 1926): 197–202; Ethel M. Johnson, "Fifteen Years of Minimum

Wage in Massachusetts," *American Federationist* 35 (October 1928): 1469–77.

12. Marius Hansome, "The Development of Workers' Education," in *Workers' Education in the United States,* ed. Theodore Brameld (New York: Harper and Brothers, Publishers, 1941), pp.48–66; Mary Van Kleeck, *Working Girls in Evening Schools: A Statistical Study* (New York: Russell Sage Foundation, Survey Associates, Inc., 1914); Pittsburgh Section, National Council of Jewish Women, *By Myself, I'm a Book! An Oral History of the Jewish Immigrant Experience* (Waltham: American Jewish Historical Society, 1972), ch. 4; Edward J. Ward, "Open the Schools," *Life and Labor* 1 (August 1911): 238–40; "The Women's Trade Union League Answers Questions of the Commissioner on Vocational Education," *Life and Labor* 4 (July 1914): 203–204; Florence H. Schneider, *Patterns of Worker Education: The Story of the Bryn Mawr Summer School* (Washington, D.C.: American Council on Public Affairs, 1941), pp.15–26.

13. Margaret Dreier Robins, "Women in Industry," *Survey* 31 (27 December 1913): 351; Elizabeth K. Adams, *Women Professional Workers: A Study Made for the Women's Educational and Industrial Union* (New York: The Macmillan Company, 1921), ch. 12; Margaret Dreier Robins, "Educational Plans of the National Women's Trade Union League," *Life and Labor* 4 (June 1914): 164–67.

14. Schneider, p.11; Lillian Herstein, Oral History Memoir, Roosevelt University, pp.119–24; Mark Starr papers, Archives of Labor History and Urban Affairs, Wayne State University; Hilda Worthington Smith, "Bryn Mawr Summer School of 1927," *American Federationist* 34 (October 1927); 1217–23; Anderson, pp.222-29; "The Industrial Experience of Women Workers at Summer Schools, 1928 to 1930," Women's Bureau, Bulletin 89 (Washington, D.C.: GPO, 1931); Andria Taylor Hourwich and Gladys L. Palmer (eds.), *I Am a Woman Worker: A Scrapbook of Autobiographies* (New York: The Affiliated Schools of Workers, Inc., 1936); Jean Carter and Hilda W. Smith, *Education and the Worker-Student: A Book about Workers' Education Based upon the Experience of Teachers and Students* (New York: Affiliated Schools for Workers, Inc., 1934); Caroline F. Ware, *Labor Education in Universities: A Study of University Programs* (New York: American Labor Education Service, Inc., 1946).

15. Fannia M. Cohn, "Twelve Years Educational Activities of International Ladies Garment Workers' Union," *American Federationist* 36 (January 1929): 105–11; Cohn, "Educational and Social Activities," *American Federationist* 36 (December 1929): 1446–52;

Cohn, "Facing the Future," *American Federationist* 42 (November 1935): 1203–1208.

16. David Cohen Brody, "American Labor Education Service, 1927–1961: An Organization in Workers' Education" (Ph.D. Diss., Cornell University, 1973); American Labor Education Service papers, Labor-Management Documentation Center, Cornell.

17. Elizabeth A. Hughes, *Living Conditions for Small-Wage Earners in Chicago* (Chicago: Department of Public Welfare, 1925), pp.14–43.

18. Robert and Helen Lynd, *Middletown* (New York: Harcourt, Brace, 1929); Harry A. A. Jebsen, "Blue Island Illinois: The History of a Working Class Suburb" (Ph.D. Diss., University of Cincinnati, 1971); John Taylor Cumbler, Jr., "Continuity and Disruption: Working-Class Community in Lynn and Fall River, Massachusetts, 1880–1950" (Ph.D. Diss., University of Michigan, 1974); Tamara K. Hareven, "The Laborers of Manchester, New Hampshire, 1912–1922: The Role of Family and Ethnicity in Adjustment to Industrial Life," *Labor History* 16 (Spring 1975): 249–65.

19. Frances R. Whitney, "What Girls Live On—and How: A Study of the Expenditures of a Sample Group of Girls Employed in Cincinnati in 1929" (Cincinnati: Consumers' League of Cincinnati, 1930); Frances Ivins Rich, "Wage-Earning Girls in Cincinnati: The Wages, Employment, Housing, Food, Recreation and Education of a Sample Group" (Cincinnati: Helen S. Troustine Foundation and YWCA, 1927); Orie Latham Hatcher, *Rural Girls in the City for Work: A Study Made for the Southern Woman's Educational Alliance* (Richmond, Va.: Garrett and Massie, Inc., Publishers, 1930).

20. Joseph A. Hill, *Women in Gainful Occupations, 1870–1920* (Washington, D. C.: GPO, 1929), pp.75–77, 148–53; "The Family Status of Breadwinning Women," Women's Bureau, Bulletin 23 (Washington, D.C.: GPO, 1922); "The Share of Wage-Earning Women in Family Support," Women's Bureau, Bulletin 30 (Washington, D. C.: GPO, 1923); "Family Status of Breadwinning Women in Four Selected Cities," Women's Bureau, Bulletin 41 (Washington, D. C.: GPO, 1925); Mary Anderson, "The Women Workers," *American Federationist* 32 (November 1925): 1073–76; Cara Cook, "Women Who Work for Wages," *American Federationist* 33 (April 1926): 454–59; Gwendolyn Salisbury Hughes, *Mothers in Industry: Wage-Earning by Mothers in Philadelphia* (New York: New Republic, Inc., 1925); Barbara Klaczunska, "Why Women Work: A Com-

parison of Various Groups in Philadelphia, 1910–1930," *Labor History* 17 (Winter 1976): 73–87.

21. Melton Alonzo McLaurin, "The Southern Cotton Textile Operative and Organized Labor, 1880–1905" (Ph.D. Diss., University of South Carolina, 1967); Jack Blicksilver, *Cotton Manufacturing in the Southeast: An Historical Analysis* (Atlanta: Bureau of Business Administration, Georgia State College of Business Administration, 1959); Matilda Robbins, "From the Notebook of a Labor Organizer," Robbins papers, Archives of Labor History and Urban Affairs, Wayne State University; "Southern Mill Hands," and "A Typical Day of a Cotton Mill Spinner," in Hourwich and Palmer, pp.37–39; John Garrett Van Osdell, Jr., "Cotton Mills, Labor, and the Southern Mind: 1880–1930" (Ph.D. Diss., Tulane University, 1966); Jennings J. Rhyne, *Some Southern Cotton Mill Workers and Their Villages* (Chapel Hill: University of North Carolina Press, 1930); Mary Anderson, "Women Workers in Textiles," *American Federationist* 36 (June 1929): 696–99; Nellie Andrews, "Organizing Women," *American Federationist* 36 (August 1929): 976–77; Liston Pope, *Millhands and Preachers: A Study of Gastonia* (New Haven: Yale University Press, 1942).

22. "Home Environment and Employment Opportunities of Women in Coal-Mine Workers' Families," Women's Bureau, Bulletin 45 (Washington, D. C.: GPO, 1925).

23. "Women Street Car Conductors and Ticket Agents," Women's Bureau, Bulletin 11 (Washington, D. C.: GPO, 1921); Anderson, pp.134–50; Lemons, pp.20–25; "Industrial Opportunities and Training for Women and Girls," Women's Bureau, Bulletin 13 (Washington, D. C.: GPO, 1920).

24. Hill, pp.7–11, 16–19, 29–41, 55–66; "The Occupational Progress of Women," Women's Bureau, Bulletin 27 (Washington, D.C.: GPO, 1922); Mary V. Dempsey, "The Occupational Progress of Women, 1910 to 1930," Women's Bureau, Bulletin 104 (Washington, D. C.: GPO, 1933); Leo Wolman, *The Growth of American Trade Unions, 1880–1923* (New York: National Bureau of Economic Research, 1924), pp.99–108.

25. Theresa Wolfson, "Wage of Organized Women Workers," *American Federationist* 32 (September 1925): 811–13; Mary Anderson, "Women's Wages," *American Federationist* 32 (August 1925): 681–83; Lillian Herstein, "Women Discuss Wages," *American Federationist* 36 (August 1929): 949–59; Bertha M. Neinburg, "Some Difficulties of Minimum Wage Commissions in Times of Business

Depression," *Life and Labor* 11 (April 1921): 99–102; Nelle Swatz, "The Trend in Women's Wages," *Annals of the American Academy of Political and Social Science* 143 (May 1929): 104–108; "Changing Jobs," Women's Bureau, Bulletin 54 (Washington, D. C.: GPO, 1926).

26. Mary Anderson, "Hours of Work," *American Federationist* 32 (September 1925): 769–72; Lucy Carmer, "Shorter Hours for Women Workers," *American Federationist* 35 (October 1928): 1246–49; Mary D. Hopkins, "The Employment of Women at Night," Women's Bureau, Bulletin 64 (Washington, D. C.: GPO, 1928).

27. Hourwich and Palmer, pp.78, 29.

28. Groves papers, Archives of Labor History and Urban Affairs, Wayne State University, 4 letters, 1968.

29. Hourwich and Palmer, pp.29, 94; Groves letters.

30. Mary Elizabeth Pidgeon and Margaret Thompson Mettert, "Employed Women and Family Support," Women's Bureau, Bulletin 168 (Washington, D. C.: GPO, 1939); Wight Bakke, *Citizens Without Work* (New Haven, Conn.: Yale University Press, 1940).

31. Ruth Shalcross, "Shall Married Women Work?" (New York: National Federation of Business and Professional Women's Clubs, n.d.); Chafe, pp.107,111; Jeanne Westin, *Making Do: How Women Survived the '30s* (Chicago: Follette Publishing Company, 1976), pp.146, 185; Frieda S. Miller, "Women's Place—What Will Determine It?" *American Federationist* 39 (March 1932): 287–90; Cecile Tipton LaFollette, "A Study of the Problems of 652 Gainfully Employed Married Women Homemakers" (New York: Bureau of Publications, Teachers College, Columbia University, 1934), pp.168–70.

32. Jane Filley and Theresa Mitchell, *Consider the Laundry Workers* (New York: League of Women Shoppers, Inc., 1937), pp.15–19, 33–36, 40–43, 48–50; "A Survey of Laundries and Their Women Workers in 23 Cities," Women's Bureau, Bulletin 78 (Washington, D. C.: GPO, 1930); "Women in Kentucky Industries, 1937," Women's Bureau, Bulletin 162 (Washington, D. C.: GPO, 1938); Elenor M. Snyder, "Job Histories of Women Workers at the Summer Schools, 1931–34 and 1938," Women's Bureau, Bulletin 174 (Washington, D. C.: GPO, 1939).

33. Harriet A. Byrne, "Women Unemployed Seeking Relief in 1933," Women's Bureau, Bulletin 139 (Washington, D. C.: GPO, 1936); Byrne and Cecile Hillyer, "Unattached Women on Relief in Chicago, in 1937," Women's Bureau, Bulletin 159 (Washington, D. C.: GPO, 1938).

34. Boone, pp.194–96; Helen Valeska Bary, Oral History Memoir, Bancroft Library, University of California–Berkeley, pp.150–54.

35. "Chronological Development of Labor Legislation for Women in the United States," Women's Bureau, Bulletin 66-II (Washington, D. C.: GPO, 1932); "Employed Women under NRA Codes," Women's Bureau, Bulletin 130 (Washington, D. C.: GPO, 1935); "Summary of State Hour Laws for Women and Minimum Wage Rates," Women's Bureau, Bulletin 137 (Washington, D. C.: GPO, 1936); Boone, pp.196–204; Agnes Nestor, *Women's Labor Leader: An Autobiography* (Rockford, Ill.: Bellevue Books, 1954), pp.264–66.

36. Wolman, pp.97–99; Theresa Wolfson, *The Woman Worker and the Trade Union* (New York: International Publishers, 1926); Clara Katzor, "Shoemaker's Story," *American Federationist* 36 (August 1929): 978–79; Fannia M. Cohn, "Women and the Labor Movement," *American Federationist* 32 (December 1925): 1186–88; William Green, "Women Wage Earners," *American Federationist* 32 (November 1925): 1004–1005; Green, "Campaign to Organize Women Wage Earners," *American Federationist* 33 (May 1926): 534; Frances Perkins, "Women Workers," *American Federationist* 36 (September 1929): 1073–79; Katherine Fisher, "Women Workers and the American Federation of Labor," *New Republic* 27 (3 August 1921): 265–67; Chafe, pp.76–79.

37. Dorothy Rabinowitz, "The Case of the ILGWU," in *The World of the Blue-Collar Worker,* ed. Irving Howe (New York: Quadrangle Books, 1972); Christine Ellis, "People Who Cannot Be Bought," in *Rank and File: Personal Histories by Working-Class Organizers,* ed. Alice and Staughton Lynd (Boston: Beacon Press, 1973), pp.18–23.

38. Margaret N. Campbell, "Organization and the Southern Worker," *Life and Labor* 10 (June 1920): 163–65; drafts of articles, Mary Heaton Vorse papers, Archives of Labor History and Urban Affairs, Wayne State University, boxes 115–18, 122, 155, 156.

39. ILGWU minutes, 1934–43, Rose Pesotta papers, New York Public Library, box 17; Hourwich and Palmer, pp. 75–76, 107, 129–32; Chafe, pp. 81–83; Boone, pp. 207–14.

40. Boone, p.207; Chafe, pp.85–86.

41. Chafe, pp.83–84.

42. Mary Heaton Vorse, *Labor's New Millions* (New York: Modern Age Books, 1938), pp.80–81, 110, 153, 205, 237; Catherine Gelles, Oral History Memoir, Institute of Labor and Industrial Relations, University of Michigan–Wayne State University, pp.1–8.

43. Chafe, pp.85–88; Rabinowitz, p.52; Ellis, pp.23–33; Robert Stuart McElvaine, "Thunder without Lightning: Working Class Discontent in the United States, 1929–1937" (Ph.D. Diss., State University of New York at Binghamton, 1974).

9. False Promises in World War II

1. William H. Chafe, *The American Woman: Her Changing Social, Economic, and Political Role, 1920–1970* (New York: Oxford University Press, 1972), p.195; Carola Woerishoffer Graduate Department of Social Economy and Social Research, *Women During the War and After: Summary of a Comprehensive Study* (Bryn Mawr: Bryn Mawr College, 1945), pp.3–11.

2. Eve Lapin, *Mothers in Overalls* (New York: Workers Library Publishers, 1943); Susan B. Anthony II, *Out of the Kitchen—Into the War: Women's Winning Role in the Nation's Drama* (New York: Stephen Day, Inc., 1943); Margaret Culkin Banning, *Women for Defense* (New York: Sloan and Pearce, 1942); "Effective Industrial Use of Women in the Defense Program," Women's Bureau, Special Bulletin 1 (Washington, D. C.: GPO, 1940); Richard R. Lingeman, *Don't You Know There's a War On?* (New York: G. P. Putnam's Sons, 1970), p.222; Frank J. Taylor, "Meet the Girls Who Keep 'Em Flying," *Saturday Evening Post* 20 (May 1942): 30.

3. Mary Anderson, with Mary N. Winslow, *Woman at Work* (Minneapolis: University of Minnesota Press, 1951), p.64; United States Bureau of the Budget, *The United States at War* (Washington, D. C.: GPO, 1946), pp.173–89; J. David Kingsley, "Manpower Muddle," *Current History* 3 (1943): 396; Mary Anderson to Rose Schneiderman, 2 October 1942, Anderson papers, Arthur and Elizabeth Schlesinger Library on the History of Women in America, Radcliffe College; Eleanor Straub, "Government Policy toward Civilian Women during World War II" (Ph.D. Diss., Emory University, 1973); Straub, "United States Government Policy Toward Civilian Women During World War II," *Prologue* 5 (Winter 1973): 240–54; National Manpower Council, *Womanpower* (New York: Columbia University Press, 1957), pp.143–66; "Womanpower Committees during World War II—United States and British Experience," Women's Bureau, Bulletin 244 (Washington, D. C.: GPO, 1953); Chester W. Gregory, *Women in Defense Work during World War II* (New York: Exposition Press, 1974), pp.15–28.

4. Austin-Wadsworth bill, *Cong. Rec.,* 89, Pt. 1, 78th Cong., 1st Sess., March 1943, 1374–75; Frances Perkins, *The Roosevelt I Knew* (New York: Viking Press, 1946), p.354.

5. "Women Workers in the Family Environment," Women's Bureau, Bulletin 183 (Washington, D. C.: GPO, 1941).

6. Beatrice Oppenheim, "Anchors Aweigh," *Independent*

Woman 22 (March 1943): 71; Katherine Glover, *Women at Work in War Time* (Washington, D. C.: Public Affairs Committee, 1943); Elizabeth H. Benham, "Employment Opportunities in Characteristic Industrial Occupations of Women," Women's Bureau, Bulletin 201 (Washington, D. C.: GPO, 1944); Gregory, pp.40–50; Augusta Clawson, *Shipyard Diary of a Woman Welder* (New York: Penguin, 1944).

7. Laura Nelson Baker, *Wanted: Women in War Industries* (New York: E. P. Dutton Company, 1943), p.9; Dorothy K. Newman, "Employing Women in Shipyards," Women's Bureau, Bulletin 192-6 (Washington, D. C.: GPO, 1944); Clawson; Elinor Morehouse Herrick papers, Schlesinger-Radcliffe; Gregory, pp.80–92.

8. Ethel Erickson, "Women's Employment in Aircraft Plants in 1942," Women's Bureau, Bulletin 192-1 (Washington, D.C.: GPO, 1942); Elizabeth Gurley Flynn, *Women in War Work* (New York: Workers Library Publishers, 1942); Dicky Meyers, *Girls at Work in Aviation* (New York: Doubleday and Company, Publishers, 1943); Gregory, pp. 76–79.

9. "Women's Work in the War," Women's Bureau, Bulletin 193 (Washington, D. C.: GPO, 1942); "Reports on Employment of Women in Wartime Industries," Women's Bureau, Bulletin 192 (Washington, D. C.: GPO, 1942–44); "Employment of Women in the War Period," *Labor Information Bulletin* 11 (December 1944): 4.

10. Joel Seidman, *American Labor from Defense to Reconversion* (Chicago: University of Chicago Press, 1953), pp.154–55; Wendell E. Whipp, "How We Put Women to Work," *American Machinist* 86 (29 October 1942): 1215.

11. United Auto Workers, War Policy Division, Women's Bureau papers, Archives of Labor History and Urban Affairs, Wayne State University, box 1: "Carry-Out Service"; Kathryn Blood, "Community Services for Women War Workers," (Washington, D. C.: GPO, 1944).

12. "Boarding Homes for Women War Workers," (Washington, D. C.: GPO, 1943).

13. "Employed Mothers and Child Care," Women's Bureau, Bulletin 246 (Washington, D. C.: GPO, 1953); Gregory, pp.51–66; Richard Polenberg, *War and Society: The United States, 1941–1945* (Philadelphia: J. B. Lippincott Company, 1972), pp.148–49.

14. "Women Workers and Their Family Environment," Women's Bureau, Bulletin 183 (Washington, D. C.: GPO, 1941).

15. Women's Bureau, Bulletin 192; Anna M. Baetjer, *Women in*

Industry: Their Health and Efficiency (Philadelphia: W. B. Saunders Company, 1946), pp.247–58.

16. "'Equal Pay' for Women in War Industries," Women's Bureau, Bulletin 196 (Washington, D. C.: GPO, 1942); *Cong. Rec.* 91, Pt. 5, 79th Cong., 21 June 1945, 6411; *Cong. Rec.,* 91, HR 526, 79th Cong., 1st Sess., 3 January 1945; "Equal Pay for Comparable Work," *Independent Woman* 24 (1945): 168; Gregory, pp.165–81; Raymond Vess, Oral History Memoir, Institute of Labor and Industrial Relations, University of Michigan–Wayne State University, pp.18–19.

17. *Congressional Quarterly* 2 (1946): 494, 759; Gregory, pp.182–91.

18. "Women Workers in Ten War Production Areas and Their Postwar Employment Plans," Women's Bureau, Bulletin 109 (Washington, D. C.: GPO, 1946); "Handbook of Facts on Women Workers: 1948," Women's Bureau, Bulletin 225 (Washington, D. C.: GPO, 1948).

19. Sheila Tobias and Lisa Anderson, "What Really Happened to Rosie the Riveter? Demobilization and the Female Labor Force, 1944–47," MSS Modular Publications, module 9 (1974).

20. "Women's Bureau 1952 Handbook of Facts on Women Workers," Women's Bureau, Bulletin 242 (Washington, D. C.: GPO, 1952).

10. Mixed Signals in Postwar Work

1. "Women Workers in Ten War Production Areas and their Postwar Employment Plans," Women's Bureau, Bulletin 209 (Washington, D. C.: GPO, 1946).

2. Jennifer Colton, "Why I Quit Working," *Good Housekeeping,* September 1951, p. 53.

3. "1975 Handbook of Women Workers," Women's Bureau, Bulletin 297 (Washington, D. C.: GPO, 1975), pp.7–19; U. S. Department of Commerce, Bureau of the Census, *A Statistical Portrait of Women in the United States,* Current Population Reports, Special Studies, Series P-23, No. 58 (Washington, D. C.: GPO, 1976), pp.26–27, 39; Valerie Kincade Oppenheimer, *The Female Labor Force in the United States: Demographic and Economic Factors Governing It* (Berkeley: University of California, Population Monograph Series, no. 5, 1970), pp.1–18; Linda Waite, "Working Wives: 1940–1960," *American Sociological Review* 41 (Fall 1976): 65–80; Alva Myrdal and Viola Klein, *Women's Two Roles: Home and Work* (London: Routledge and Kegan Paul, Ltd., 1956, 1969), pp. x–xi, 59–66; Abbott

L. Ferriss, *Indicators of Trends in the Status of American Women* (New York: Russell Sage Foundation, 1971), pp. 85–91; National Manpower Council, *Womanpower* (New York: Columbia University Press, 1957); Mary Dublin Keyserling, "The Economic Status of Women in the United States," *American Economic Review* 66 (May 1976): 205–12.

4. *1975 Handbook*, pp.19–25; U. S. Department of Labor, Employment Standards Administration, Women's Bureau, "Why Women Work" (1975); *Womanpower*, pp.71–74; Michelle Fascardi, "Besides, I Needed the Money," *Women: A Journal of Liberation* 4 (Spring 1975): 12–15; William J. Serow and Julia H. Martin, *Virginia's Population: A Decade of Change: The Status of Women* (Charlottesville: Tayloe Murphy Institute, University of Virginia, 1974).

5. *1975 Handbook*, pp.83–101; "Women in the Workplace: A Special Section," *Monthly Labor Review* 97 (May 1974); *Statistical Portrait*, p.34; Ferris, pp.108–14.

6. Elinor Langer, "The Women of the Telephone Company," *New York Review of Books,* 12 and 26 March 1970; Brenda and Peggy, "Dial 'O' for Oppression," in "Working Women: Our Stories and Struggles" (New York: Center for United Labor Action, 1972), pp.24–25; *1975 Handbook*, p.146; Nikki Green, "Don't Think, Type," in "Working Women," pp.22–23.

7. Josephine Hulett and Janet Dewart, "Household Help Wanted —Female," *MS Magazine* 1 (February 1972): 45–49; Ethlyn Christensen, "Household Employment: Restructuring the Occupation," *Issues in Industrial Society* 2 (1971): 47–53; Edith B. Sloan, "Keynote Address, First National Conference of Household Workers," *NCHE News* 2 (July 1971).

8. Mary Welles, "The Waitress," in *The Workers: Portraits of Nine American Jobholders,* ed. Kenneth Lasson (New York: Grossman Publishers, 1971), pp.185–86; Elizabeth Ross, "Waitressing— All You Have to Take for a Tip," in "Working Women," pp.6–7; Bernard Rosenberg and Saul Weinman, "An Interview with Myra Wolfgang: Young Women Who Work," in *The World of the Blue Collar Worker,* ed. Irving Howe (New York: Quadrangle Books, 1972), pp.23–25.

9. *1975 Handbook*, p.98; Sharon Ellis, "Hospital Workers—Sheets, Mops, and Bedpans," in "Working Women," pp.12–13.

10. *1975 Handbook*, pp.96, 99, 115, 166–69; Barbara Garson, *All the Livelong Day: The Meaning and Demeaning of Routine Work* (Garden City: Doubleday, 1975), pp.56–72; Esther Young, "Individuality

in a Factory," *American Behavioral Scientist* 16 (September–October 1972): 65–74.

11. 1975 Handbook, pp.241–77; Laura Rohrlich and Ethel L. Vatter, "Women in the World of Work: Past, Present, and Future," *Women's Studies* 1 (1973): 263–77; Patricia Marshall, "Look Who's Wearing Lipstick," *Manpower Magazine* 4 (December 1972): 2–9.

12. U. S. Department of Labor, Employment Standards Administration, Women's Bureau, "The Myth and the Reality," May 1974; Joy F. Sokeitous and Kathy McFadden, "Myths about Working Women" (Pittsburgh: KNOW, Inc., n.d.); Myrdal and Klein, pp.94–96, 106–10; William F. Barnes and Ethel B. Jones, "Manufacturing Quit Rates Revisited: A Cyclical View of Women's Rights," *Monthly Labor Review* 96 (December 1973): 53–56; Paul A. Armknecht and John F. Early, "Manufacturing Quit Rates Revisited: Secular Changes and Women's Quits," *Monthly Labor Review* 96 (December 1973): 56–58.

13. 1975 Handbook, pp.123–49, 166–69; *Statistical Portrait,* pp.45–46; Elizabeth Waldman and Beverly J. McEaddy, "Where Women Work—An Analysis by Income and Occupation," *Monthly Labor Review* 57 (May 1974): 7, 10; U. S. Department of Labor, Employment Standards Administration, Women's Bureau, "The Earnings Gap: Median Earnings of Year-Round Fulltime Workers, by Sex," March 1975; Richard B. Mancke, "Lower Pay for Women: A Case of Economic Discrimination?" *Industrial Relations* 10 (October 1971): 1316–26; Ronald L. Oaxaca, "Male-Female Wage Differential in Urban Labor Markets" (Princeton: University Industrial Relations Section, 1971).

14. Judith Long-Laws, "Causes and Effects of Sex Discrimination in the Bell System," testimony, Federal Communications Commission, Docket No. 19143, 1972, pp.1–52; Ethel Chipcase, "Discrimination against Women," *Free Labour World* 285 (May 1973): 17–20; U.S. Department of Labor, Wage and Hour Division, Workplace Standards Administration, publications 1209 and 1320.

15. Mary Stevenson, "The Determinants of Low Wages for Women Workers" (Ph.D. Diss., University of Michigan, 1974); Barry Bluestone, William H. Murphy, and Mary Stevenson, *Low Wages and the Working Poor* (Ann Arbor: Institute of Labor and Industrial Relations, University of Michigan, 1973); Oppenheimer, pp.65–120; Ferris, pp.114–17; Jerolyn R. Lyle and Jane L. Ross, *Women in Industry: Employment Patterns of Women in Corporate America* (Lexington, Mass.: D. C. Heath and Company, 1973); Adele Simmons

et al., *Exploitation from 9 to 5: Report of the Twentieth Century Fund Task Force on Women and Employment* (New York: Twentieth Century Fund, 1975); Janice Fanning Madden, *The Economics of Sex Discrimination* (Lexington, Mass.: D. C. Heath and Company, 1973).

16. 1975 Handbook, pp.50–64; Virginia E. O'Leary, "Some Attitudinal Barriers to Occupational Aspiration in Women," *Psychological Bulletin* 81 (November 1974): 809–26.

17. 1975 Handbook, pp.64–81; Ferris, pp.121–35; *Annual Report of the Council of Economic Advisers, Economic Report of the President, January 1973* (Washington, D. C.: GPO, 1973), pp.96–100; Curtis L. Gilroy, "Job Losers, Leavers, and Entrants: Traits and Trends," *Monthly Labor Review* 96 (August 1973): 3–15; Carolyn Shaw Bell, "The Economics of Might-Have-Been," *Monthly Labor Review* 97 (November 1974): 40–42.

18. 1975 Handbook, pp.25–33; "Who Are the Working Mothers?" Women's Bureau, Leaflet 37 (Washington, D. C.: GPO, 1972); Ferris, pp.103–108; H. T. Groat, R. L. Workman, and A. G. Neal, "Labor Force Participation and Family Formation: A Study of Working Mothers," *Demography* 13 (Fall, 1976): 115–25; Sandra L. Bem and Daryl J. Bem, "Training the Woman to Know Her Place: The Social Antecedents of Women in the World of Work" (Harrisburg: Pennsylvania Department of Education, 1973); James A. Sweet, "Labor Force Reentry by Mothers of Young Children," *Social Science Research* 1 (June 1972): 189–210; C. Etaugh, "Effects of Maternal Employment on Children: A Review of Recent Research," *Merrill-Palmer Quarterly* 20 (April 1974): 71–98; R. J. Schonberger, "Inflexible Working Conditions Keep Women 'Unliberated,'" *Personal Journal* 50 (November 1971): 834–37; Janice Neipert Hedges and Jeanne K. Barnett, "Working Women and the Division of Household Tasks," *Monthly Labor Review* 95 (April 1972): 9–13.

19. 1975 Handbook, pp.33–41; U. S. Senate, Committee on Finance, *Child Care: Data and Materials* (Washington, D. C.: GPO, 1974); Mary Dublin Keyserling, "Day Care," *Parents' Magazine,* April 1972, p.12; Carol Kleinman, "A Crying Need for Day Care," *Progressive Woman* 2 (May 1972): 11.

20. Kenneth Morris, Oral History Memoir, Institute of Labor and Industrial Relations, University of Michigan–Wayne State University, p.40; Dorothy Haener, "What Is Labor Doing about Women in the Work Force?" in *Women in the Work Force: Proceedings of a Conference Sponsored by the Division of Personnel Psychology of*

the New York State Psychological Association (New York: Behavioral Publications, Inc., 1972), pp.43–52; "Proceedings, 15th Annual Constitutional Convention, Union of Auto, Aerospace and Agricultural Implement Workers of America (UAW–CIO)," Cleveland, 27 May–1 April 1955.

21. U. S. Congress, Senate, Committee on Labor and Public Welfare, *Labor Management Relations in the Southern Textile Manufacturing Industry,* 81st Cong., 2nd Sess., 21–24 August 1950.

22. 1975 Handbook, p.76; Ferris, pp.176–79; Simons, pp.119–25; Barbara M. Wertheimer and Anne H. Nelson, *Trade Union Women: A Study of their Participation in New York City Locals* (New York: Praeger Publishers, 1975), pp.7–11.

23. Wertheimer and Nelson, pp.60–63; Dorothy Rabinowitz, "The Case of the ILGWU," in *World of the Blue-Collar Worker,* ed. Howe, pp.55–57.

24. Wertheimer and Nelson, pp.49–53, 56–60; "Trade Union Leader Speaks: An Interview with Doris Turner," *Women's Rights Law Reporter* 1 (Fall 1972/1973):73–76.

25. Bessie Hillman, "Gifted Women in the Trade Unions," in *American Women: The Changing Image,* ed. Beverly Benner Cassara (Boston: Beacon Press, 1962), pp.99–115; Wertheimer and Nelson, pp. viii–ix, 144–45.

26. Susan Davis, "Organizing from Within," *MS Magazine* 1 (August 1972): 92–98.

27. Shultz v. Wheaton Glass Co., 398 U.S. 905 (1970); Brennan v. Prince William Hospital, 503 F. 2d 282 (1974); Corning Glass Works v. Brennan, 417 U.S. 188 (1974); John G. Burns and Catherine G. Burns, "Analysis of the Equal Pay Act," *Labor Law Journal* 24 (Fall 1973): 92–94.

28. Leo Kanowitz, *Women and the Law: The Unfinished Revolution* (Albuquerque: University of New Mexico Press, 1969), pp.100–48; *Journal of Reprints of Documents Affecting Women* 1, no. 1 (July 1976), docs. 1–22; William Brown, III, "The Equal Employment Opportunity Act of 1972—the Light at the Top of the Stairs," *Personnel Administration* 35 (June 1972): 4; Mary Eastwood, "Fighting Job Discrimination: Three Federal Approaches," *Feminist Studies* 1 (Summer 1972): 75–103; "Case Summaries," *Women's Rights Law Reporter* 1 (Fall–Winter 1972–1973): 34–71; Elliott Abrams, "The Quota Commission," *Commentary* 54 (October 1972): 54–57; Barbara Yaffe and Byron Yaffe, "State Protective Legislation: An Anachronism under Title VII?" *Issues in Industrial Society* 2

(1971): 54–61; Arthur B. Smith, "The Impact on Collective Bargaining of Equal Employment Opportunity Remedies," *Industrial and Labor Relations Review* 28 (April 1975): 376–94.

29. 1975 Handbook, pp.281–338, 361–63; Kanowitz, pp.192–96; Rosenberg and Weinman, pp.23–25.

11. Postwar Challenges to Home and Community

1. Mary Wills, "The Waitress," in *The Workers: Portraits of Nine American Jobholders,* ed. Kenneth Lasson (New York: Grossman Publishers, 1971), pp.181–206.

2. U. S. Department of Commerce, Bureau of the Census, *A Statistical Portrait of Women in the United States,* Current Population Reports, Special Studies, Series P-23, No. 58 (Washington, D. C.: GPO, 1976), pp.3–4; Fabian Linden and Helen Axel, *Women: A Demographic, Social and Economic Presentation* (New York: The Conference Board, 1973); Abbott L. Ferriss, *Indicators of Trends in the Status of American Women* (New York: Russell Sage Foundation, 1971), pp.4–5.

3. Lee Rainwater, Richard P. Coleman, and Gerald Hanley, *Workingman's Wife: Her Personality, World, and Life Style* (New York: Oceana Publications, Inc., 1959), pp.17–18.

4. William H. Chafe, *The American Woman: Her Changing Social, Economic, and Political Role, 1920–1970* (New York: Oxford University Press, 1972), p.189.

5. Stanley Aronowitz, *False Promises: The Shaping of American Working Class Consciousness* (New York: McGraw-Hill, Publishers, Inc., 1973), p.92; Nona Glazer-Malbin, "Capitalism and the Class Crisis for Women," paper, Pacific Sociological Association, 1976; Albert Szymanski, "Race, Sex, and the U. S. Working Class," *Social Problems* 21 (June 1974): 706–25.

6. Wills, pp.181–206.

7. "I Denied My Sex," *True Romance,* April 1954; Betty Friedan, *The Feminine Mystique* (New York: W. W. Norton and Company, 1963), ch. 2.

8. Rainwater et al., pp.67–78.

9. Lee Rainwater, *And the Poor Get Children: Sex, Contraception, and Family Planning in the Working Class* (Chicago: Quadrangle Books, Inc., 1960), pp.62–81; Mirra Komarovsky, *Blue Collar Marriage* (New York: Random House, 1962), pp.24–26, ch. 10; E. E. LeMasters, *Blue-Collar Aristocrats: Life-Styles at a Working-Class*

Tavern (Madison: University of Wisconsin Press, 1975), pp.81–88; Rainwater et al., *Workingman's Wife,* pp.67–78; Cornelia Butler Flora, "The Passive Female: Her Comparative Image by Class and Culture in Women's Magazine Fiction," *Journal of Marriage and the Family* 33 (August 1971): 435–44.

10. *Statistical Portrait,* p.15; LeMasters, p.100; Joseph T. Howell, *Hard Living on Clay Street: Portraits of Blue Collar Families* (Garden City, N. Y.: Anchor Press, Doubleday, 1973), pp.2–3.

11. Rainwater, pp.81–91; Rainwater et al., pp. 30–32, 88–102; Komarovsky, pp.73–76; Aronowitz, p.91; Sar A. Levitan, *Blue-Collar Workers: A Symposium on Middle America* (New York: McGraw-Hill Book Company, 1971), p.159.

12. *Statistical Portrait,* p.18; Rainwater, pp.25–27, 46–49, 54–57, 163–71; Jack O. Balswick, "Attitudes of Lower Class Males Toward Taking a Male Birth Control Pill," *Family Coordinator* 21 (April 1972): 195–99; William B. Clifford, II, and A. Clarke Davis, "Socioeconomic Status, Residence Background, Value Orientations, and Fertility Preferences," *Rural Sociology* 37 (June 1972): 228–35.

13. Social Research, Inc., "Working-Class Women in a Changing World: A Review of Recent Research Findings" (New York: McFadden-Bartell Corporation, 1973), pp.14–15, 22–25.

14. Rainwater et al., pp.26–30, 126–41, 184–202; Komarovsky, ch. 3; Diane Leech, "Diary of a Tired Mother," in "Working Women: Our Stories and Struggles" (New York: Center for United Labor Action, 1972), pp.17–18; "Diary of Marion Hudson," in *America's Working Women,* ed.Rosalyn Baxandall, Linda Gordon and Susan Reverby (New York: Random House, 1976), pp.336–40; "Changing World," pp.17–19.

15. Rainwater et al., pp.32–40, 103–13; Komarovsky, pp.27–33, 43–44, and ch. 11, 12, 14; LeMasters, pp. 151–55; George S. Rosenberg and Donald F. Anspach, *Working Class Kinship* (Lexington, Mass.: D. C. Heath and Company, 1973).

16. Nancy Seifer, "Absent from the Majority: Working Class Women in America" (New York: National Project on Ethnic America, National Jewish Committee, 1973), pp.47–49.

17. Levitan, pp.295, 367–68; Levison, pp.12, 13, 22–25, 30–38; Seifer, pp.5–6, 10–12; Ferriss, pp. 137–54; Pamela Roby (ed.), *The Poverty Establishment* (Englewood Cliffs: Prentice-Hall, Inc., 1974), p.2.

18. Ferriss, pp.151–56; Beverly Johnson McEaddy, "Women Who Head Families: A Sociological Analysis," *Monthly Labor Review* 99

(June 1976): 3–9; Heather L. Ross and Isabel V. Sawhill, *Time of Transition: The Growth of Families Headed by Women* (Washington, D. C.: The Urban Institute, 1975); Paul and Sandy DeVivo, "Help for the Woman Breadwinner," *U. S. Manpower* 5 (February 1973): 9–14.

19. Rainwater et al., pp.145–83, 205–15; "Changing World," pp.13–15, 45–48; John Kenneth Galbraith, "The Economics of the American Housewife," *Atlantic* 232 (August 1973): 79–83.

20. Alva Myrdal and Viola Klein, *Women's Two Roles: Home and Work* (London: Routledge and Kegan Paul, Ltd., 1956, 1968), pp.41–45, 75–90; Levison, pp.49–50; National Manpower Council, *Womanpower* (New York: Columbia University Press, 1957), pp.125–29; Clarence D. Long, *The Labor Force under Changing Income and Employment* (Princeton: Princeton University Press, 1958), pp.54–57; Michael Jett, "The Return of Rosie: Blue Collar Occupations Attract More Women, Mainly for the Money," *Wall Street Journal,* 16 April 1973; Michael J. Boskin, "The Effects of Government Expenditures and Taxes on Female Labor," *American Economic Review* 44 (May 1974): 251–56; Ferriss, pp.95–103; Seifer, p.16.

21. Richard Centers, *The Psychology of Social Classes* (Princeton: Princeton University Press, 1949), pp.145–46; Jean A. Dowdell, "Jobs and Families: Social Status Differences in Women's Attitudes toward Employment," paper, Southwestern Sociological Association, San Antonio, Texas, 28 March 1975; Levitan, pp.84, 159–60; Komarovsky, pp.61–73; Patricia and Brendon Sexton, *Blue Collars and Hard Hats* (New York: Random House, 1971); Seifer, pp.26–32, 42–47; Myrdal and Klein, pp.1–25; Jean D. Dowdall, "Women's Attitudes Toward Employment and Family Role," *Sociological Analysis* 35 (Winter 1974): 251–62.

22. Sar A. Levitan and William B. Johnston, *Work Is Here To Stay, Alas* (Salt Lake City: Olympus Publishing Company, 1973), pp.50, 131; Rainwater et al., p.30; Seifer, pp.37–41; Joann Vanek, "Time Spent in Housework," *Scientific American* 231 (November 1974): 116–20.

23. Robert Noel Whitehurst, "Employed Mothers' Influences on Working-Class Family Structure" (Ph.D. Diss., Purdue University, 1963); Howard Hayghe, "Families and the Rise of Working Wives —An Overview," *Monthly Labor Review* 99 (May 1976): 12–19; Seifer, pp.16–18, 50–55; Jean Catherine Darian, "Labor Force Participation of Married Women in the United States: An Investigation of the Role of Occupation" (Ph.D. Diss., University of Pennsylvania,

1972); Harold Feldman and Margaret Feldman, "Preferences by Low-income Women about Day Care," *Human Ecology Forum* 4 (Autumn 1973): 16–18.

24. Edwin Russell Coover, "Status and Role Change Among Women in the United States, 1940–1970: A Quantitative Approach" (Ph.D. Diss., University of Minnesota, 1973); Harold Sheppard and Neal Q. Herrick, *Where Have All the Robots Gone?* (New York: The Free Press, 1972); U. S. Department of Labor, Employment Standards Administration, Women's Bureau, "Highlights of Women's Employment and Education," June 1974; *Statistical Portrait,* p.21.

25. Seifer, pp.50–55; Douglas W. Bray, "The Assessment Center Opportunities for Women," *Personnel* 48 (September–October 1971): 30–34; U. S. Department of Labor, Employment Standards Administration, Women's Bureau, "Steps in Opening the Skilled Trades to Women," 1974; Norma Briggs, "Women Apprentices: Removing the Barriers," *Manpower* 1 (December 1974): 3–11; Better Jobs for Women, Denver, Colorado; Women in Apprenticeship, Madison, Wisconsin; Women and Girls Employment Enabling Services (WAGES), Memphis, Tennessee; Female Job Placement Program, Chattanooga, Tennessee; Advocates for Women, San Francisco, California; Apprenticeship Outreach Program for Women, Manpower Administration.

26. Seifer, pp.32–35; Pamela Roby, ed., *Child Care—Who Cares? Foreign and Domestic Infant and Early Childhood Development Policies* (New York: Basic Books, 1973).

27. Groves letters, Archives of Labor History and Urban Affairs, Wayne State University, 19 November 1968.

28. Seifer, pp.12–13; Rainwater et al., pp.44–66; Howell, pp.263–352; Levison, "Changing World," pp.20–21; Arthur B. Shostak, *Blue Collar Life* (New York: Random House, 1966), pp.30–194; Richard Sennett and Jonathan Cobb, *Hidden Injuries of Class* (New York: Vintage Books, 1972), pp.7, 75, 158; Patricia Cayo Sexton, "Speaking for the Working-Class Wife," *Harper's Magazine* 225 (October 1962): 129–33; Lee Rainwater, "Making the Good Life: Working-Class Family and Life-Styles," in Levitan, pp.204–29.

29. Seifer, pp.15, 22, 25; Irving Levine and Judith Herman, *The Life of White Ethnics: Toward More Effective Class Strategies* (New York: Institute on Human Relations, 1972); Stanley Feldstein and Lawrence Costello (eds.), *The Ordeal of Assimilation: A Documentary History of the White Working Class* (New York: Doubleday/Anchor, 1974); Mary Wills, "The Waitress," in Lasson, pp.181–206.

30. Margaret Benston, "The Political Economy of Women's Liberation," *Monthly Review,* September 1969; Seifer, pp.1, 3; "Changing World," pp.27–30, 34–37; Victoria Samuels, "Nowhere to Be Found: A Literature Review and Annotated Bibliography on White Working Class Women," Working Paper Series No. 13 (New York: American Jewish Committee, Institute on Pluralism and Group Identity, Project on Group Life and Ethnic America, 1975), pp.1–3.

31. Samuels, pp.8–9; Seifer, pp.56–62; "Changing World," pp.5–13, 31–33, 39–44; Susan Jacoby, "What Do I Do for the Next Twenty Years?" *New York Times Magazine,* 17 June 1973; "Sexism and Racism: Feminist Perspectives," *Civil Rights Digest* 6 (Spring 1974); Barbara Peters and Victoria Samuels (eds.), "Dialogue on Diversity: A New Agenda for American Women" (New York: Institute on Pluralism and Group Identity of the American Jewish Committee, 1976).

32. *Statistical Portrait,* p.10; Bennett Berger, *Working-Class Suburb: A Study of Auto Workers in Suburbia* (Berkeley and Los Angeles: University of California Press, 1960); Irving Levine and Judith Herman, "Search for Identity in Blue Collar America," *Civil Rights Digest* 4 (Winter 1972); "Changing World," p.21.

33. Komarovsky, pp.323–24; Rainwater et al., pp.114–25; Howell, p.6.

34. Seifer, pp.6–8, 18–25; "Here Come the Ethnics," *Newsweek,* 3 April 1972, p.86; "Changing World," pp.5, 9, 12; Studs Terkel, "The Challenge of Being the Woman in One of America's Scorned Families," *Today's Health,* February 1972, pp.49–53, 72; Kathleen McCourt, *Working-Class Women and Grass-Roots Politics* (Bloomington: Indiana University Press, 1977).

12. Contemporary Beginnings of Awareness

1. Nancy Seifer, "Barbara Mikulski and the Blue Collar Woman," *MS Magazine* 3 (November 1973): 70–74, 108.

2. National Center for Urban Ethnic Affairs, reprints.

3. National Congress of Neighborhood Women, newsletters.

4. Joyce Maupin, "Working Women and Their Organizations—150 Years of Struggle" (Berkeley: Union Wage, 1974), pp.26–30.

5. Olga Madar papers, Archives of Labor History and Urban Affairs, Wayne State University.

6. Lee Rainwater, Richard P. Coleman, and Gerald Hanley, *Workingman's Wife: Her Personality, World, and Life Style* (New York: Oceana Publications, Inc., 1959).

7. Social Research, Inc., "Working-Class Women in a Changing World: A Review of Research Findings" (New York: MacFadden-Bartell Corporation, 1973).

8. Victoria Samuels, "Nowhere to Be Found: A Literature Review and Annotated Bibliography on White Working Class Women," Working Paper Series No. 13 (New York: American Jewish Committee, Institute on Pluralism and Group Identity, Project on Group Life and Ethnic America, 1975), pp.10–12; Nancy S. Tedesco, "Patterns in Prime Time," *Journal of Communications,* Spring 1974, p.120.

9. For example, William H. Form, *Man, Work, and Society: A Reader in the Sociology of Occupations* (New York: Basic Books, 1962); Peter L. Berger, *The Human Shape of Work: Studies in the Sociology of Occupations* (New York: The Macmillan Company, 1964); Arthur B. Shostak and William Gomberg, eds., *Blue Collar World* (Englewood Cliffs, N.J.: Prentice-Hall, Publishers, Inc., 1964); Eli Ginzberg and H. Berman, *The American Worker in the Twentieth Century* (New York: Free Press, 1963).

10. For example, Jessie Bernard, *Academic Women* (University Park, Pa.: Pennsylvania State University, 1964); Cynthia Fuchs Epstein, *Woman's Place: Options and Limits in Professional Careers* (Berkeley: University of California Press, 1970); Margaret Cussler, *The Woman Executive* (New York: Harcourt, Brace, 1958); Amital Etzioni, ed., *The Semi-Professions and Their Organization: Teachers, Nurses, Social Workers* (New York: The Free Press, 1969).

11. Wertheimer and Nelson, *Trade Union Women: A Study of Their Participation in New York City Locals* (New York: Praeger Publishers, 1975); Connie Kopelov (ed.), "Proceedings, First New York Trade Union Women's Conference, January 19, 1974" (New York: New York State School for Industrial and Labor Relations, Cornell University, 1974).

12. Seifer, "Absent from the Majority: Working Class Women in America" (New York: National Project on Ethnic America, National Jewish Committee, 1973).

13. Roby, "The Condition of Women in Blue Collar, Industrial, and Service Jobs: A Review of Research and Proposal for Research, Action, and Policy," draft prepared for Russell Sage Foundation's Social Science Frontiers Publication Series, September 1974.

14. Barbara Peters and Victoria Samuels, eds., "Dialogue on Diversity: A New Agenda for American Women" (New York: Insti-

tute on Pluralism and Group Identity of the American Jewish Committee, 1976).

15. U.S. Department of Labor, Employment Standards Administration, Women's Bureau, "The Women's Bureau: Its Roles and Goals," October 1974.

16. "What Next for U.S. Women," *Time,* 5 December 1977, pp.19–26; "Women March on Houston," *Time,* 28 November 1977, pp.12–14; *New York Times,* 18–22 November 1977.

Bibliography

Manuscripts

Abbott, Edith and Grace. University of Chicago.

Addams, Jane. Sophia Smith Collection, Smith College.

American Association for Labor Legislation. Labor-Management Documentation Center, New York State School of Industrial and Labor Relations, Cornell University.

American Labor Education Service. Labor-Management Documentation Center, New York State School of Industrial and Labor Relations, Cornell University.

Anderson, Mary. Arthur and Elizabeth Schlesinger Library on the History of Women in America, Radcliffe College.

Ballard, Russell Ward. University of Illinois at Chicago Circle.

Barrett, Kate Waller. Library of Congress.

Beasley, Olive. Archives of Labor History and Urban Affairs, Wayne State University.

Beffel, John. Archives of Labor History and Urban Affairs, Wayne State University.

Benton House. Chicago Historical Society.

Beyer, Clara Mortenson. Arthur and Elizabeth Schlesinger Library on the History of Women in America, Radcliffe College.

Bishop, Dorothy Hubbard. Archives of Labor History and Urban Affairs, Wayne State University.

Blankenhorn, Ann Washington Craton. Archives of Labor History and Urban Affairs, Wayne State University.

Boltwood Family. Burton Historical Collections, Detroit Public Library.

Bowen, Louise Hadduck de Koven. Chicago Historical Society.

Breckinridge, Sophonisba P. Library of Congress.

Brewer, Grace D. Archives of Labor History and Urban Affairs, Wayne State University.

Brotherhood of Sleeping Car Porters, International Ladies Auxiliary. Chicago Historical Society.

Brown, Dorothy Kirchwey. Arthur and Elizabeth Schlesinger Library on the History of Women in America, Radcliffe College.

Catholic Council on Working Life. Chicago Historical Society.
Chapin Hall for Children. Chicago Historical Society.
Chicago Commons. Chicago Historical Society.
Chicago Exchange for Woman's Work. Chicago Historical Society.
Chicago Federation of Labor. Chicago Historical Society, in papers of Victor Olander and John Fitzpatrick.
Chicago Woman's Aid. University of Illinois at Chicago Circle.
Christopher House. Chicago Historical Society.
Cigar Makers Union No. 130, Saginaw, Michigan. Archives of Labor History and Urban Affairs, Wayne State University.
Cohn, Fannia. New York Public Library, Manuscript Division, Annex.
Collier, Phyllis. Archives of Labor History and Urban Affairs, Wayne State University.
Columbia Religious and Industrial School for Jewish Girls. American Jewish Historical Society.
Connelly, Polly. Chicago Historical Society.
Consumers' League of Connecticut. Arthur and Elizabeth Schlesinger Library on the History of Women in America, Radcliffe College.
Consumers' League of Massachusetts. Arthur and Elizabeth Schlesinger Library on the History of Women in America, Radcliffe College.
Consumers' League of New York. Labor-Management Documentation Center, New York State School of Industrial and Labor Relations, Cornell University.
Cooke, Flora Juliette. Chicago Historical Society.
Denison House. Arthur and Elizabeth Schlesinger Library on the History of Women in America, Radcliffe College.
Dewson, Mary W. Arthur and Elizabeth Schlesinger Library on the History of Women in America, Radcliffe College.
Diekmann, Annetta. University of Illinois at Chicago Circle.
Edelman, John. Archives of Labor History and Urban Affairs, Wayne State University.
Edwards, Thyra. Chicago Historical Society.
Ellickson, Katherine Pollack. Archives of Labor History and Urban Affairs, Wayne State University.
Emerson House. Chicago Historical Society.
Erie Neighborhood House. Chicago Historical Society.
Flynn, Elizabeth Gurley. Archives of Labor History and Urban Affairs, Wayne State University.

Frankfurter, Felix. Library of Congress.

Friendship House. Chicago Historical Society.

Gads Hill Center. Chicago Historical Society.

German Aid Society, Chicago. University of Illinois at Chicago Circle.

Gibson, Margaret Purdy. John M. Olin Library, Cornell University.

Gilman, Charlotte Perkins. Arthur and Elizabeth Schlesinger Library on the History of Women in America, Radcliffe College.

Goldmark Family. Arthur and Elizabeth Schlesinger Library on the History of Women in America, Radcliffe College.

Goldstein, Jonah J. American Jewish Historical Society.

Groves, Phyllis. Archives of Labor History and Urban Affairs, Wayne State University.

Hamilton, Alice. Arthur and Elizabeth Schlesinger Library on the History of Women in America, Radcliffe College.

Henrotin, Ellen Martin. Arthur and Elizabeth Schlesinger Library on the History of Women in America, Radcliffe College.

Herrick, Elinore Morehouse. Arthur and Elizabeth Schlesinger Library on the History of Women in America, Radcliffe College.

Herstein, Lillian. Chicago Historical Society.

Hull House Association. Jane Addams' Hull House.

Illinois Humane Society. University of Illinois at Chicago Circle.

Immigrants' Protective League. University of Illinois at Chicago Circle.

Industrial Workers of the World. Archives of Labor History and Urban Affairs, Wayne State University.

International Federation of Working Women. Arthur and Elizabeth Schlesinger Library on the History of Women in America, Radcliffe College.

International Typographical Union, Local 6, New York. New York Public Library, Manuscript Division.

Italian Welfare Council. Chicago Historical Society.

Jewish Community Centers of Chicago. Chicago Historical Society.

Johnson, Ethel M. Arthur and Elizabeth Schlesinger Library on the History of Women in America, Radcliffe College.

Kadish, Jack. Archives of Labor History and Urban Affairs, Wayne State University.

Kohn, Esther Loeb. University of Illinois at Chicago Circle.

Lauck, W. Jett. Special Collections, Alderman Library, University of Virginia.

League of Women Voters of the United States. Library of Congress.

Lens, Sidney. Chicago Historical Society.
Leopold, Alice Koller. Arthur and Elizabeth Schlesinger Library on the History of Women in America, Radcliffe College.
McDowell, Mary Eliza. Chicago Historical Society.
Madar, Olga. Archives of Labor History and Urban Affairs, Wayne State University.
Marillac House. Chicago Historical Society.
Mencken, Alice Davis. American Jewish Historical Society.
Miller, Frieda Segelke. Arthur and Elizabeth Schlesinger Library on the History of Women in America, Radcliffe College.
Mitchell, John. Catholic University of America.
Moore, Ruth. Chicago Historical Society.
Morgan, Thomas J. University of Chicago.
Nathan, Maud. Arthur and Elizabeth Schlesinger Library on the History of Women in America, Radcliffe College.
National Consumers' League. Library of Congress.
National Women's Trade Union League of America. Library of Congress; Arthur and Elizabeth Schlesinger Library on the History of Women in America, Radcliffe College; Sophia Smith Collection, Smith College.
Nestor, Agnes. Chicago Historical Society.
Olivet Community Center. Chicago Historical Society.
Onward Neighborhood House. University of Illinois at Chicago Circle.
O'Reilly, Leonora. Arthur and Elizabeth Schlesinger Library on the History of Women in America, Radcliffe College.
Parkway Community House. Chicago Historical Society.
Paulson, Eveline Belden. University of Illinois at Chicago Circle.
Pemberton Mills Relief Committee, Lawrence, Massachusetts. Merrimack Valley Textile Museum.
Perkins, Frances. Columbia University.
Pesotta, Rose. New York Public Library.
Pinchot, Cornelia Elizabeth Bryce. Library of Congress.
Planned Parenthood Federation of America. Library of Congress; Sophia Smith Collection, Smith College.
Powderly, Terence William. Catholic University of America.
President's Commission on the Status of Women. Arthur and Elizabeth Schlesinger Library on the History of Women in America, Radcliffe College.
Rich, Adena Miller. Jane Addams' Hull House.
Rich, Charles and Albina. The Newberry Library.

Richmond, Mary. Columbia University.

Robbins, Matilda Rabinowitz. Archives of Labor History and Urban Affairs, Wayne State University.

Robinson, Harriet Jane Hansen. Arthur and Elizabeth Schlesinger Library on the History of Women in America, Radcliffe College.

Rose, Florence. Sophia Smith Collection, Smith College.

Rutland Corner House. Arthur and Elizabeth Schlesinger Library on the History of Women in America, Radcliffe College.

Sanger, Margaret Higgins. Library of Congress; Sophia Smith Collection, Smith College.

C. G. Sargents Sons, Graniteville, Massachusetts. Merrimack Valley Textile Museum.

Schneider, Anna Weinstock. Labor-Management Documentation Center, New York State School for Industrial and Labor Relations, Cornell University.

Schneiderman, Rose. Tamiment Library, New York University.

Sherwood, Lillian. Archives of Labor History and Urban Affairs, Wayne State University.

Simkovich, Mary Kingsbury. Arthur and Elizabeth Schlesinger Library on the History of Women in America, Radcliffe College.

Smith, Hattie H. Arthur and Elizabeth Schlesinger Library on the History of Women in America, Radcliffe College.

Smith, Hilda Worthington. Arthur and Elizabeth Schlesinger Library on the History of Women in America, Radcliffe College.

Smith, Margaret N. Arthur and Elizabeth Schlesinger Library on the History of Women in America, Radcliffe College.

Starr, Ellen Gates. Sophia Smith Collection, Smith College.

Starr, Mark and Helen. Archives of Labor History and Urban Affairs, Wayne State University.

Stevens Mills, North Andover, Massachusetts. Merrimack Valley Textile Museum.

Swiss Benevolent Society of Chicago. University of Illinois at Chicago Circle.

Taylor, Lea Demarest. Chicago Historical Society; University of Illinois at Chicago Circle.

Travelers Aid Society of Chicago. University of Illinois at Chicago Circle.

United Auto Workers. Archives of Labor History and Urban Affairs, Wayne State University.

United Charities of Chicago. Chicago Historical Society.

United States Department of Labor, Women's Bureau. National Archives, Record Group 86.

Van Kleeck, Mary. Archives of Labor History and Urban Affairs, Wayne State University; Sophia Smith Collection, Smith College.

Visiting Nurse Association of Chicago. Chicago Historical Society.

Vittum, Harriet E. University of Illinois at Chicago Circle.

Vorse, Mary Heaton. Archives of Labor History and Urban Affairs, Wayne State University.

Wagner, Robert F. Georgetown University.

Wald, Lillian. Columbia University; New York Public Library.

Watson, Amy. Labor-Management Documentation Center, New York State School of Industrial and Labor Relations, Cornell University.

Welfare Council of Metropolitan Chicago. Chicago Historical Society.

White, Eva Whiting. Arthur and Elizabeth Schlesinger Library on the History of Women in America, Radcliffe College.

Wiley, Anna Kelton. Library of Congress.

Winslow, Mary E. Arthur and Elizabeth Schlesinger Library on the History of Women in America, Radcliffe College.

Wolf, Herman. Archives of Labor History and Urban Affairs, Wayne State University.

The Women's Educational and Industrial Union. Arthur and Elizabeth Schlesinger Library on the History of Women in America, Radcliffe College.

Women's Trade Union League, Chicago. University of Illinois at Chicago Circle.

Woodward, Ellen S. Arthur and Elizabeth Schlesinger Library on the History of Women in America, Radcliffe College.

Oral Histories

Albrier, Frances. Institute of Labor and Industrial Relations, University of Michigan and Wayne State University.

Bary, Helen Valeska. Bancroft Library, University of California at Berkeley.

Gelles, Catherine. Institute of Labor and Industrial Relations, University of Michigan and Wayne State University.

Herstein, Lillian. Roosevelt University, Chicago.

Morris, Ken. Institute of Labor and Industrial Relations, University of Michigan and Wayne State University.

Oliver, William. Institute of Labor and Industrial Relations, University of Michigan and Wayne State University.

Vess, Raymond. Institute of Labor and Industrial Relations, University of Michigan and Wayne State University.

Books

Abbott, Edith. *Immigration: Select Documents and Case Records.* Chicago: University of Chicago Press, 1924.

———. *Women in Industry: A Study in American Economic History.* New York: D. Appleton and Co., 1910.

———. *The Tenements of Chicago, 1908–1935.* Chicago: University of Chicago Press, 1936.

Abbott, Grace. *The Immigrant and the Community.* New York: The Century Company, 1917.

———. *Workers on Relief.* New Haven: Yale University Press, 1939.

Addams, Jane. *A New Conscience and an Ancient Evil.* New York: The Macmillan Company, 1913.

Anderson, Mary, and Winslow, Mary N. *Woman at Work.* Minneapolis: University of Minnesota Press, 1951.

Andres, Carol. *Sex and Caste in America.* Englewood Cliffs, N.J.: Prentice-Hall, Publishers, 1971.

Andrews, John B., and Bliss, W. D. P. *History of Women in Trade Unions.* Vol. X of *Report on Conditions of Woman and Child Wage Earners in the United States.* Washington, D.C.: Government Printing Office, 1911.

Anthony, Katherine. *Mothers Who Must Earn.* Russell Sage Foundation, West Side Studies. New York: Survey Associates, 1914.

Anthony, Susan B. II. *Out of the Kitchen—Into the War: Woman's Winning Role in the Nation's Drama.* New York: Stephen Day, Inc., 1943.

Aronowitz, Stanley. *False Promises: The Shaping of American Working Class Consciousness.* New York: McGraw-Hill Book Company, 1973.

Arthur, Julietta K. *Jobs for Women over Thirty-five.* New York: Prentice-Hall, Inc., 1947.

Baetjer, Anna M. *Women in Industry: Their Health and Efficiency.* Philadelphia: W. B. Saunders Company, 1946.

Baker, Elizabeth Faulkner. *Protective Labor Legislation.* Columbia

Studies in History, Economics, and Public Law, vol. CXVI, pp.201–667. New York: Columbia University Press, 1925.

———. *Technology and Woman's Work.* New York: Columbia University Press, 1964.

Banning, Margaret Culkin. *Women for Defense.* New York: Duell, Sloan & Pearce, 1942.

Barrett, Kate Waller. *Some Practical Suggestions on the Conduct of a Rescue Home.* Washington, D.C.: National Florence Crittenton Mission, 1903.

Baum, Charlotte; Hyman, Paula; and Michel, Sonya. *The Jewish Woman in America.* New York: The Dial Press, 1976.

Baxandall, Rosalyn; Gordon, Linda; and Reverby, Susan (eds.). *America's Working Woman.* New York: Random House, 1976.

Beard, Mary R. *On Understanding Women.* New York: Grosset & Dunlap, Publishers, 1931.

Berger, Bennett. *Working-Class Suburb: A Study of Auto Workers in Suburbia.* Berkeley and Los Angeles: University of California Press, 1960.

Bird, Caroline, with Briller, Sara Welles. *Born Female: The High Cost of Keeping Women Down.* New York: David McCay Company, Inc., 1968, 1970.

———. *Everything a Woman Needs to Know to Get Paid What She's Worth.* Edited by Helene Mandelbaum. New York: David McKay Company, Inc., 1973.

Blicksilver, Jack. *Cotton Manufacturing in the Southeast: An Historical Analysis.* Atlanta, Ga.: Bureau of Business and Economic Research, School of Business Administration, Georgia State College of Business Administration, 1959.

Bloor, Ella R. *We Are Many: An Autobiography.* New York: International Publishers, 1940.

Blumberg, Dorothy Rose. *Florence Kelley: The Making of a Social Pioneer.* New York: Augustus M. Kelley, Publishers, 1966.

Blumenthal, Walter Hart. *Brides from Bridewell: Female Felons Sent to Colonial America.* Rutland, Vermont: Charles Tuttle Co., Inc., 1962.

———. *Women Camp Followers of the American Revolution.* Philadelphia: George S. McManus Company, 1952. New York: Arno Press, 1974.

Boone, Gladys. *The Women's Trade Union Leagues in Great Britain and the United States of America.* New York: Columbia University Press, 1942.

Brameld, Theodore, ed. *Workers' Education in the United States.* New York and London: Harper and Brothers Publishers, 1941.

Brandeis, Louis D., and Goldmark, Josephine. *The Case Against Nightwork for Women; The People of the State of New York, Respondent, against Charles Schweinler Press, a Corporation, Defendant-Appellant; Summary of "Facts of Knowledge" submitted on Behalf of the People.* [1914] New York: National Consumers League [1918].

―――. *Women in Industry: Decision of the United States Supreme Court in Curt Muller vs. State of Oregon Upholding the Constitutionality of the Oregon Ten Hour Law for Women and Brief for the State of Oregon.* New York: Reprinted for the National Consumers' League, 1908.

Brissenden, Paul. *Earnings of Factory Workers, 1899–1927: An Analysis of Pay-Roll Statistics.* Washington, D.C.: Government Printing Office, 1929.

Brownlee, W. Eliot, and Brownlee, Mary M. *Women in the American Economy: A Documentary History, 1675–1929.* New Haven: Yale University Press, 1976.

Bryner, Edna. *Dressmaking and Millinery.* Cleveland: The Survey Committee of the Cleveland Foundation, 1916.

Budish, Jacob M., and Soule, George. *The New Unionism in the Clothing Industry.* New York: Harcourt, Brace & Howe, 1920.

Butler, Elizabeth Beardsley. *Saleswomen in Mercantile Stores: Baltimore, 1909.* New York: Russell Sage Foundation, Survey Association, Inc., 1912.

―――. *Women and the Trades: Pittsburgh, 1907–1908.* New York: Charities Publication Committee, 1909.

Campbell, Helen. *Prisoners of Poverty: Women Wage-Workers, Their Trades and Their Lives.* Boston: Robert Brothers, 1887.

―――. *Women Wage-Earners: Their Past, Their Present, and Their Future.* Boston: Robert Brothers, 1893.

Cantor, Milton, and Laurie, Bruce, eds. *Class, Sex, and the Woman Worker.* Westport, Conn.: Greenwood Press, Inc., 1977.

Carola Woerishoffer Graduate Department of Social Economy and Social Research. *Women During the War and After: Summary of a Comprehensive Study.* Bryn Mawr: Bryn Mawr College, 1945.

Carola Woerishoffer: Her Life and Work. Bryn Mawr: Bryn Mawr College, Class of 1907, 1912.

Carsel, Wilfred. *A History of the Chicago Ladies' Garment Workers' Union.* Chicago: Normandie House, 1940.

Carter, Jean, and Smith, Hilda W. *Education and the Worker-Student: A Book about Workers' Education Based upon the Experience of Teachers and Students.* New York: Affiliated Schools for Workers, Inc., 1934.

Cassara, Beverly Benner. *American Women: The Changing Image.* Boston: Beacon Press, 1963.

Cavalleri, Rosa. *Rosa: The Life of an Italian Immigrant.* Edited by Marie Hall Ets. Minneapolis: University of Minnesota Press, 1970.

Chafe, William H. *The American Woman: Her Changing Social, Economic, and Political Role, 1920–1970.* New York: Oxford University Press, 1972.

———. *Women and Equality: Changing Patterns in American Culture.* New York: Oxford University Press, 1977.

Chamberlain, Neil H; Pierson, Frank C.; and Wolfson, Theresa. *A Decade of Industrial Relations Research, 1946–1956.* New York: Harper, 1958.

Chambers, Clarke A. *Seedtime of Reform: American Social Service and Social Action, 1918–1933.* Minneapolis: University of Minnesota Press, 1963.

Clark, Alice. *Working Life of Women in the Seventeenth Century.* New York: E. P. Dutton & Co., 1919.

Clark, Sue Ainslie, and Wyatt, Edith. *Making Both Ends Meet: The Income and Outlay of New York Working Girls.* New York: The Macmillan Company, 1911.

Clawson, Augusta H. *Shipyard Diary of a Woman Welder.* New York: Penguin, 1944.

Clinebell, Charlotte Holt. *Meet Me in the Middle: On Becoming Human Together.* New York: Harper and Row, Publishers, 1973.

Commons, John R., et al. *History of Labor in the United States.* 4 vols. New York: The Macmillan Company, 1921–1935.

Cott, Nancy F., ed. *Roots of Bitterness: Documents of the Social History of American Woman.* New York: E. P. Dutton & Co., 1972.

Cross, Susan Deller. *The Rights of Women: The Basic ACLU Guide to Woman's Rights.* New York: Avon Books, 1973.

Delzell, Ruth. *The Early History of Women Trade Unionists in America.* Chicago: National Women's Trade Union League of America, 1919.

Demos, John. *A Little Commonwealth: Family Life in Plymouth Colony.* New York: Oxford University Press, 1970.

Dodge, Grace H. *A Bundle of Letters to Busy Girls on Practical Matters.* New York: Funk & Wagnalls, 1887.

———, ed. *Thoughts of Busy Girls.* New York: Cassell Publishing Co., 1892.

Donovan, Frances R. *The Saleslady.* Chicago: University of Chicago Press, 1929.

———. *The Woman Who Waits.* Boston: Richard G. Bader, The Gorham Press, 1920.

Dreier, Mary E. *Margaret Dreier Robins: Her Life, Letters, and Work.* New York: Island Press Cooperative, Inc., 1950.

Feldstein, Stanley, and Costello, Lawrence. *The Ordeal of Assimilation: A Documentary History of the White Working Class.* Garden City, N.Y.: Anchor Press/Doubleday, 1974.

Ferriss, Abbott L. *Indicators of Trends in the Status of American Women.* New York: Russell Sage Foundation, 1971.

Fetherling, Dale. *Mother Jones, the Miners' Angel: A Portrait.* Carbondale and Edwardsville: Southern Illinois University Press, 1974.

Filene, Catherine, ed. *Careers for Women: New Ideas, New Methods, New Opportunities to Fit a New World.* Boston: Houghton Mifflin Company, n.d.

Filley, Jane, and Mitchell, Therese. *Consider the Laundry Workers.* New York: League of Women Shoppers, Inc., 1937.

Flexner, Eleanor. *Century of Struggle: The Women's Rights Movement in the United States.* Cambridge, Mass.: Harvard University Press, 1959.

Flynn, Elizabeth Gurley. *I Speak My Own Piece: Autobiography of "The Rebel Girl."* New York: Masses and Mainstream, 1955.

———. *The Rebel Girl, An Autobiography: My First Life (1906–1926).* New York: International Publishers, 1973.

Foner, Philip S. *History of the Labor Movement in the United States.* Vol. IV: *The Industrial Workers of the World, 1905–1917.* New York: International Publishers, 1965.

Foster, Colin, and Tucker, G. S. L. *Economic Opportunity and White American Fertility Ratios, 1800–1860.* New Haven: Yale University Press, 1972.

Garson, Barbara. *All the Livelong Day: The Meaning and Demeaning of Routine Work.* Garden City, N.Y.: Doubleday and Company, Inc., 1975.

Ginzberg, Eli, and Berman, Hyman. *The American Worker in the Twentieth Century: A History through Autobiographies.* New York: The Free Press, 1963.

Glanz, Rudolf. *The Jewish Woman in America: Two Female Immi-*

grant Generations, 1820–1929. Vol. I: *The Eastern European Jewish Woman.* New York: Ktav Publishing House and National Council of Jewish Women, 1976.

Goldmark, Josephine. *Fatigue and Efficiency: A Study in Industry.* New York: Russell Sage Foundation, Survey Associates, 1912.

———. *Impatient Crusader: Florence Kelley's Life Story.* Urbana: University of Illinois Press, 1953.

Gregory, Chester W. *Women in Defense Work During World War II: An Analysis of the Labor Problem and Women's Rights.* New York: Exposition Press, 1974.

Gutman, Herbert G. *Work, Culture, and Society in Industrializing America: Essays in American Working-Class and Social History.* New York: Alfred A. Knopf, 1976.

Hatcher, Orie Latham. *Rural Girls in the City for Work: A Study made For the Southern Woman's Education Alliance.* Richmond: Garrett and Massie, Inc., Publishers, 1930.

Henry, Alice. *The Trade Union Woman.* New York: D. Appleton and Company, 1915.

———. *Women and the Labor Movement.* New York: George H. Doran Company, 1923.

Herron, Belva Mary. *The Progress of Labor Organizations Among Women, Together with Some Considerations Concerning their Place in Industry.* Urbana: University of Illinois Press, 1905.

Hill, Caroline M. *Mary McDowell and Municipal Housekeeping: A Symposium.* Chicago: Millar Publishing Company, n.d.

Hill, Joseph A. *Women in Gainful Occupations, 1870–1920.* Washington, D.C.: Government Printing Office, 1929.

Hourwich, Andria Taylor, and Palmer, Gladys L., eds. *I Am a Woman Worker: A Scrapbook of Autobiographies.* New York: The Affiliated Schools for Workers, Inc., 1936.

Howe, Irving. *World of Our Fathers.* New York: Simon & Schuster, 1976.

———, ed. *The World of the Blue-Collar Worker.* New York: Quadrangle Books, 1972.

Howell, Joseph L. *Hard Living on Clay Street: Portraits of Blue Collar Families.* Garden City, N.Y.: Anchor Press/Doubleday, 1973.

Hughes, Gwendolyn Salisbury. *Mothers in Industry: Wage-Earning by Mothers in Philadelphia.* New York: New Republic, Inc., 1925.

Hutchinson, Emilie J. *Women's Wages: A Study of the Wages of Industrial Women and Measures Suggested to Increase Them.* New York: Columbia University Press, 1919.

Jacobs, Sue-Ellen. *Women in Perspective: A Guide for Cross Cultural Studies.* Urbana: University of Illinois Press, 1974.

Johnsen, Julia E. *Special Legislation for Women.* New York: H. W. Wilson Company, 1926.

Jones, Mary. *Autobiography of Mother Jones.* Chicago: Charles H. Kerr & Co., 1925.

Josephson, Hannah. *The Golden Threads: New England's Mill Girls and Magnates.* New York: Duell, Sloan and Pearce, 1949.

Kennedy, David M. *Birth Control in America: The Career of Margaret Sanger.* New Haven: Yale University Press, 1970.

Kessner, Thomas. *The Golden Door: Italian and Jewish Immigrant Mobility in New York City, 1880–1915.* New York: Oxford University Press, 1977.

Komarovsky, Mirra. *Blue Collar Marriage.* New York: Random House, 1962.

Larcom, Lucy. *A New England Girlhood.* New York: Houghton, Mifflin, 1889.

Lasson, Kenneth. *The Workers: Portraits of Nine American Jobholders.* New York: Grossman Publishers, 1971.

Lattimore, Eleanor L., and Trent, Ray S. *Legal Recognition of Industrial Women.* New York: Industrial Committee of War Work Council of National Board Of YWCA, 1919.

Laughlin, Clara E. *The Work-a-Day Girl: A Study of Some Present-Day Conditions.* New York: Fleming H. Revell Company, 1913. Reprint: New York: Arno Press, 1974.

LeMasters, E. E. *Blue-Collar Aristocrats: Life-Styles at a Working-Class Tavern.* Madison: University of Wisconsin Press, 1975.

Lemons, J. Stanley. *The Woman Citizen: Social Feminism in the 1920s.* Urbana: University of Illinois Press, 1973.

Lerner, Gerda. *The Woman in American History.* Reading, Mass.: Addison-Wesley Publishing Company, 1971.

———, ed. *The Female Experience: An American Documentary.* Indianapolis: Bobbs-Merrill Company, 1977.

Levison, Andrew. *The Working-Class Majority.* New York: Coward, McCann & Geoghegan, 1974.

Levitan, Sar A., ed. *Blue-Collar Workers: A Symposium on Middle America.* New York: McGraw-Hill, 1971.

———, and Johnston, William B. *Work Is Here To Stay. Alas.* Salt Lake City: Olympus Publishing Co., 1973.

Linden, Fabian, and Axel, Helen. *Women: A Demographic, Social, and Economic Presentation.* New York: The Conference Board, 1973.

Little, Frances. *Early American Textiles.* New York: Century Co., 1931.

Lobsenz, Johanna. *The Older Woman in Industry.* New York: Charles Scribner's Sons, 1929.

Long, Clarence D. *Wages and Earnings in the United States: 1860–1890.* Princeton: Princeton University Press, 1960.

Long, Priscilla. *Mother Jones, Woman Organizer.* Cambridge, Mass.: Red Sun Press, 1976.

Lyle, Jerolyn R., and Ross, Jane L. *Women in Industry: Employment Patterns of Women in Corporate America.* Lexington, Mass.: D.C. Heath and Company, 1973.

Lynd, Alice, and Lynd, Staughton. *Rank and File: Personal Histories by Working-Class Organizers.* Boston: Beacon Press, 1973.

McCourt, Kathleen. *Working-Class Women and Grass-Roots Politics.* Bloomington: Indiana University Press, 1977.

MacLean, Annie Marion. *Wage-Earning Women.* New York: The Macmillan Co., 1910.

———. *Women Workers and Society.* Chicago: A. C. McClurg & Co., 1916.

Madden, Janice Fanning. *The Economics of Sex Discrimination.* Lexington, Mass.: D. C. Heath and Company, 1973.

Marot, Helen. *American Labor Unions.* New York: Holt & Co., 1914.

Matthews, Lillian R. *Women in Trade Unions in San Francisco.* Berkeley: University of California Press, 1913.

Metzger, Isaac, ed. *A Bintel Brief: Sixty Years of Letters from the Lower East Side to the Jewish Daily Forward.* Garden City, N.Y.: Doubleday & Co., 1971.

Meyer, Annie Nathan, ed. *Woman's Work in America.* New York: H. Holt & Co. 1891.

Morris, Richard. *Government and Labor in Early America.* New York: Octagon Books, Farrar, Strauss & Giroux, Inc., 1946.

Myrdal, Alva, and Klein, Viola. *Women's Two Roles: Home and Work.* London: Routledge & Kegan Paul Ltd., 1956, 1968.

Myrdal, Gunnar. *An American Dilemma: The Negro Problem and Modern Democracy.* New York: Harper & Bros., Publishers, 1944.

Naden, Corrine J. *The Triangle Shirtwaist Fire, March 25, 1911: The Blaze that Changed an Industry.* New York: Franklin Watts, 1971.

Nathan, Maud. *Once Upon a Time and Today.* New York: G. P. Putnam's Sons, 1933.

———. *The Story of an Epoch-Making Movement.* Garden City: Doubleday, Page & Co., 1926.

National Manpower Council. *Womanpower.* New York: Columbia University Press, 1957.

Neidle, Cecyle S. *America's Immigrant Women.* Boston: Twayne Publishers, G. K. Hall & Co., 1975.

Nestor, Agnes. *Woman's Labor Leader: An Autobiography.* Rockford, Ill.: Bellevue Books, 1954.

Oates, Mary J. *The Role of the Cotton Textile Industry in the Economic Development of the American Southeast: 1900–1940.* New York: Arno Press, 1975.

Odencrantz, Louise C. *Italian Women in Industry: A Study of Conditions In New York City.* New York: Russell Sage Foundation, 1919.

O'Neill, William L. ed. *Women at Work.* Chicago: Quadrangle Books, 1972.

Oppenheimer, Valerie Kincade. *The Female Labor Force in the United States: Demographic and Economic Factors Governing its Growth and Changing Composition.* Berkeley: University of California Population Monograph Series, no. 3, 1970. Westport, Conn.: Greenwood Press, Publishers, 1976.

Penny, Virginia. *The Employment of Women: A Cyclopaedia of Woman's Work.* Boston: Walker, Wise, and Company, 1863.

Perry, Lorinda. *The Millinery Trade in Boston and Philadelphia: A Study of Women in Industry.* Binghamton, N.Y.: The Vail-Ballou Co., 1916.

Persons, Charles E.; Parton, Mabel; Moses, Mabelle; et al. *Labor Laws and Their Enforcement, with Special Reference to Massachusetts.* Edited by Susan M. Kingsbury. New York: Longmans, Green and Co., 1911.

Pesotta, Rose. *Bread upon the Waters.* Edited by John Nicholas Beffel. New York: Dodd, Mead and Co., 1944.

Pittsburgh Section, National Council of Jewish Women. *By Myself, I'm a Book! An Oral History of the Jewish Immigrant Experience.* Waltham: American Jewish Historical Society, 1972.

Porter, Rev. James. *The Operative's Friend, and Defence: or, Hints to Young Ladies, Who Are Dependent on Their Own Exertions.* Boston: Charles H. Peirce, 1850.

Rainwater, Lee. *And the Poor Get Children: Sex, Contraception, and Family Planning in the Working Class.* Chicago: Quadrangle Books, Inc., 1960.

———; Coleman, Richard P.; and Hanley, Gerald. *Workingman's Wife: Her Personality, World and Life Style.* New York: Oceana Publications, Inc., 1959.

Rhyne, Jennings J. *Some Southern Cotton Mill Workers and Their Villages.* Chapel Hill: University of North Carolina Press, 1930.

Richardson, Dorothy. *The Long Day: The Story of a New York Working Girl.* New York: The Century Company, 1905. Reprinted in *Women at Work,* edited by William L. O'Neill. Chicago: Quadrangle Books, 1972.

Richmond, Mary E., and Hull, Fred S. *A Study of Nine Hundred and Eight-five Widows Known to Certain Charity Organization Societies in 1910.* New York: Charity Organization Department of the Russell Sage Foundation, 1913.

Riegel, Robert E. *American Women: A Story of Social Change.* Rutherford, N.J.: Fairleigh Dickinson University Press, 1970.

Roby, Pamela, ed. *The Poverty Establishment.* Englewood Cliffs, N.J.: Prentice-Hall, Inc., 1974.

Rosenberg, George S., and Anspach, Donald F. *Working Class Kinship.* Lexington, Mass.: D. C. Heath and Company, 1973.

Ross, Heather L., and Sawhill, Isabel V. *Times of Transition: The Growth of Families Headed by Women.* Washington, D.C.: The Urban Institute, 1975.

Ryan, Joseph A., ed. *White Ethnics: Life in Working-Class America.* Englewood Cliffs, N.J.: Prentice-Hall, Inc., 1973.

Ryan, Mary P. *Womanhood in America: From Colonial Times to the Present.* New York: New Viewpoints, Franklin Watts, 1975.

Sanger, Margaret. *Margaret Sanger: An Autobiography.* New York: W. W. Norton & Co., 1938.

Schneider, Florence H. *Patterns of Worker Education: The Story of the Bryn Mawr Summer School.* Washington, D.C.: American Council on Public Affairs, 1941.

Schneiderman, Rose, with Goldthwaite, Lucy. *All for One.* New York: Paul S. Eriksson, Inc., 1967.

Scott, Anne Firor. *The Southern Lady: From Pedestal to Politics, 1830–1930.* Chicago: University of Chicago Press, 1970.

———, ed. *The American Woman: Who Was She?* Englewood Cliffs, N.J.: Prentice-Hall, Publishers, 1971.

Seidman, Joel. *American Labor from Defense to Reconversion.* Chicago: University of Chicago Press, 1953.

Serow, William J., and Martin, Julia H. *Virginia's Population: A*

Decade of Change; The Status of Women. Charlottesville: Tayloe Murphy Institute, University of Virginia [1974].

Simkhovitch, Mary Kingsbury. *The City Worker's World in America.* New York: The Macmillan Co., 1917.

Simmons, Adele, et al. *Exploitation from 9 to 5: Report of the Twentieth Century Fund Task Force on Women and Employment.* New York: Twentieth Century Fund, 1975.

Smith, Page. *Daughters of the Promised Land: Women in American History.* Boston: Little, Brown and Company, 1970.

Smuts, Robert W. *Women and Work in America.* New York: Columbia University Press, 1959.

Somers, Gerald G., ed. *The Next Twenty-five Years of Industrial Relations.* Madison, Wisc.: Industrial Relations Research Association, 1973.

Spruill, Julia Cherry. *Women's Life and Work in the Southern Colonies.* N.P.: University of North Carolina Press, 1938. New York: W. W. Norton & Company, Inc., 1972.

Stein, Leon, ed. *Out of the Sweatshop: The Struggle for Industrial Democracy.* New York: Quadrangle, 1977.

Stevens, George A. *New York Typographical Union No. 6: A Study of a Modern Trade Union and its Predecessors.* Albany: J. B. Lyon Company, 1913.

Sumner, Helen. *History of Women in Industry in the United States.* Vol. IX of *Report on Conditions of Woman and Child Wage-Earners in the United States.* Washington, D.C.: Government Printing Office, 1910–13.

Sweet, James A. *Women in the Labor Force.* New York: Seminar Press, 1973.

Thompson, Roger. *Women in Stuart England and America: A Comparative Study.* Boston: Routledge & Kegan Paul, 1974.

Trotsky, Leon. *Women and the Family.* New York: Pathfinder Press, 1970.

United States President's Commission on the Status of Women. *American Women: The Report of the President's Commission on the Status of Women and other Publications of the Commission.* Edited by Margaret Meade and Francis B. Kaplan. New York: Charles Scribner's Sons, 1965.

Van Kleeck, Mary. *Artificial Flower Makers.* New York: Russell Sage Foundation, Survey Associates, Inc., 1913.

———. *A Seasonal Industry: A Study of the Millinery Trade in New York.* New York: Russell Sage Foundation, 1917.

————. *Women in the Bookbinding Trade.* New York: Russell Sage Foundation, Survey Associates, Inc., 1913.

————. *Working Girls in Evening Schools. A Statistical Study.* New York: Russell Sage Foundation, Survey Associates, Inc., 1914.

Van Vorst, Mrs. John [Bessie], and Van Vorst, Marie. *The Woman Who Toils: Being the Experiences of Two Gentlewomen as Factory Girls.* New York: Doubleday, Page and Company, 1903.

Vorse, Mary Heaton. *Labor's New Millions.* New York: Modern Age Books, 1938.

Ware, Caroline F. *The Early New England Cotton Manufacture: A Study in Industrial Beginnings.* Boston: Houghton, Mifflin, 1934. Reprint. New York: Russell & Russell, 1966.

————. *Labor Education in Universities: A Study of University Programs.* New York: American Labor Education Service, Inc., 1946.

Ware, Norman. *The Industrial Worker, 1840–1860: The Reaction of American Industrial Society to the Advance of the Industrial Revolution.* Boston: Houghton, Mifflin Company, 1924.

Werstein, Irving. *Labor's Defiant Lady: The Story of Mother Jones.* New York: Thomas Y. Crowell Company, 1969.

Wertheimer, Barbara M. *We Were There: The Story of Working Women in America.* New York: Pantheon Books, 1977.

————, and Nelson, Anne H. *Trade Union Women: A Study of Their Participation in New York City Locals.* New York: Praeger Publishers, 1975.

Westin, Jeane. *Making Do: How Women Survived the '30s.* Chicago: Follette Publishing Company, 1976.

Willett, Mabel Hurd. *The Employment of Women in the Clothing Trade.* New York: Columbia University Press, 1902.

Woods, Robert A., and Kennedy, Albert J., eds. *Young Working Girls: A Summary of Evidence from Two Thousand Social Workers.* Boston: National Federation of Settlements, Houghton Mifflin, 1913.

Wright, Carroll D. *The Working Girls of Boston: From the Fifteenth Annual Report of the Massachusetts Bureau of Statistics of Labor for 1884.* Boston: Wright and Potter, 1889.

Zapoleon, Marguerite Wycoff. *Occupational Planning for Women.* New York: Harper & Brothers, Publishers, 1961.

Pamphlets

Bem, Sandra L., and Bem, Daryl J. *Training the Woman to Know Her Place: The Social Antecedents of Women in the World of Work.* Harrisburg: Pennsylvania Department of Education, 1973.

Davis, Rebecca Harding. "Life in the Iron Mills; or the Korl Woman" *Atlantic Monthly,* April 1861. Reprint. New York: The Feminist Press, 1972. (With extensive afternote by Tillie Olsen.)

Kingsbury, Susan M., and Moses, Mabelle. *Licensed Workers in Industrial Home Work in Massachusetts.* Commonwealth of Massachusetts, State Board of Labor and Industry, Industrial Bulletin No. 4. Boston: Wright and Potter, Printing Co., 1915.

La Follette, Cecile Tipton. *A Study of the Problems of 652 Gainfully Employed Married Women Homemakers.* New York: Bureau of Publications, Teachers College, Columbia University, 1934.

Langer, Elinor. "The Women of the Telephone Company." *New York Review of Books,* XIV (March 12 and 16, 1970). Reprinted by New England Free Press. Also reprinted in *Women at Work,* edited by William L. O'Neill (Chicago: Quadrangle Books, 1972).

Mason, Lucy Randolph. *The Shorter Day and Women Workers.* Richmond: Virginia League of Women Voters, 1922.

———. *Standards for Workers in Southern Industry.* N.P.: National Consumers' League, 1931.

Maupin, Joyce. *Labor Heroines: Ten Women Who Led the Struggle.* Berkeley, California: Union WAGE Educational Committee, 1974.

———. *Working Women and their Organizations: 150 Years of Struggle.* Berkeley, Calif.: Union WAGE Educational Committee, 1974.

Robinson, Harriet H. *Early Factory Life in New England.* Boston: Wrights & Potter Printing Co., 1883.

Samuels, Victoria. *Nowhere to be Found: A Literature Review and Annotated Bibliography on White Working Class Women.* Working Paper Series No. 13. New York: American Jewish Committee, Institute on Pluralism and Group Identity, Project on Group Life and Ethnic America, 1975.

Schweitzer, David J. *A Brief Summary of Investigations and Inquiries Made Between the Years of 1905 and 1915 by Government and Private Agencies into typical Industries Prevalent in the State of New York and Affording Work to Large Numbers of Women.* New York: Council of Jewish Women, Department of Immigrant Aid, 1916.

Seifer, Nancy. *Absent from the Majority: Working Class Women in America.* New York: National Project on Ethnic America, National Jewish Committee, 1973.

Social Research, Inc. *Working-Class Women in a Changing World: A Review of Research Findings.* New York: MacFadden-Bartell Corporation, 1973.

Studley, Jeanette. *A Standard Budget for Women Workers in Connecticut.* Hartford: The Consumers' League of Connecticut, 1938.

Van Kleeck, Mary. *Facts about Wage-Earners in the United States Census.* New York: The New York School of Philanthropy, 1915.

————. *Industrial Investigations of the Russell Sage Foundation.* New York: Russell Sage Foundation, Committee on Women's Work, 1915.

Vogel, Lise. *Women Workers: Some Basic Statistics.* Somerville, Mass.: New England Free Press, n.d.

Waugh, Catherine G. *Women's Wages.* Rockford, Ill.: Daily Gazette Book and Job Office, 1888.

Periodicals

American Federationist.
American Journal of Sociology.
Annals of the American Academy of Political and Social Science.
Civil Rights Digest.
Current Opinion.
Feminist Studies.
Journal of Political Economy.
Journal of Women's Work.
Labor History.
Life and Labor.
Lowell Offering.
Monthly Labor Review.
Nation.
New Republic.
Outlook.
Prologue.
Radical America.
Survey.
The Woman Worker.
Selected articles in single issues of other journals, as indicated in footnotes.

Government Documents

Citizens' Advisory Council on the Status of Women. *Women in 1970. 1971. 1972. 1973.* Washington, D.C.: Government Printing Office, 1971, 1972, 1973, 1974.

New York State Factory Investigating Commission, *Fourth Report of the Factory Investigating Commission, 1914.* 5 vols. Transmitted to the Legislature February 15, 1915. Albany: J. B. Lyon Company, 1915.

New York State Factory Investigating Commission. *Preliminary Report of the Factory Investigating Commission, 1912.* Transmitted to the Legislature March 1, 1912. Albany: The Argus Company, 1912.

New York State Factory Investigating Commission. *Second Report of the Factory Investigating Commission, 1913.* Transmitted to the Legislature January 15, 1913. Albany: J.B. Lyon Company, 1913.

New York State Factory Investigating Commission. *Third Report of the Factory Investigating Commission, 1914.* Transmitted to the Legislature February 14, 1914. Albany: J. B. Lyon Company, 1914.

U.S. Bureau of Labor. *Report on Conditions of Woman and Child Wage-Earners in the United States.* 19 vols. Washington, D.C.: Government Printing Office, 1910–13.

U.S. Department of Commerce, Bureau of the Census. *A Statistical Portrait of Women in the United States.* Current Population Reports, Special Studies, Series P-23, No. 58. Washington, D.C.: Government Printing Office, 1976.

U.S. Department of Labor, Women's Bureau. Bulletins 1–293. Washington, D.C.: Government Printing Office, 1919–66.

Theses and Dissertations

Anderson, James Russell. "The New Deal Career of Frances Perkins, Secretary of Labor, 1933–1939." Ph.D. dissertation, Case Western Reserve University, 1968.

Barkey, Frederick Allan. "The Socialist Party in West Virginia from 1898 to 1920 as a Study in Working Class Radicalism." Ph.D. dissertation, University of Pittsburgh, 1971.

Berman, Hyman. "Era of the Protocol: A Chapter in the History of the International Ladies' Garment Workers' Union, 1910–1916." Ph.D. dissertation, Columbia University, 1956.

Bloomberg, Susan Eleanor Hirsch. "Industrialization and Skilled Workers: Newark, 1826 to 1860." Ph.D dissertation, University of Michigan, 1974.

Boulding, Elise Marie Niorn-Hansen. "The Effects of Industrialization on the Participation of Women in Society." Ph.D. dissertation, University of Michigan, 1969.

Brody, Doris Cohen. "American Labor Education Service, 1927–

1962: An Organization in Workers' Education." Ph.D. dissertation, Cornell University, 1973.

Buell, Charles Chauncey. "The Workers of Worcester: Social Mobility and Ethnicity in a New England City, 1850–1880." Ph.D. dissertation, New York University, 1974.

Buhle, Mari Jo. "Feminism and Socialism in the United States, 1830–1920." Ph.D. dissertation, University of Wisconsin, 1974.

Coover, Edwin Russell. "Status and Role Change Among Women in the United States, 1940–1970: A Quantitative Approach." Ph.D. dissertation, University of Minnesota, 1973.

Cumbler, John Taylor. "Continuity and Disruption: Working-Class Community in Lynn and Fall River, Massachusetts, 1880–1950." Ph.D. dissertation, University of Michigan, 1974.

Daly, Sister John Marie. "Mary Anderson, Pioneer Labor Leader." Ph.D. dissertation, Georgetown University, 1968.

Darian, Jean Catherine. "Labor Force Participation of Married Women in the United States: An Investigation of the Role of Occupation." Ph.D. dissertation, University of Pennsylvania, 1972.

Davis, Stephen Robert. "From Plowshares to Spindles: Dedham, Massachusetts, 1790–1840." Ph.D. dissertation, University of Wisconsin, 1973.

Dickinson, Joan Younger. "The Role of the Immigrant Women in the U.S. Labor Force, 1890–1910." Ph.D. dissertation, University of Pennsylvania, 1975.

Dublin, Thomas Louis. "Women at Work: The Transformation of Work and Community in Lowell, Massachusetts, 1826–1860." Ph.D. dissertation, Columbia University, 1975.

Dye, Nancy Schrom. "The Women's Trade Union League of New York, 1903–1920." Ph.D. dissertation, University of Wisconsin–Madison, 1974.

Garfinkle, Stuart H. "Tables of Working Life for Women." Ph.D. dissertation, The American University, 1958.

Garlock, Jonathan Ezra. "A Structural Analysis of the Knights of Labor: A Prolegomenon to the History of the Producing Classes." Ph.D. dissertation, University of Rochester, 1974.

Gregory, Chester Woodrow. "The Problem of Labor During World War II: The Employment of Women in Defense Production." Ph.D. dissertation, The Ohio State University, 1969.

Hodges, James Andrew. "The New Deal Labor Policy and the Southern Cotton Textile Industry, 1933–1941." Ph.D. dissertation, Vanderbilt University, 1963.

Howe, Frances Hovey. "Leonora O'Reilly, Socialist and Reformer, 1870–1927." Honors thesis, Radcliffe College, 1952.

Jensen, Harry A. A. "Blue Island, Illinois: The History of a Working Class Suburb." Ph.D. dissertation, University of Cincinnati, 1971.

Kleinberg, Susan J. "Technology's Stepdaughters, the Impact of Industrialization upon Working Class Women, Pittsburgh, 1865–1890."Ph.D. dissertation, University of Pittsburgh, 1973.

Krivy, Leonard Philip. "American Organized Labor and the First World War, 1917–1918: A History of Labor Problems and the Development of a Government War Labor Program." Ph.D. dissertation, New York University, 1965.

Kugler, Israel. "The Woman's Rights Movement and the National Labor Union (1866–1872): What Was the Nature of the Relationships between the National Labor Union and the Woman's Rights Movement and What May Serve to Explain Periods of Cooperation and Subsequent Divergence?" Ph.D. dissertation, New York University, 1954.

Laurie, Bruce Gordon. "The Working People of Philadelphia, 1827–1853." Ph.D. dissertation, University of Pittsburgh, 1971.

Lieberman, Jacob Andrew. "Their Sisters' Keepers: The Women's Hours and Wages Movement in the United States, 1890–1925." Ph.D. dissertation, Columbia University, 1971.

McElvaine, Robert Stuart. "Thunder without Lightning: Working Class Discontent in the United States, 1929–1937." Ph.D. dissertation, State University of New York at Binghamton, 1974.

McLaurin, Melton Alonzo. "The Southern Cotton Textile Operative and Organized Labor, 1880–1905." Ph.D. dissertation, University of South Carolina, 1967.

McMahon, Theresa Schmidt. "Women and Economic Evolution, or The Effects of Industrial Changes upon the Status of Women." Ph.D. dissertation, University of Wisconsin, 1908.

Mattis, Mary Catherine. "The Irish Family in Buffalo, New York, 1855–1875: A Socio-Historical Analysis." Ph.D. dissertation, Washington University, 1975.

Pernicone, Carol Groneman. " 'The Bloody Ould Sixth': A Social Analysis of a New York City Working-class Community in the Mid-nineteenth Century." Ph.D. dissertation, University of Rochester, 1973.

Reznick, Allan Edward. "Lillian D. Wald: The Years at Henry Street." Ph.D. dissertation, University of Wisconsin, 1973.

Sayin, Afife Fevzi. "Industrial Home Work in Pennsylvania: A Study of the Home Work System in the Knitted Outerwear and the Women's Apparel Industries." Ph.D. dissertation, Bryn Mawr College, 1945.

Shlakman, Vera. "Economic History of a Factory Town: A Study of Chicopee, Massachusetts." Smith College Studies in History, vol. 20, no. 1, 1935.

Straub, Eleanor Ferguson. "Government Policy Toward Civilian Women during World War II." Ph.D. dissertation, Emory University, 1973.

Sweet, James Arthur. "Family Composition and the Labor Force Activity of Married Women in the United States." Ph.D. dissertation, University of Michigan, 1968.

Toporoff, Ralph. "Generating Role Types Concerning the Occupational Participation of Women in the Twentieth Century." Ph.D. dissertation, Washington State University, 1972.

Van Osdell, John Garrett, Jr. "Cotton Mills, Labor, and the Southern Mind." Ph.D. dissertation, Tulane University, 1966.

Walkowitz, Daniel Jay. "Working Class Culture in the Gilded Age: The Iron Workers of Troy, New York, and the Cotton Workers of Cohoes, New York—1855–1884." Ph.D. dissertation, University of Rochester, 1972.

Weil, Mildred Wishnatt. "A Study of the Factors Affecting the Role and Role Expectations of Women Participating or Planning to Participate in the Labor Force." Ph.D. dissertation, New York University, 1959.

Whitehurst, Robert Noel. "Employed Mother's Influences on Working-Class Family Structure." Ph.D. dissertation, Purdue University, 1963.

Unpublished Papers

Blewett, Mary. "The 'Newer Woman' and Trade Unionism: Haverhill, Massachusetts and the Formation of the Boot and Shoe Workers' Union, 1895." Third Berkshire Conference on History of Women. Bryn Mawr College, 11 June 1976.

Buhle, Mari Jo. "Socialist Women and Class Organization, 1900–1920." Conference on Class and Ethnicity in Women's History, SUNY-Binghamton, 22 September 1976.

Dubnoff, Stephen. "Mill Women of Lowell, Massachusetts in the 1860s." Third Berkshire Conference on the History of Women, Bryn Mawr College, 11 June 1976.

Dye, Nancy Schrom. "Creating a Feminist Alliance: 'Sisterhood' and Class Conflict in the New York Women's Trade Union League, 1903–1914." Conference on Class and Ethnicity in Women's History, SUNY-Binghamton, 22 September 1974.

Groneman, Carol. "She Earns as a Child; She Pays as a Man: Women Workers in a Mid-Nineteenth Century New York City Community." Conference on Immigrants in Industrial Life, 1850–1920, Eleutherian Mills Historical Library and the Balch Institute, 2 November 1973.

Hareven, Tamara K. "Industrial Work and the Family Cycle." Conference on Class and Ethnicity in Women's History, SUNY-Binghamton, 21 September 1976.

Kessler-Harris, Alice. "Organizing the Unorganizable: Jewish Women and Their Unions." Conference on Class and Ethnicity in Woman's History, SUNY-Binghamton, 22 September 1974.

————. "Wage-earning Women." Third Berkshire Conference on the History of Women, Bryn Mawr College, 9 June 1976.

Levine, Sue. " 'Strive for Your Rights, Oh Sisters Dear': The Carpet Weavers' Strike and the Knights of Labor, 1885." Third Berkshire Conference on History of Women, Bryn Mawr College, 11 June 1976.

Martelet, Penny. "Women's Land Army." National Archives 1976 Conference on Women's History, Washington, D.C., 23 April 1976.

Nisonoff, Laurie. "Bread and Roses: The Proletarianisation of Women Workers in New England Textile Mills, 1827–1848." Conference on Class and Ethnicity in Women's History, SUNY-Binghamton, 21 September 1974.

Roby, Pamela. "The Conditions of Women in Blue Collar, Industrial and Service Jobs: A Review of Research and Proposal for Research, Action and Policy." Draft prepared for Russell Sage Foundation's Social Science Frontiers Publication Series, September 1974.

Seller, Maxine. "The Education of the Immigrant Woman, 1890–1935." Third Berkshire Conference on the History of Women, Bryn Mawr College, 10 June 1976.

Shorter, Edward. "Women's Work: What Difference Did Capitalism Make?" Conference on Class and Ethnicity in Women's History, SUNY-Binghamton, 21 September 1974.

Smith, Judith. "Work Patterns of Italian Emigrant Women in Early Twentieth Century Providence, Rhode Island." Third Berkshire

Conference on History of Women, Bryn Mawr College, 10 June 1976.

Straub, Eleanor F. "Women in the Civilian Labor Force." National Archives 1976 Conference on Women's History, Washington, D.C., 23 April 1976.

Tentler, Leslie. "Occupational Segregation and the Female Work Experience, 1900–1930." Third Berkshire Conference on History of Women, Bryn Mawr College, 10 June 1976.

Vinovskis, Maris. "Women's Employment and Fertility Patterns." Conference on Class and Ethnicity in Women's History, SUNY-Binghamton, 21 September 1974.

Yans-MacLaughlin, Virginia. "Italian Women and Work: Experience and Perception." Conference on Class and Ethnicity in Women's History, SUNY-Binghamton, 21 September 1976.

Index